FIFTH EDITION

The World News Prism

FIFTH EDITION

The World News Prism

Changing Media of International Communication

William A. Hachten

With the collaboration of Harva Hachten

Iowa State University Press / Ames

WILLIAM A. HACHTEN is professor emeritus of journalism and mass communication at the University of Wisconsin–Madison.

HARVA HACHTEN is a journalist and author. She has collaborated on previous editions of this book.

© 1999, 1996, 1992 William A. Hachten
© 1987, 1981 Iowa State University Press
All rights reserved

Iowa State University Press
2121 South State Avenue, Ames, Iowa 50014

Orders: 1-800-862-6657
Office: 1-515-292-0140
Fax: 1-515-292-3348
Web site: www.isupress.edu

♾ Printed on acid-free paper in the United States of America

First edition, 1981
Second edition, 1987
Third edition, 1992
Fourth edition, 1996
Fifth edition, 1999

International Standard Book Number: 0-8138-2319-6

Library of Congress Cataloging-in-Publication Data

Hachten, William A.
      The world news prism : changing media of international communication /
   William A. Hachten : with the collaboration of Harva Hachten.—5th ed.
        p.   cm.
   Includes bibliographical references and index.
   ISBN 0-8138-2319-6
      1. Foreign news.   2.   Communication, International.   3.   Journalism—
   Political aspects.   I. Hachten, Harva.   II. Title.
   PN4784.F6H3   1999
   070.4′332—dc21   98–49238

The last digit is the print number: 9 8 7 6 5 4 3 2

Contents

Preface to the Fifth Edition

Global events of this last decade have had a dramatic impact on modern history as well as on the news media that report the "first draft" of history. Distant datelines—Moscow, Berlin, Warsaw, Beijing, Prague, Sarajevo, Baghdad, Jerusalem, Belfast, Mogadishu, Johannesburg—have appeared on front pages, and vivid images of momentous events from those places have flickered on television screens everywhere.

In the truly historic year of 1989, the world watched on television in dazzled amazement as Communist regimes were toppled in Poland, East Germany, Hungary, Czechoslovakia, Bulgaria, and Romania. Two years later, the Soviet Union itself, after a right-wing coup had failed, went through a convulsive revolution of its own, outlawing the Communist Party and its media as well as dismantling the Soviet Union itself.

With the collapse of Communist political economies came the withering away of the Communist theory of the press and the disappearance of many Communist news media. The Communist concept of journalism in Eastern Europe and the Soviet Union became a remnant of history rather than a viable way to organize news and mass communication.

These historic events also heralded the end of the Cold War and with it the demise of the propaganda or information "wars" that had enlivened international communication for 45 years. The shrill ideological rhetoric between East and West sharply decreased as the peoples of Eastern Europe and the reconstituted USSR opted for developing democratic governments, market economies, and Western-style media systems.

But the post–Cold War world of the 1990s has proved to be a harsh and forbidding place. The forces of intense nationalism and unleashed ethnic animosities have led to civil wars, genocide, political instability, and economic and social chaos starkly evident in the prolonged and agonizing strife engaging the Bosnian Muslims, Croatians, and Serbs of the former Yugoslavia. Elsewhere, various experiments in democracy and market economies sputtered and foundered. Still, in China and throughout East and South Asia, economies grew at spectacular rates.

But as 1997 ended, several of those economies—Thailand, South Korea, Malaysia, and Indonesia—were in serious trouble: plummeting currencies and stock markets in free fall sent shock waves around the world. Even Japan's economy had severe problems. In our new post–Cold War world with its increasingly globalized economy, economic concerns often took precedence over political concerns.

In other arenas, over 80,000 innocent civilians have died in an irrational six-year civil war in Algeria, Laurent Kabila's ragtag rebel army ousted dictator Mobutu in Zaire and renamed it Congo, genocide flared up again in Rwanda and Burundi, and in Israel a peaceful settlement with the Palestinians still seemed beyond reach. Saddam Hussein's Iraq continued to annoy and vex the United States and United Nations, North Korea's erratic and starving Communist regime worried the West, and Bosnia continued its uneasy truce. But these events were perceived as regional, not global, problems, and none of those hot spots made America's top ten news stories for 1997.

The rapid pace of interrelated political and economic upheaval continued into 1998. After violent student protests, and rioting amid economic collapse in Indonesia, President Suharto bowed to people power and resigned. More ominously, the threat of nuclear war again hung over the world when both India and Pakistan tested nuclear devices in a highly charged political standoff. This specter of a possible religious nuclear war in South Asia more than offset the encouraging news from Ireland, where both Ulster and the Irish Republic resoundingly voted to support a plan that offered the hope of ending sectarian violence.

But for the U.S. public, the biggest news story from abroad in recent years was the death and funeral of Princess Diana, which, of course, was not really foreign news. Rather it was a human-interest tale of the tangled life, spectacular death, and ceremonial funeral of the world's best-known celebrity that just happened to take place abroad. The overwhelming, sentimental, at times mawkish, sustained coverage—by all media—was itself an indictment of Western journalism for increasingly placing celebrity, sensation, and gossip ahead of serious news coverage.

Our recent concern about Princess Di, and such stories as the "nanny" trial, the Iowa septuplets, and especially the Clinton sex scandals, may have reflected, in part, a period of relative prosperity and uneasy peace in places where the absence of armed conflict must be counted as an achievement. But more troubling were clear indications that Americans had much less interest in what was happening abroad, and the news media themselves responded by reporting a good deal less foreign news. With diminished nuclear threat or little fear of global warfare, polls showed Americans were more comfortable with the post–Cold War era. But as much of twentieth-century history reminds us, the world can change very quickly.

International communication in general was affected by world events as it continued to expand. International broadcasting has become less propagandistic and more informative. In most countries, journalists enjoyed greater access to news. New independent and outspoken publications and broadcast outlets sprouted like mushrooms in spring. Communication satellites transmitting news and pop culture have proliferated, and audiences have greatly expanded, especially in Asia.

Divisive issues between North and South, such as the prolonged debate over a new world information order, receded as many millions around the globe tacitly accepted Western-style communications. Ideological conflicts between competing media concepts and differing news values abated as cooperation rather than confrontation became more common in international news exchanges.

International television reporting came into its own during the events in the Persian Gulf, from Iraq's invasion of Kuwait to Iraq's sound military defeat. Through high-technology global television (especially the Cable News Network) and high-speed news dissemination, many millions of viewers learned of events (or thought they did) as they were occurring. Thanks to television's global reach, viewers watched dramatic pictures of the bombing of Baghdad and Scud missile attacks on Tel Aviv. When U.S. bombers again struck Iraq in late 1998, such coverage seemed routine.

When U.S. bombers again struck Iraq in late 1998, such coverage seemed routine.

The same media technology, as well as CNN and the British Broadcasting Corporation's World Service television, brought vivid television reports from the rioting in Jakarta and war in Bosnia and from the U.S. interventions in Somalia, Rwanda, and later, Haiti. Global television, whether at Tiananmen Square or Baghdad, clearly became a major player in diplomacy and world politics.

Incisive Western reporting of recent economic turmoil and political upheavals in Asia brought angry denunciations from autocratic rulers of Malaysia, Indonesia, and Thailand, but underscored the fact that reliable news and information are essential, in fact, indispensable, to the effective functioning of a global economy.

Further, personalized media—videos, VCRs, audiocassettes, personal computers with modems, and fax machines—continued their rapid global penetration, as did cablevision and the Internet. Western Europe has been going through its own regional communication revolution with transnational competition between commercial cable and satellite systems as it moves haltingly toward economic integration.

The ongoing rush of technological developments in international communication accelerated. Direct broadcasting from portable transmitters to satellites and then back to dish antennas—bypassing complicated, expensive ground installations—has become commonplace. Small portable earth terminals, for example, have enabled broadcast journalists reporting remote news events to send their video reports directly to satellites and thus to the whole world. Any news development in Bosnia or, for that matter, in almost any faraway troubled area, can instantly become a global media event, riveting millions to their television screens to watch the drama unfold.

In just a few years, the Internet has become a player in international communication of great and ominous potential for both journalism and as a device that lets people share ideas freely on a global network.

The rush to media consolidation has accelerated also. In late 1995, three multi-billion-dollar mergers involving six major American media companies surprised Wall Street—and the world. Time Warner and Turner Broadcasting (owner of CNN) combined forces, as did the Disney Company and Capital Cities/American Broadcasting Co., and Westinghouse Electric bought out Columbia Broadcasting System, once the crown jewel of American radio and television. The three communications giants are now positioning themselves to compete for the expanding overseas markets for news, television, motion pictures, and recordings.

In this age of information, communications systems are at the leading edge of social, economic, and political changes. With the unprecedented growth in global telecommunications, an informed public has developed a more immediate concern with both world news and the symbiotic relationship between events and those who report them.

For this fifth edition, the text has been thoroughly revised, with new material added to every chapter. I thank my wife, Harva Hachten, a skilled writer who carefully edited the manuscript and made useful suggestions. I alone am responsible for the judgments and any errors in the book.

—W.A.H.

Introduction

> After years of global fretfulness about the brute effectiveness of modern armaments, it turned out during one of the most pervasively revolutionary years of the 20th century, if not of all recorded history, that the most potent single weapon in nearly every conflict was the video camera. In nation after nation, vastly superior military forces were stood off and frequently compelled to retreat before the symbolic and testimonial power of televised images.
>
> —William A. Henry III

As our tragic and war-stained century (and millennium) comes to an end, we are reminded both of the changes as well as continuities that have marked journalism and international communications in our times. In 1900, all the elements were in place—great metropolitan newspapers, rotary presses and linotypes, the typewriter, the telegraph and the undersea cable, the Associated Press and cooperative news gathering—as building blocks for the changes to come. News was recognized as a valued and useful commodity in itself and as an essential means of comprehending and coping with a strange and distant world. At the same time, sensationalism and trivia were already abundant in the press.

But no one could have foreseen the political and social changes to come in our tumultuous century as a result of the greatly enhanced speed, volume, and reach of international news and "public knowledge" in the second half of the twentieth century.

Journalists and broadcasters jetting about the globe with camcorders, comsat phones, and laptop computers reported great events instantly via satellite networks and, in so doing, often became participants and catalysts in global news stories.

When Princess Diana was killed in a shocking auto crash, she was being pursued through Paris by paparazzi seeking ever more photos of the most recognized woman on earth. Afterward, much of the public and some in the media condemned the photographers for providing what that same public had so eagerly received for years, thus reflecting the public's ever-ambivalent attitudes toward the press.

From the Spanish-American War to the Gulf War, the press has reported news from abroad, but it has been only in the last three decades that we have seen how great events abroad vividly illustrate the technetronic age, the melding of technology and electronics, that planet earth has entered. It is a new era of information whose potential we but dimly perceive; whose complicated gadgetry only few of us totally grasp; whose social, political, and economic consequences are accelerating change and cleavages among the nations of the world.

For the world we live in today is changing rapidly, in no small part because worldwide television, communication satellites, high-speed transmission of news and data, and other computer and electronic hardware and software (including the Internet) have transformed the ways that nations and peoples communicate with one another. The fact that a news event can be transmitted almost instantaneously to newsrooms and onto television and computer screens around the world can be as important as the event itself. Long-distance mass communication has become a rudimentary central nervous system for our fragile, shrinking, and increasingly interdependent world.

Yet, there can be disconcerting side effects. The accelerating speed and efficiency of news media technology has often created severe strains on the standards and ethics of responsible journalism. The news eruption that followed President Clinton's alleged ties with Monica Lewinsky in 1998 illustrated how news now breaks 24 hours a day, around the clock, instead of at the more leisurely pace that prevailed before the rise of 24-hour cable television news and news sources on the Internet. As fierce competitors such as MSNBC and talk shows have proliferated on cable and on-line, news organizations have relaxed their rules on checking and verifying sources in the race to break news first. There is a growing sense that getting it first is more important than getting it right. A result is journalism that is sometimes shaky, or worse, and with it, a loss of public trust in news media.

High among the various factors contributing to the collapse of Communist regimes (and their press) was certainly the impact of Western communications in all their diversity and seductive appeal. For throughout the 1980s, two great groundswells rolled through the seas of international communication. On an incoming tide, the methods of organizing and distributing news and mass culture developed in Western democracies have washed inexorably over the globe, driven by innovations in media technology and expanding audiences along with a resurgence of market economies on a global scale.

On an outgoing tide, the theory and practices of Communist or Marxist/Leninist public communication have become widely discredited by the many millions living under Communist regimes, as well as their own journalists and rulers. The resounding rejection was directly related, of course, to the worldwide failures of socialist political economies and, particularly, the rejection of Communist political rule in Eastern Europe. The crowds that protested Communist regimes in Warsaw, Beijing, East Berlin, Prague, Budapest, Sofia, and Moscow in 1989 were also calling for more open and free media systems—the kind they knew about from images and sounds from the West. Expanding waves from these astonishing events radiated to the former Third World. Even as far away as Africa, several one-party states—Zambia, Kenya, Gabon, Zaire, and the Ivory Coast—felt pressures for multiparty democracy.

So far, such high hopes have generally not been realized. Africa—beset by economic stagnation; drought and famine; political unrest; and civil wars in Sudan, Somalia, Mozambique, Liberia, Congo (formerly Zaire), and Rwanda—has in fact retrogressed. Hopes for meaningful democracy in Kenya, Zimbabwe, and Congo have all been dashed recently. Today's unipolar world, with the United States as its uncertain and often indecisive leader, is plagued with new problems, many associated with resurgent nationalism, racism, and/or religious fundamentalism.

This book describes and analyzes the altered role of transnational news media in our evolving technetronic age and their impact on rapidly changing news events.

News has increasingly become a powerful political and diplomatic force. U.S. television shows stark pictures of starving Somali mothers and children, American public opinion becomes concerned, and the White House watches, hesitates, and then sends in the marines to help feed the starving and keep the peace. A few months later, a dozen American soldiers are killed in an ambush, and the U.S. public is outraged at seeing on television the body of an American soldier dragged through the streets of Mogadishu. Soon the White House announces that troops will be withdrawn.

In late 1995, after unrelenting media coverage of Bosnia's bitter civil war, the United States and its NATO allies intervened with a bombing campaign that led to a tenuous peace accord. With American troops involved in enforcing the peace, the public's perceptions on how well or how badly things are going in Bosnia has been influenced by the news coverage. News, instantaneous and vivid, speeds up history as it directly influences diplomacy and government policy. At the same time, in this age of satellites, the Internet, and shortwave radio, tyrants find it impossible to keep unflattering news about their regimes from reaching their own people.

On the one hand are the technological and operational changes taking place in the international news media, with their enhanced capability for global communication that is reshaping "spaceship earth." Wider communication often seems to exacerbate political and cultural conflicts between the West and Islam, between rich and poor nations. Also, there are the frictions and the problems these changes have wrought, including conflicts over transnational news gathering and dissemination and the impact of television programming, motion pictures, videos, radio broadcasting, and other aspects of mass culture, much of it coming out of the United States.

Another source of concern is that serious international news seems often to be pushed aside at times by profit-making and entertainment considerations. "Infotainment"—scandal, sensation, celebrities—is becoming more and more the staple of American and British media.

Network television news programs, from which most Americans get their news, have sharply cut back on the amount of foreign news on the major networks. Similar trends are seen among the newsmagazines. This reflects (or explains) why Americans have been showing a declining interest in news from abroad.

This book deals with various facets of the changing media and their impact on transnational journalism and mass communication. It is intended to provide some insights into how and why international news communication is evolving and where it is headed.

Few of us can appreciate, much less fully understand, the meaning of the global information revolution we are living through. The major components of this quiet revolution are the computer and telecommunications, principally the communication satellite plus other sophisticated electronic devices that have become as much a part of our lives as the electric light. Journalism and mass communication recently have made quantum leaps in scope and reach because of application of this new technology to the gathering, production, and dissemination of news throughout the globe.

We may not be aware of how our perceptions of the world are being changed by the transformed news system, but we quickly learn to take that system for granted. If there is another seizure of American hostages somewhere, a new outbreak of terrorism in the Middle East, or another civil war in Africa, we expect to see live television reports the same day or on a 24-hour news channel, such as CNN, within the same hour via satellite. We are fascinated but not surprised to see detailed, computer-refined pictures of the exploration of planet Mars or the dramatic saga of repairs to the *Mir* spacecraft. We no longer marvel that we and half the human race are more or less simultaneously linked as viewers of the Olympic Games on television every four years.

In a broader context, the fact that information of all kinds, including urgent news, can now be communicated almost instantly to almost anywhere has profound implications for international organization and interaction. News of Iraq's invasion of Kuwait, for example, had an almost immediate impact on the price of gas at the pump and initiated an international diplomatic reaction resulting in mass movement of U.S. military forces. And the world's subsequent perceptions of the crisis and war were certainly shaped and, at times, distorted by the flickering images on television screens. Instant information is not necessarily the truth or the whole picture and on occasion can distort the images that people receive.

Still, global news has many uses. The financial media's close day-to-day reporting in 1998 of the continuing economic crises in Asian stock markets and currencies and their effects on stock markets and economies of Japan, Europe, and America illustrates how many millions around the world, including small stockholders, rely on fast, accurate information in their daily lives.

A new global society of sorts is emerging rapidly and inexorably, though experts disagree about its nature. The media of mass communication, along with global telecommunications, air transportation, and growing interdependence of national economies, are providing the essential linkages that make interaction and cooperation—and dangerous frictions—possible.

Full understanding of the nature of this new society requires that today's students of international communication be conversant with world affairs, including recent history, and be quick to recognize significant trends as they occur. Further, they must understand national and cultural differences and keep up with technological innovations in communication media, such as the Internet, and with changing journalistic practices.

Communication satellites are just one example of the truly revolutionary impact that communication technology has had on the modern world. The earlier role of transistor radios in the Third World was another; today the small hand-held video camcorder is having news effects undreamed of. As we will see, the Internet is beginning to be perceived as yet another technological marvel that may dramatically alter international communication, but so far, no one seems to know exactly how and when it will happen. Finally, students of international communication must be attuned to the roles and functions of mass communication in changing the political and social relationships of the world's peoples.

The interplay of these elements makes the study of international communication fascinating and important. The major emphasis throughout this book is on the journalistic aspects of international communication—the new challenges and perils of reporting the news, the important but imperfect and controversial ways that journalists and mass communicators keep the world informed.

Several chapters concern the changing media—the ways that international journalism is adapting to altering global conditions, changing concepts of news, and utilizing the new hardware of our information age. Some of the fundamental changes that are bringing all peoples of the world—for better or worse—much closer together are broadly outlined.

Today, for the first time in history, all nations, however remote, have stepped onto the stage of the modern world. What happens in Rwanda or Indonesia, Kosovo or Iraq, can have global significance and often sends repercussions around the world, in part because those events are reported. More importantly, a much greater degree of interdependence among all peoples and nations has developed. Americans, perhaps, are much slower than others to recognize this. Since our families, jobs, and local communities are of primary and immediate concern, most people, including many leaders, do not perceive the rapid and fundamental changes taking place, changes directly related to our expanded powers of long-distance communication.

For the world has been evolving an international news system that moves information and mass culture ever faster and in greater volume to any place on earth where an antenna can be put on a shortwave radio receiver, where dish antennas can receive television programs from a communication satellite, or increasingly where there is a personal computer with a modem hooked onto the Internet. Although politics, economic disparities, cultural and linguistic differences, and ideology keep us apart on many issues, the international news system has on occasion made us one community if only for a few brief moments—as when Neil Armstrong took that "one giant leap for mankind" in 1969. An estimated 600 million people throughout the world watched that first walk on the moon, and they sat before their television sets not as Americans, French, Africans, or Japanese but as earthlings watching in awe as one of their kind first stepped onto another planet.

Actually, the reportage of Armstrong's walk has further relevance to this book because the new information age is partly an outgrowth of the exploration of space. The communication satellite, high-speed data transmission, and miniaturized computer technology are by-products of space technology, and all are playing integral roles in the transformation of international communication and transnational journalism.

The modern world's practices of globally collecting and distributing news are only about a hundred years old and were initiated by news agencies of the United States and the great imperial powers: Britain and France. Today, the world agencies—the Associated Press (United States), Reuters (Britain), and Agence France-Presse (France)—are still the principal, but not the only, conduits of transnational news, although they and other media have been transformed by the new space-age technology.

Change has been coming so quickly that it is often difficult to stay current with the ways in which news is being moved. And to understand the future potential of these space-age gadgets is like trying to perceive in 1905 what the absurd horseless carriage or the telephone would do in time to the cities and lifestyles of the twentieth century.

Furthermore, technology and global reach are modifying some of the institutions of transnational communication. Subtly and almost imperceptibly, various media, including the news agencies, are evolving from national to increasingly international, or better, to supranational institutions of mass communication. The successful *International Herald Tribune* reaches a sophisticated non-American readership from Paris to Hong Kong; *Time* and *Newsweek* publish special editions truly international in outlook; the *Asian Wall Street Journal* is widely read by Asian businesspeople; and CNN is viewed in over 140 countries. Some may deplore this trend, but there is no doubt that it is a response to the informational needs of a shrinking world. Concomitantly, English is clearly the world's media language. The logic of mass communication requires that sender and receiver understand a common language, and so far, English, the language of science and technology—and computers—is it.

Modern media, especially shortwave radio, are utilized by many nations for purposes of "international political communication"—a polite term for propaganda. The international broadcasters—BBC World Service, Voice of America, Radio Moscow, Deutsche Welle, Radio Cairo, and many others, including small national services in developing nations—use the airwaves to voice their interpretations and reactions to world events. "Propaganda warfare" appears in a variety of manifestations of international politics, including economic competition, but with the demise of the Cold War, advocacy is giving way to more information in international radio. Propagandistic or not, shortwave radio conveys news to untold millions, especially in the poorer nations.

The international news media, furthermore, are unevenly distributed among nations, creating serious frictions between the haves and have-nots in mass communication. The explosion of communication technology has coincided with the post–World War II decolonization of the Third World, and the penetration of Western news and mass culture into the newly independent nations, as well as into the former Communist bloc, has been perceived by some as a new attempt to reassert the domination of the former colonial powers.

Part of this book focuses on the differences that frustrate and at times inhibit the flow of international news and divide journalists and mass communicators: political and ideological differences, economic disparities, geographic and ethnic divisions. Africa, in particular, lies on the periphery of world news flow and presents formidable challenges to Western reporters.

The conflicts and frictions in international communication arise from divergent concepts of mass communication. In the concept of the press that has evolved in Western democratic nations, which dominate international news flow, the journalist and the press are relatively independent of government, free to report directly to the public that uses the information to understand the world and to assess its governors. This view is unacceptable to authoritarian nations which control and manipulate their media to serve better the goals of the state and their unelected leaders. The Communist press concept is now largely defunct. (See Chapter 2, "Changing Ideologies.") In numerous, mostly impoverished nations, a similar theory—the Developmental concept—has emerged, which holds that mass media must be mobilized to serve the goals of nation building and economic development.

The clashes between these media concepts and various debates on controls on the flow of news reverberated for years through international organizations such as the United Nations Educational, Scientific, and Cultural Organization (UNESCO) and international professional media and press groups. Although efforts to reconcile these conflicting approaches to global journalism have been slow, the controversy has clearly diminished.

Nonetheless, Western journalists believe that their ability to gather news abroad is frequently impaired as some nations frustrate and block the activities of foreign reporters. Authoritarian governments with controlled press systems resent what they consider to be the negative reporting of Western media and, as a result, do not permit foreign reporters to enter or report from their countries. For their part, many non-Western nations resent what they consider to be the domination of the world news flow by a few Western media. They see a kind of "media imperialism" imposing alien values on developing societies through a one-way flow of news.

The deep differences between the media-rich and media-poor nations reflect closely other differences between rich and poor nations. Despite the impressive gains in the technical ability to communicate more widely and quickly, the disturbing evidence is that in some ways the world may be growing further apart rather than closer together. Most of the benefits of the communication and information revolution have accrued to the industrialized nations of the West and to Japan and the Pacific Rim nations. For an individual to benefit fully from the news media, he or she ideally should be literate, educated, and affluent enough to have access to a variety of news sources. Unfortunately, in our unfair world, the largest share of such individuals are found in the few industrialized democracies. Technological change in communication seems to race far ahead of our political skills to use it for the greatest good of all.

The world's system of distributing news can be likened to a crystal prism. What in one place is considered the straight white light of truth travels through the prism and is refracted and bent into a variety of colors and shades. One person's truth becomes, to another, biased reporting or propaganda, depending on where the light strikes the prism and where it emerges. As we understand and accept the optics of a prism for measuring the spectrum of light, so must we understand and accept the transecting planes of different cultural and political traditions that refract divergent perceptions of our world.

I must acknowledge how the light refracts for me. In considering the problems of international communication, I have tried to be sympathetic to the views and frustrations of non-Western nations and the enormous difficulties they face.

Journalism is a highly subjective pursuit, tempered and shaped by the political conditions and cultural traditions of the particular society where it is practiced; the news and the world do look different from Beijing, Lagos, or Baghdad than they do from New York City or London.

As a product of the Western press tradition, I believe journalists should be suspicious of, and disagree at times with, political leaders and with other journalists and the owners of the media. For me, the essence of journalism is diversity of ideas and the freedom to express them. I find it difficult to disagree with Albert Camus, who wrote that "a free press can of course be good or bad, but certainly without freedom, it will never be anything but bad. ... Freedom is nothing else but a chance to be better, whereas enslavement is a certainty of the worse."

And in the dangerous, strife-ridden world of the late twentieth century, I believe that the billions of people inhabiting this planet deserve to know more about the events and trends that affect their lives and well-being. Only journalists who are free and independent of authoritarian controls and other constraints can begin the difficult task of reporting the news and information we all need to know.

The World News Prism

CHAPTER 1

News Communication for an Interdependent World

> By every indication the global human society is entering a period of change of historical proportions. Some call it the era of limited resources; some see it as the start of the new world economic order; some call it the communications age, or the postindustrial society or the information age; but nearly every discipline and sector of society senses the shift taking place. By whatever name, ... we are moving along a trajectory leading to a global human culture in which events across the world affect us with the same speed and impact as if they happened next door.
>
> —Representative George E. Brown (*D-California*)

Foreign news stories and pictures come in all sizes and shapes. Sometimes there may be just several short "filler" items from the Associated Press in our afternoon paper. Another time it may be a dramatic news photo, say, of Pope John Paul II meeting Fidel Castro in, of all places, Havana, Cuba.

Perhaps one of the most significant photographs of modern times was taken during the *Apollo 11* mission to the moon. The astronauts photographed the earthrise as seen from the moon, and there was our planet, like a big, cloudy, blue, agate marble. The widely reprinted picture illuminated the fragility and cosmic insignificance of our spaceship earth.

That stunning image coincided with the worldwide concern about ecology and global pollution; even more, it made it easy to grasp why many scientists already treat that cloudy, blue marble as a complete biological system in which change in one part will inevitably affect other parts.

Certainly in the years since, concerned persons around the world have become more aware of our global interdependence. Although some experts disagree, an important trend of our times is that the world is becoming a single, rudimentary community. Today's world is faced with urgent and complex problems, most of them interrelated: overpopulation, poverty,

3

famine, depletion of natural resources (especially energy), pollution of the biosphere, regional political disputes, continuing arms buildup including the nuclear threat, and the widening gap between rich and poor nations, which seems exacerbated by economic integration.

Change seems to be the only constant in our fast-moving world. The prolonged East-West crisis known as the Cold War had no sooner ended than it was followed by the Persian Gulf War as well as numerous regional armed clashes based on nationalism, ethnicity, and religion.

Such global crises ebb and flow on the world's news agenda, but they are truly international in scope; the amelioration, much less solution, of any of them requires cooperation and goodwill among nations. To achieve that, there first must be information and understanding of these challenges, for these are crises of interdependence. No one nation or even combination of nations can deal effectively with such global concerns as international monetary crises, pollution of the air and oceans, population control, terrorism, regional warfare, and widespread famine and food shortages, yet the blinders of nationalism and modern tribalism continue to influence political leaders everywhere to react to international problems with narrow and parochial responses.

Few events illustrate this modern dilemma more vividly than the accident at the Chernobyl nuclear station near Kiev in April 1986. Radiation levels rose significantly first in Scandinavia and Eastern Europe and then in parts of Western Europe, contaminating crops and milk. People in the affected areas outside of Russia demanded full information and were outraged when the Soviet government at first tried to minimize the accident and then withheld details about the exact readings and extent of radiation contamination. But nuclear accidents of this scope are truly international catastrophes in which the fullest sharing of reliable information—news—to all people affected is the first imperative.

Lester Brown, an authority on global needs, described the problems of the late twentieth century as "unique in their scale." Previous catastrophes—famines, floods, earthquakes, volcanic eruptions—were local and temporary. But now, the world's more pressing concerns can be solved only through multinational or global cooperation, yet the institutions to cope with them are largely national. And since each technological innovation seems to create new problems but not the political will capable of resolving them, Brown saw global conditions worsening in the years immediately ahead.

Brown's view of world problems, shared by people in many nations, is still not understood by any great numbers of them. We Americans, for example, periodically turn inward and become self-absorbed, failing to comprehend how domestic problems have roots in events that occur thousands of miles away.[1]

But then, events such as those in the late 1980s and early 1990s reawakened Americans' interest, at least temporarily, in foreign affairs. The collapse of communism, with its resulting confusion and disarray, and the ominous crisis over Iraq and Kuwait all altered American public opinion sharply, as did subsequent U.S. incursions into Somalia, Rwanda, and Haiti.

Americans and some leaders of developing countries were becoming aware that population growth is putting intolerable pressures on the earth's land, water, and energy resources as well as its economies.

Pressures of Population

In 1994, the United Nations (UN) Population Fund estimated the world's population at 5.66 billion and growing at the rate of 94 million people a year. (In 1950, the world had 2.5 billion people.) By the year 2025, total population is projected to be 8.5 billion. Because of the difficulty of predicting fertility rates, various projections for the year 2050 were set at 7.8 billion (low), 10 billion (medium), and 12.5 billion (high).

The Population Institute in 1998 reported that at least 74 countries—including Nigeria, Iran, Ethiopia, Iraq, and Guatemala—will probably double their populations in 30 years; that 33 countries, 25 of them in Africa, still have a fertility rate of six children per woman; and that 3 billion women—the equivalent of the world's population in 1960—will enter their childbearing years in the next few years.

Thomas Merrick, president of the Population Reference Bureau, a private, nonprofit group, said, "For the developing nations it is a question of whether they will evolve into a kind of permanent underclass at the bottom of a two-tiered world economy. For the more developed nations, now approaching population stabilization, it may be difficult to continue to be islands of prosperity in a sea of poverty in a world made smaller by modern transportation and communication."[2] This separation will be more difficult to maintain if these imbalances generate waves of immigration.

Even without these ominous developments, the very nature of the problems of the late twentieth century—transnational in scope and beyond the ability of this or any single nation to solve—may be changing America's traditional provincialism.

The world's political structures, many believe, must be reshaped to enable us to cope with these global challenges. Hence, the great importance, despite their shortcomings, of international organizations such as the United Nations and its attendant agencies. The end of the Cold War and the newfound cooperation between the West and the former Communist nations seemed to have helped revive the United Nations. Tangible proof was provided by the Security Council's near unanimity in condemning Iraq's invasion of Kuwait and imposing sanctions on Saddam Hussein. However, later there was much concern over the failures of UN peace-keeping efforts in Bosnia, Rwanda, Kosovo, Iraq, and Somalia.

The late Edwin Reischauer, former U.S. ambassador to Japan, felt the response to American provincialism must start by changing individuals through a profound reshaping of education. Proliferating communication technology, he felt, is fast destroying the cushioning that once existed between the different nations and cultures of the world. This in turn rapidly increases not only interdependence, but tensions as well.

"While the world is in the process of becoming a single great mass of humanity—a global community, as it is sometimes called," Reischauer wrote, "the very diverse national and cultural groupings that make up the world's population retain attitudes and habits more appropriate to a different technological age."

In the United States, he said, education "is not moving rapidly enough in the right directions to produce the knowledge about the outside world and the attitudes toward other peoples that may be essential for human survival within a generation or two. This, I feel, is a much greater international problem than the military balance of power that absorbs so much of our attention today."[3]

Public opinion polls show that many Americans are uninformed about international affairs. For example, a Gallup Poll found that half of all Americans did not know that the United States had to import petroleum to meet its needs.

Professor Robert Ward has described the extent of our current neglect of international education at all levels as shocking. He might have added that most American news media pay too little attention to news from abroad. What worries experts in this field is that ignorance and apathy about the world beyond America's borders may undermine this country's political, diplomatic, and economic influence. The next generation of Americans will be ill-prepared to grapple with global problems.

As important as formal education is, its influence sometimes does not change attitudes or improve understanding until a generation or two later.

In immediate terms, the media flow of information and news throughout the globe will have a greater impact than education on the world's ability to understand its problems and dangers.

Since World War II, an intricate and worldwide network of international news media has evolved, providing an expanded capability for information flows. This relationship between the capacity and the need to communicate rapidly has resulted from the interaction of two long-term historical processes: the evolution toward a single global society and the movement of civilization beyond four great benchmarks of human communication—speech, writing, printing, and electronic communications (telephone and radio)—into a fifth era of long-distance instant communication based on telecommunications (mainly satellites) and computer technology.

Harold Lasswell believed that the mass-media revolution has accelerated the tempo and direction of world history. What would have happened later has happened sooner, and changes in timing may have modified substantive developments.[4]

The toppling of President Ferdinand Marcos from power in the Philippines in 1986 provided a cogent example of the power of international news media to influence international politics. From the assassination of opposition leader Benigno Aquino through the election campaign, the U.S. news media took a close interest in Marcos' affairs, reporting extensively on Marcos' "hidden wealth," including New York City real estate, as well as his dubious war record. This scrutiny helped the cause of candidate Corazon Aquino and galvanized U.S. public opinion and the Congress. The Reagan White House in turn was pushed to urge Marcos to step down after full media glare showed his election victory to be a fraud.

As Thomas Griffith of *Time* wrote, "The visuals on American TV did Marcos in. It wasn't Dan Rather or George Will. It was the pictures—the nuns, and the crowds wearing a touch of yellow, blocking the path of the armored cars. It was the sight of ballot boxes being dumped. In a few precarious days, it was the total collapse of Marcos' American support that sped the end. TV proved its awesome power."[5]

Commenting on the episode, Walter B. Wriston observed, "This is a brand new situation in the world. The global electronic network that has evolved in the last decade is forcing us to redefine our ideas of sovereignty. The rapid transmission of information has become a radical force for change, encouraging the growth of political and economic freedom. Marcos's demise is not an isolated instance."[6] The revolutionary year of 1989 provided further examples of the power of modern communications in the uprisings from Berlin and Prague to Tiananmen Square. (See Chapter 5, "Global Impact of Western News and Pop Culture.")

In another example, the world's reactions to the widespread racial conflict and state of emergency in South Africa during 1985–86 was greatly accelerated by the intense news coverage abroad. In 1960, after police killed 69 blacks and injured 180 others in Sharpeville township, similar reactions occurred toward the imposition of martial law, continued racial unrest, worldwide condemnation, and flight of capital. But in the mid-1980s, the foreign reactions, including protests and widespread condemnation, the imposition of sanctions and the flight of capital, were much faster and more intense because the world was now seeing nightly color television reports of black protesters being attacked by white soldiers and police. Not surprisingly, South Africa in November 1985 banned all foreign photographic coverage by television and news photographers reporting racial violence in black townships. U.S. television coverage fell markedly after visuals were no longer available, and international pressures on South Africa lessened—even though the violence continued unabated. Nonetheless, the momentum for political change, fueled by foreign-media pressures, led to the release from prison of Nelson Mandela in 1990 and to his subsequent election in 1994 as the president of South Africa.

Intense global media attention to Indonesia in May 1998 probably contributed to the bloodless coup that toppled President Suharto.

Paradoxically, even with this greatly enhanced capability of involvement in world affairs, comparatively few people are well informed or even care much about what happens beyond their borders. Many who follow the news on television have only a superficial knowledge of events such as a cancellation of an election in Nigeria or a stock-market crash in Indonesia. But for those comparative few who do follow public affairs closely (and they are found in every nation), perceptions of the world are being formed and reshaped by this revolution in long-distance instant communications.

Our ability, or lack of it, to use the fruits of this technological revolution is directly related to our success or failure to act decisively and in concert as a world community. International experts worry whether the world can organize itself and deal effectively with what have been called the seven major interrelated world problems: mass poverty, population, food, pollution, energy, military expenditure, and the world monetary system. To organize, though, we must communicate, since communication is the neural system of any organization. The extent of its ability to communicate determines the boundaries of any community—be it a primitive tribe in Papua New Guinea or a global society—and only expanded and more effective communication can make possible a viable global community.

The technology to circulate that information exists, but the barriers of illiteracy, poverty, and political constraints keep too many people in the world from receiving it. The illiteracy situation is particularly vexing. However, there has been improvement. On International Literacy Day, September 8, 1997, Federico Mayor, director general of the United Nations Educational, Scientific, and Cultural Organization (UNESCO), reported that the tide of worldwide illiteracy is turning: the illiteracy rate, estimated at 45 percent 50 years ago, had fallen to 23 percent. This was a remarkable achievement, considering that world population continued to rise during that period. The average rate, however, masked significant disparities. In 1995, nineteen nations had an illiteracy rate equal to or higher than 70 percent, 14 of them in Africa. Moreover, UNESCO reported that the number of illiterates is rising in Southern Asia, sub-Saharan Africa, and the Arab states.

Literacy is the key skill for modernization, education, and use of mass media. Illiteracy is widespread in Africa, so it is no wonder that there are only about 125 daily newspapers in all of Africa compared with more than 1,770 in the United States. In any country, therefore, the proportion of people able to receive news and information will vary greatly according to the availability of mass media and the ability of people to use the media.

Those living in such "information societies" as Japan, Western Europe, or the United States are overwhelmed with information and news, while throughout the many poor nations only a tiny fraction of persons are able to participate in the international news flow, due in large part to the lack of news media. Regardless of where they live, however, too few people take advantage of opportunities to acquire and use information in the solution of urgent transnational problems.

Importance of Foreign News—and Its Decline

Much of the essential information we need for our personal lives comes from the news media. Our economy, our society, and our government would have difficulty functioning without the flow of reliable news and information. An open democratic society without independent news media is impossible to imagine.

Foreign news is a special genre of news. Serious journalists and editors have long held that important information from overseas should be reported capably and thoroughly, even though most people are primarily concerned about what happens in their own communities or to themselves personally.

Throughout our turbulent century, events beyond our borders have directly affected, and disrupted, many American lives—World War I, a worldwide depression, the rise of Hitler and Stalin, World War II, the Korean and Vietnam Wars and the Cold War, and, more recently, our interdependent global economy. In an open democratic society, the public must know what is happening in the outside world in order to judge how well its own government responds to threats from abroad. The history of American journalism clearly shows that the best and most responsible news media have *always* given high priority to foreign news. This is still true today, especially for a handful of great daily newspapers.

Yet for many Americans, foreign news does not seem as important today as it did before the Cold War ended and the nuclear threat receded. Who is to blame: the press or the public? Perhaps both. Without a crisis demanding our attention—famine and civil war in Sudan, civil strife and genocide in Bosnia and Kosovo—the average daily paper carries usually only about six short items—unless American soldiers or hostages are involved.

Most Americans rely on television for their news, yet anyone regularly watching network news is aware that foreign news has been typically reduced to several short items ("And now the news from abroad ...") unless some video with violent footage is available. (Fifty percent of television's foreign coverage does portray violence.) Critics say that serious foreign news on television has been pushed aside in favor of more personalized, self-help, and advice stories—so-called "you news."

The public apparently does not mind. A 1996 survey of the American public by the Pew Research Center found that among regular users of the news media, the topics of most interest were, in order, crime, local news about people and events, and health news. International news ranked ninth, well behind sports, local government, science, religion, and political news.

The Associated Press, the principal source of foreign news for most U.S. news media, conducts an annual poll of 700 editors and found that the top 10 stories of 1997 did not include any serious international stories unless one included the death of Princess Diana (no. 1) or the death of Mother Teresa (no. 3).

Most foreign news consists of political and economic events that highlight policy issues. Except for 1989 and the collapse of Communist states, coverage of international news in U.S. media has steadily declined since the late seventies. Michael Emery of California State University found in 1989 that only 2.6 percent of the nonadvertising space in 10 leading newspapers was devoted to news from abroad. (See Chapter 8, "Changes in Foreign Coverage," for further discussion.)

Other surveys conducted by the Pew Research Center in 1997 found that the percentage of people following foreign news dropped from 80 percent in the 1980s to 20 percent in 1990. The decline was most precipitous among young people, who were turned off by such traditional categories as international politics, security, war, and peace. The relatively few serious news stories that attract the attention of adult Americans are those that deal with national calamities or the use of American military force. Only one in four Americans (25 percent) followed the average story closely. Of 480 stories reported over five years, the survey found that most attention went to natural or man-made disasters, such as the *Challenger* spacecraft explosion, and stories about war and terrorism involving American citizens. Most notably, only 5 percent of Americans paid very close attention in 1991 to news about the outbreak of civil war in Yugoslavia.

I agree with Stephen Hess of the Brookings Institution, who argues that we have become a nation with a two-media system, especially in regard to foreign news. Hess wrote, "Our society is awash in specialized information (including foreign news) available to those who have the time, interest, money, and education to take advantage of it. The other society encompasses the vast majority of Americans, who devote limited attention to subjects far removed from their necessary concerns (again, foreign news). They are content to turn to the top stories of television networks' evening news programs and their community's daily newspapers for the information."[7]

Yet perhaps this diminished interest in international events is not as dismal as it would seem. Recent polls show that while the public is turned off by some foreign news, the public does crave engagement in the world's crises, but not in ways defined by government, academics, and the media. For example, a University of Maryland poll found that 74 percent of people wanted a sharing of power internationally while only 13 percent wanted the United States to assert itself as the only superpower. Also, while Congress refuses to approve $1.5 billion in overdue assessments for the United Nations, a Pew Center survey found that Americans hold the organization in high regard. The Pew survey found broad support for cooperative action to halt global warming, even if it meant applying fuel consumption standards leading to higher U.S. gasoline prices.

In short, the public seems much concerned about issues they see as directly affecting their lives. These include immigration and trade negotiations that could impact on their jobs and taxes, environmental issues like resource depletion, health threats, drug trafficking, and other cross-border crime.[8]

Moving Together or Apart?

Whether the problem is pollution of the seas or proliferation of nuclear weapons, the fact remains that international society is marked by the absence of collective procedures, by competition rather than cooperation, and by the lack of a commitment to a common goal—in other words, a situation that approaches anarchy. The world is ruled by nation-states, not by an effective international organization, and each state will usually act according to its own interests and needs. In several African nations, such as Somalia, Liberia, and Sierra Leone, an even more discouraging trend has emerged—the complete breakdown of a nation into warring camps without a coherent central government.[9] Political scientist Robert Tucker reminds us that

> the prospects for an emergent global community cannot appear promising today. Instead of a universal conscience in the making, throughout most of the world we can observe discrete national consciences in the making. The vision of shared community that, once internalized, could prompt people to sacrifice on behalf of a common good remains at best embryonic. For the time being, the global challenges posed by nuclear weapons, grinding poverty, and burgeoning populations—to mention only the most pressing—will have to be dealt with by a world that is, in many respects, as divided as ever.[10]

Some academics argue that the apparent thrust toward global unity is actually misleading. Political scientist Steven Krasner of Stanford University believes the idea that the world has fundamentally changed lacks historical perspective. The international transfer of ideas, trade, and capital has been going on for 400 to 500 years, he says. Others agree that global integration has been overblown and that we are not yet up to the late-nineteenth-century standard of integration. They argue that the current globalization is a return to a process interrupted by two world wars.[11]

Others feel that the world is both converging and diverging at the same time. In 1993, the *New York Times* listed 48 nations where long-suppressed ethnic, religious, and sectional conflicts had surfaced. Policymakers say the ethnic conflicts are actually the third wave of this century, with the first having taken place after World War I and the second with the explosion of anticolonial movements in Africa and Asia after World War II.[12] Most of these nations' ancient rivalries and bigotry have remained largely unaffected by communication technology.

On the other hand, powerful technetronic forces are binding the world together—circulating news, ideas, and information faster and in greater volume than ever before. These technologies are transforming many economic enterprises into truly global businesses.

So, while global integration may seem both real and illusory, there may be encouragement perhaps in the futuristic views of science-fiction writer Arthur C. Clarke expressed over 25 years ago regarding the communication satellite:

> What we are now doing—whether we like it or not—indeed, whether we wish it or not—is laying the foundation of the first global society. Whether the final planetary authority will be an analogue of the federal systems now existing in the United States or the USSR I do not know. I suspect that, without any deliberate planning, such organizations as the world meteorological and earth resources satellite system and the world communications satellite system (of which INTELSAT is the precursor) will eventually transcend their individual components. At some time during the next century they will discover, to their great surprise, that they are really running the world.
>
> There are many who will regard these possibilities with alarm or distaste and may even attempt to prevent their fulfillment. I would remind them of the story of the wise English king, Canute, who had his throne set upon the seashore so he could demonstrate to his foolish courtiers that even the king could not command the incoming tide.
>
> The wave of the future is now rising before us. Gentlemen, do not attempt to hold it back. Wisdom lies in recognizing the inevitable—and cooperating with it. In the world that is coming, the great powers are not great enough.[13]

Some signs of this trend are visible; a slow but perceptible movement toward internationalization of the world's news media is taking place. The world's news agencies, a few newspapers and magazines, and both radio and television broadcasting are transcending the national states from which they arose. With this has come from the West a pervasive popular culture.

Such a transition will be welcomed by some as a contribution to better world understanding or resented by others as efforts by some nations to impose their models of mass communication and pop culture on everyone.

The technological capability for worldwide communication has never been greater, but then never have truly global problems and challenges seemed more urgent. Not enough people anywhere understand these problems or are in a position to cooperate with others in resolving them.

Serious questions can be posed about the quality and adequacy of today's system of global news communication, but no doubts exist about the importance to the world of the newspapers, news agencies, and broadcasters that report the world's news to itself. And yet, as we shall see, profound political and ideological differences separate the journalists and mass communicators who staff the world's news media.

CHAPTER 2

Changing Ideologies: Five Press Concepts

A journalist is a grumbler, a censurer, a giver of advice, a regent of sovereigns, a tutor of nations. Four hostile newspapers are more to be feared than a thousand bayonets.

—Napoleon

Abuses of the freedom of speech ought to be repressed, but to whom dare we commit the power of doing it?

—Benjamin Franklin

The impressive technological improvements in international news exchanges cannot give editors and broadcasters any real control over how news will be perceived as it emerges from the global news prism, whose planes and surfaces have been cut and polished by diverse and frequently antagonistic political and social systems. As the news passes through the prism, what one journalist considers to be truthful, objective reporting can bend into what another journalist elsewhere in the world considers to be distortion or propaganda.

Despite our impressive technological expertise, political differences and cultural conflicts prevent the international news process from working smoothly and harmoniously. More and faster news communication across national borders does not automatically lead to better understanding; often it results in enmity and distrust, since the profound cultural and social differences that characterize the world community preclude agreement on what is legitimate news. One person's truth is another person's propaganda and vice versa.

As a result, international journalism has often been the subject of rancor and mutual suspicion. Mass communication's powerful ability to publicize, to expose, to glorify, to criticize, to sensationalize, to denigrate, and to mislead or propagandize is universally recognized and often feared. At one time or another, government leaders in every land become unhappy or

15

dismayed with the press and often do something about it. In the West, a president or prime minister may complain bitterly that his or her programs are unfairly reported by press opponents and try to bring pressure to bear on the offending publication.

In an African country, an offending foreign correspondent may be thrown into jail or expelled from the country. In Iraq, Farzad Bazoft, an Iranian-born journalist with a British newspaper and carrying a British passport, was executed in Iraq after he investigated an explosion at a secret chemical plant. Under duress, and perhaps torture, Bazoft confessed to spying for Israel. The incident illustrated the often narrow line between espionage and journalism in Iraq, as elsewhere. Throughout the world today, journalists have become the victims of violence from those who do not want some particular information reported.

The differing perceptions about the nature and role of journalism and mass communication are rooted in divergent political systems and historical traditions and are broadly reflected in five political concepts of the press found in the world today: (1) Authoritarian, (2) Western, (3) Communist, (4) Revolutionary, and (5) Developmental.[1] These are normative concepts that reflect how the media ideally should perform under certain political conditions and social values. I believe that an understanding of these contrasting approaches to the role and function of transnational journalism can clarify some of the issues that divide the world's press.

Authoritarianism is the oldest and most pervasive concept and has spawned two twentieth-century modifications: the Communist and Developmental concepts. The Western concept, under which the press in Western democracies with market economies generally functions, represents a fundamental alternative to the Authoritarian concept and contains elements of both eighteenth-century political liberalism and twentieth-century views of Social Responsibility. The Revolutionary concept has one trait in common with the Western: they both try to operate outside of governmental controls. The Developmental concept is an emerging pattern associated with the new nations of the developing world, most of which lack adequate media resources.

Newspapers, television, and other mass media, always and everywhere, function within some kinds of governmental, societal, and economic constraints. Even the "freest" or most independent press system must deal with varying degrees of regulation by political authority. In the relationship between government and mass communication, the basic question is not whether government controls the press but the *nature* and *extent* of those controls. All press systems exist somewhere along a continuum from complete controls (absolute authoritarianism) at one end to no controls (pure libertarianism) on the other. Absolute freedom of expression is a myth. Beyond that, controls on the press are so varied and complex that it is difficult, if not impossible, to compare press freedom in one nation with that in another. In one country, newspapers may be under harsh, arbitrary political restraints; in another, they may be under more subtle, yet real, economic and corporate restrictions.

A basic tenet of the following analysis is that all press systems reflect the *values* of the political and economic systems of the nations within which they operate. The trend toward internationalization notwithstanding, print and broadcast systems are still controlled and regulated by their own national governments. And in this era of increasing transnational communication, journalists from an open society often must work and collect news abroad in a closed or autocratic society, thereby increasing opportunities for friction between divergent concepts.

Authoritarian Concept

Authoritarian political systems were the norm at the time the printing press was invented by Gutenberg in the mid-fifteenth century and, in the years since, more people have lived under an authoritarian press concept than under any other. The basic principle of authoritarianism is quite simple: the press is always subject to direct or implied control by the state or sovereign. A printing press (or, later, a broadcasting facility) cannot be used to challenge, criticize, or in any way undermine the sovereign. The press functions from the top down: the king or ruler decides what shall be published because truth (and information) is essentially a monopoly of those in authority.

There is much in Western political philosophy, developed over many centuries, that stresses the central importance of authority in political theory. From Plato's *Republic* through Hobbes's *Leviathan* to Hegel and Marx, the all-powerful state is given both the right and duty to sustain and protect itself in any way necessary for its survival.

To the authoritarian, diversity of views is wasteful and irresponsible, dissent is an annoying nuisance and often subversive, and consensus and standardization are logical and sensible goals for mass communication. There is a certain compelling logic behind this.

As that great eighteenth-century Englishman Dr. Samuel Johnson wrote,

Every society has a right to preserve public peace and order, and therefore has a good right to prohibit the propagation of opinions which have
a dangerous tendency. To say the magistrate has this right is using an inadequate word: it is the society for which the magistrate is the agent. He
may be morally and theologically wrong in restraining the propagation
of opinions which he thinks dangerous but he is politically right.[2]

To many in authority around the world today, these views are not un-
reasonable, certainly not to leaders of poverty-stricken developing nations
faced with monumental tasks of political integration and economic development. Why, under such circumstances, should government tolerate
what it considers disruptive and seditious views? Why should it permit foreign journalists to enter its country and then write critical and negative reports to the outside world, thus undermining the authority and prestige of
the ruling government?

Under traditional authoritarianism, the press operates outside of government and is permitted to gather and publish news, but it must function
for the "good of the state." The government usually leaves the press alone
as long as it does not criticize authority or challenge the leadership in any
way. If the press does attack authority, then the political authority inter-
venes, imposing censorship or even closing down publications and jailing
editors. Under the Authoritarian concept, the constraint of potential censorship, if not actual prior restraint itself, always exists. Editors and reporters exercise a good deal of self-censorship, but never know for sure just
how far they can go without triggering official disfavor and intervention.
They must support the status quo and neither advocate change, criticize
the nation's leadership, nor give offense to the dominant moral or political
values.

So wherever governments arbitrarily intervene and suppress independent newspapers and broadcasters, there the Authoritarian concept flourishes. For example, in November 1990, the Suharto government barred
from Indonesia a *New York Times* correspondent, Steven Erlanger, for a
published story about the business interests of Suharto's children and their
success in winning government contracts. The *International Herald Tribune,* which carried the story in Asia, was barred from circulating in Indonesia.[3] Yet again, in November 1994, the Indonesian government barred
foreign reporters from visiting East Timor after the largest antigovernment
demonstrations in years.[4]

In July 1995, the Singapore courts ordered the *International Herald
Tribune* to pay libel damages of $670,000 to the country's top three lead-

ers for a story that would have been mild political comment in the West.

The Authoritarian concept is alive and well today in other South Asian nations, especially Singapore, Malaysia, and Thailand. Singapore, despite its prosperity and economic ties to the West, has been unusually hostile to foreign publications, having restricted or banned distribution of the *Asian Wall Street Journal, Time, Asiaweek,* and *Far Eastern Economic Review* at various times.

Authoritarianism is widespread today, especially if, as some scholars aver, the Communist and Developmental concepts are understood to be variations of traditional authoritarianism.

Other nations recently under Authoritarian press controls include Algeria, China, Cuba, Nigeria, Belarus, Burma, Ethiopia, Syria, Turkey, and Iraq. Many so-called democratic nations, with political parties and elected presidents, are not in fact very democratic because rulers often act arbitrarily, dissidents and minorities lack legal rights, and local journalists operate under strict controls, including harassment, torture, and imprisonment. The Committee to Protect Journalists lists these leaders as among the 10 worst enemies of the press: China's President Jiang Zemin, Cuba's Fidel Castro, and Albania's President Sali Berisha.

Moreover, authoritarian practices cannot always be clearly delimited. Democracies in time of war or crisis (Britain during World War II, for example) sometimes adopt authoritarian controls on the press. And democratic France, under Charles de Gaulle and several of his successors, suffered under heavy-handed authoritarian control of its television system. In many nations, especially in Latin America, the media have moved back and forth between freedom and controls as the governments changed from military to democratic regimes and back again.

Foreign correspondents pose a special challenge to authoritarian regimes, and Western journalists often encounter a variety of difficulties: entry visas are denied; stories are censored; telephone and Comsat facilities are refused; and sometimes reporters are harassed, mistreated, jailed, or expelled.

Western Concept

The Western concept represents a distinct deviation from the traditional authoritarian controls and evolved during the rise of democracies in Europe and North America. During the long constitutional struggle in Britain among the crown, the courts, and the Commons and, later, in the

United States, a press relatively free of arbitrary government controls slowly evolved.

In fact, one definition of freedom of the press is the right of the press to report, comment on, and criticize its own government without retaliation or threat of retaliation from that government. This has been called the "right to talk politics." Historically, seditious libel meant criticism of government, laws, or officials. The absence of seditious libel as a crime has been regarded as the true pragmatic test of a country's freedom of expression, since politically relevant speech is what press freedom is mostly about.

By this demanding test—the right to talk politics—the Western concept is comparatively rare in today's world, although many authoritarian governments give it lip service. A free or independent press is usually found in only a dozen or more Western nations that share these characteristics: (1) a system of law that provides meaningful protection to individual civil liberties and property rights (here, common-law nations, such as the United States and Britain, seem to do better than nations, such as France or Italy, with civil law traditions); (2) high average levels of per capita income, education, and literacy; (3) governance by constitutional parliamentary democracy or at least with legitimate political oppositions; (4) sufficient capital or private enterprise to support media of news communication, that is, market economies; and (5) an established tradition of independent journalism.

Any list of nations meeting these criteria for a Western press today would certainly include the United States, the United Kingdom, Canada, Sweden, Germany, France, the Netherlands, Belgium, Australia, New Zealand, Norway, Denmark, Austria, Iceland, Ireland, Israel, Italy, and Switzerland. In addition to these Western nations, highly developed and westernized Japan surely should be added. And India, the world's largest democracy, has enjoyed a remarkably free press despite its diverse problems.

Journalists in many other nations support and practice the Western concept but, because of political instability, their media over the years have swung back and forth between freedom and control. Such nations, among others, include Spain, Greece, Portugal, Colombia, Brazil, Argentina, Chile, Turkey, and Venezuela, and happily, most are recently counted among the democracies.

By and large, the Western nations that meet the criteria include the handful that do most of the world's news gathering from other nations and whose correspondents most often come in conflict with authoritarian regimes, for the Western concept holds most strongly that a government—

any government, here or abroad—should not interfere in the process of collecting and disseminating news. The press, in theory, must be independent of authority and, of course, exist outside of government and be well protected by law and custom from arbitrary government interference. And so an independent press usually means one situated in a democratic, capitalist economy and enjoying the same autonomy as other private business enterprises.

The ideals of Western libertarian journalism are, to a large extent, a by-product of the Enlightenment and the liberal political tradition reflected in the writings of John Milton, John Locke, Thomas Jefferson, and John Stuart Mill. Primarily, there must be a diversity of views and news sources available—a "marketplace of ideas" from which the public can choose what it wishes to read and believe, for no one or no authority, spiritual or temporal, has a monopoly on truth. United States Judge Learned Hand expressed it well:

> That [newspaper] industry serves one of the most vital of all general interests: the dissemination of news from as many different sources, and with as many different facets as is possible. ... It presupposes that right conclusions are more likely to be gathered out of a multitude of tongues than through any kind of authoritarian selection. To many this is, and always will be, folly; but we have staked upon it our all.[5]

Underlying this diversity of views is the faith that citizens will somehow make the right choices about what to believe if enough voices are heard and government keeps its hands off.

In American Constitutional theory, this libertarian view is based upon certain values deemed inherent in a free press: (1) by gathering public information and scrutinizing government, the press makes self-government and democracy possible; (2) an unfettered press ensures that a diversity of views and news will be read and heard; (3) a system of free expression provides autonomy for individuals to lead free and productive lives; and (4) it enables an independent press to serve as a check on abuses of power by government.[6]

Carried over to the international context, the Western concept argues that there must be a free flow of information unimpeded by any intervention by any nation. ("Free flow," it is argued, does not necessarily mean a balanced or two-way flow of news, as desirable as that may be.) No government anywhere should obstruct the gathering and dissemination of legitimate news. Only news media free of official restraints will be credible to readers and viewers here and abroad.

Advocates say the Western concept serves the cause of global news flow in several important ways. Firstly, it makes possible the gathering and dissemination of reliable and accurate news.

Then, it provides news and important information to peoples living in authoritarian regimes that censor their own media. International short-wave radio broadcasters—BBC (British Broadcasting Corporation) World Service, Voice of America, Deutsche Welle, and others—relay news from Western news gatherers. During upheavals, people in non-Western nations often turn to shortwave radio to learn what is happening in their own country. (See Chapter 7, "Public Diplomacy and Propaganda.")

Furthermore, by serving as a "surrogate press" for peoples denied access to news, the Western media contribute to the promotion of human rights by publicizing the fate of political prisoners, including imprisoned journalists. Amnesty International has lauded this role of the international press in publicizing human-rights violations, whether in Argentina, China, Saudi Arabia, Turkey, or elsewhere, and believes that a political prisoner is more likely to survive and be released if his or her imprisonment is known to the outside world. Sometimes that news comes from local journalists courageous enough to defy their own authoritarian governments.

Western news media are not without their shortcomings. Critics charge that too many news media have become submerged into giant, entertainment-oriented conglomerates such as Time Warner, Disney, and Murdoch's News Corporation, all primarily concerned with turning a profit. And, to do so, Western media are accused of slighting serious news in favor of sensation, scandal, and the cult of celebrity. Furthermore, Western media certainly are not immune from pressures from their own governments. Political freedom does not preclude economic and corporate interference with journalistic practices. A privately owned media system will, in varying degrees, reflect the interests and concerns of its owners. Yet to stay independent of outside controls, including government, the publishers and broadcasters must be financially strong and profitable. Journalistic excellence and profitability are not identical goals, although some of the best news media are also very profitable; for some owners, however, making money is the primary purpose of journalism, and independence and public service mean little.

Then, too, diversity at both national and international levels appears to be in decline, and the marked increase of media conglomerates and ownership concentration has reduced the number of independent voices heard in the marketplace.[7]

In some democracies, such as Norway and Sweden, the government maintains diversity of political views by providing subsidies to the newspapers of the various political parties, a practice not without potential danger to press independence.

Some modifications of the Western concept fall under the rubric of Social Responsibility. This view holds that the media have clear obligations of public service that transcend moneymaking. Public service implies professional standards for journalists as well as reliable and objective reporting. The media are obligated, in addition, to ensure that all voices and views in the community are heard. Further, government is granted a limited role in intervening in media operations and in regulating conditions if public interests are not being adequately served. Government regulation of broadcasting in the United States, for example, in earlier years offered an example of the Social Responsibility position.

Two other related modifications are the Democratic Socialist concept and the Democratic Participant concept. Expressing fears concerning the abuses of private ownership, the Democratic Socialist says state action is needed to institute new forms of ownership and management and to intervene in the economics of the media.[8]

Similarly, Democratic Participant theory reflects a reaction against commercialization and monopolization of the privately owned media as well as against the centralism and bureaucratization of public broadcasting. Dennis McQuail summarized several of its principles: (1) media should exist primarily for their audiences and not for media organizations, professionals, or clients of media; (2) individual citizens and minority groups have rights of access to media (rights to communicate) and rights to be served by media according to the peoples' own determination of need; (3) organization and content of the media should not be subject to centralized political or state bureaucratic control; and, finally, (4) small-scale, interactive, and participative media forms are better than large-scale, professionalized media.[9]

These evolving views, which represent some disillusionment with mass-media performance, are found throughout Western democracies but especially in Northern Europe. The major disadvantage of these attitudes is that such decentralized, small-scale media are less able to check the abuses of government power, whether at home or abroad. But this debate illustrates a built-in advantage of the Western concept: it enjoys the freedom to criticize and reform its own media system through democratic processes—something lacking in the other concepts.

Finally, the Western press concept, with its emphasis on the individual's rights to send and receive information, is best suited as a conceptual framework for the new "personalized media"—computers with modems, faxes, interactive television, videocassettes, and the Internet—that are now playing a growing role in international communication. (See Chapter 4, "Comsats, Internet, and New Media.")

Rise and Fall of the Communist Concept

In some places in the world, the Western concept is regarded as a culture-bound by-product of industrialized capitalist nations and, as such, is irrelevant to the needs and problems of Socialist and developing nations. Furthermore, some consider it fallacious to judge the press of non-Western nations by Western standards.

For over 70 years, the Western concept of the press had been under direct challenge by advocates of the Communist press theory just as capitalism itself was under assault by Marxist/Leninist economic doctrines. Lenin had written that "'freedom of the press' of a bourgeois society consists in freedom of the rich systematically, unceasingly, and daily in the millions of copies to deceive, corrupt, and fool the exploited and oppressed mass of the people, the poor."[10]

Many intellectuals and writers were convinced that the Western liberal democracies and their press were outdated and doomed and that the USSR's Communism and its party-controlled media were the wave of the future. Even among its critics, the Leninist theory was seen as something new and different—certainly more positive and meaningful than the traditional Authoritarian concept that the world had long known.

Mass media controlled and directed by the Communist Party, Lenin argued, can concentrate on the serious task of nation building by publishing news relating to the entire society's policies and goals as determined by the top party leadership. To Lenin, the press was an integral part of the Communist Party, which was itself seen as a teacher to instruct the masses and lead the proletariat.

The basic postulates of the theory deriving from Marx and Engels with rules of application of Lenin were summarized by McQuail:

> Media should serve the interests of, and be in control of, the working class and should not be privately owned. Media should serve positive functions for society by socialization to desired norms, education, information, motivation, and mobilization. Within their overall task for soci-

ety, the media should respond to wishes and needs of their audiences. Society has a right to use censorship and other legal measures to prevent, or punish after the event, anti-societal publication. Media should provide a complete and objective view of society and the world according to Marxist-Leninist principles. Media should support progressive movements at home and abroad.[11]

Aside from normative theory, the characteristics of the Soviet press concept that set it apart from Western journalism were these: it was, first, a planned and completely government- and party-controlled system that permitted no competing private media. As Lenin said, there is no freedom for the enemies of socialism; his concept would avoid the abuses of the capitalist press. Second, this one-party press enjoyed a monopoly on news, both coming in and going out. Information was controlled by the state; the Party version of events was all that mattered. This condition lasted through the Stalin years, when foreign broadcasts were jammed and foreign publication barred at the borders.

Third, news itself was defined by "positive" information that furthers the goals of the Party, not information of direct interest or relevance to the lives of the Soviet people themselves. A plane crash or a nuclear accident was not news; a government farm report or a new tractor factory was.

Finally, the press, in concert with the Communist Party and secret police, was used to control the people as well as to promote government policies and prepare the public for future policy changes.[12]

The Communist media faithfully served the Party's ruling elite, but their fatal flaw was that they did not serve the interests of the people themselves. As the peoples under Communist regimes in Central and East Europe, deprived of political freedoms, saw their economies crumble and fall behind the West, they became increasingly disillusioned with their own mass media, which spoke only for authority and failed to criticize or report weaknesses in the ruling Communist elites. In the USSR, much of the same disillusionment existed, but it can be argued that some impetus for reform came from above as Gorbachev's *glasnost* policies led to media changes beginning in 1985, well before the upheaval of 1991.

Over time, the mass media in the USSR and Eastern bloc backed off from all of Lenin's journalistic precepts, just as Marx and Lenin have been repudiated on broader theoretical issues of political economy. Interestingly, the changes in Communist media practice were mainly in the direction of those followed by Western journalism.

The Communist press theory unraveled over a number of years. First came loss of faith in Leninist ideology: the slogans and buzzwords became increasingly empty and hollow. From the 1970s onward, Marxist press advocates no longer extolled the superiority of Communist theory and focused instead on criticizing Western media.

The *practices* of Communist mass communication, especially as a means of controlling and leading public opinion, continued with some modifications into the 1980s but without the old ideological fervor. In its final stages, the Communist media were reduced to playing a role similar to that of the secret police—another means of controlling the people.

Concurrently, Western mass communication kept intruding on the closed societies of the East and appears to have facilitated the demise of Communist regimes. Soviet media's monopoly on news began to crack early in the Cold War. BBC World Service, Voice of America, Radio Free Europe, and other Western broadcasters were widely heard. East Germans watched Western television beamed from West Berlin and the Federal Republic of Germany. Alternative and unofficial forms of publication flourished in the USSR, and the West learned a new word, *samizdat* ("self-publishing" in Russian).[13] Despite efforts to keep them out, Western rock music and videocassettes found their way into Communist cultures and became hugely successful. Rambo, the fictional anti-Communist avenger, became a folk hero with Russian video fans. Because of its stagnant economy and a long tradition of barring individual control over and access to communications, the Soviet Union was slow to join the information revolution.

The nuclear accident at Chernobyl in April 1986 signaled a change in the Soviet media's handling of a major "bad news" story. At first, the Soviet government made an extraordinary effort to deny any catastrophe had occurred and restricted information even while airborne radiation was detected in Scandinavia and Poland. This reflexive retreat into secrecy illustrated the Kremlin's traditional unwillingness to concede any failings before its people and the world. But abroad, the Kremlin was harshly criticized for failing to provide prompt information about the radioactivity spreading across Europe and for neglecting to warn its own citizens. Gradually, Soviet media were forced, by Western media coverage, to report details even though they were released weeks after the event.

The news void on Chernobyl was filled in part by Radio Free Europe and Radio Liberty, which provided breaking news to Communist bloc listeners. In such emergencies, Eastern Europeans were likely to turn to Western radio for information unavailable elsewhere. To obtain information by radio, Voice of America officials reported, people traveled out of the cities to rural areas where jamming was ineffective.

Finally, four years later, in April 1990, the Soviet Union finally acknowledged that the medical, environmental, and political consequences of the Chernobyl disaster had been much greater than the Kremlin had ever frankly discussed.[14]

As the Chernobyl disaster showed, the Communist media could not deal with foreign competition, something unforeseen in Lenin's closed-system press theory.

With Mikhail Gorbachev's proclamation of *glasnost* and *perestroika* in the mid-1980s, changes in media theory and practice accelerated.

A Soviet weekly, *Argumenti i Fakti,* with a circulation of over 20 million, published in 1989 the most detailed account of Stalin's victims yet presented to a Soviet mass audience, indicating that about 20 million Soviet citizens died in labor camps, forced collectivization, famine, and executions.

The same year in Warsaw, the first independently published daily newspaper in the Eastern bloc appeared: *Gazeta* supported the newly legalized Solidarity trade union. And, in East Germany, the Communist media turned on their former masters and behaved like Western investigative reporters. *Neues Deutschland,* the main Communist paper, *Berliner Zeitung,* and *Junge Welt* all published accusations of corruption and profiteering by high Communist officials under Erich Honecker. East German television, a week earlier a subservient tool of the Honecker regime, ran a series of 16 reports depicting the high living of the top Communists. These revelations scandalized the public and reinforced the outcry that forced the Honecker regime from power.

After 70-plus years of Leninist mass communication, the Soviet Union, in a period of five years, made these profound modifications in its news media: The Communist Party's monopoly on mass communication was broken up. The principle of diversity—news from diverse and competing sources—was recognized. Principles of press freedom were proclaimed, ending censorship and providing protection of law for journalists from government repression. Journalists and others were permitted to publish the "bad news" of Soviet society—crime and social problems, hidden historical crimes such as Stalin's purges, political and economic malfeasance, and man-made disasters such as Chernobyl and air crashes. The Western principle of free flow of information was recognized by ending both the jamming of foreign radio broadcasts and border censorship of publications, thus discarding the last remnants of the Iron Curtain. Restrictions and harassment of foreign journalists eased greatly as reporters enjoyed greater freedom to roam and report.

From East Berlin to Warsaw to Prague to Budapest to Moscow, the Communist theory of the press has been left in shambles, in effect, tossed in the much-utilized dustbin of history.

Recently, as Roger Cohen has reported, "Journalism has been reinvented in Eastern Europe as a craft involving independence and objectivity, but politicians remain uneasy and sometimes ruthless about the new press freedom. Through satellite dishes, cable systems and a wide range of publications, the people of the former East Bloc have access to a range of information and entertainment unthinkable under Communism."[15] This is not say that authoritarian or even totalitarian controls will not return from time to time to some of the news media of Central and Eastern Europe.

News processing has become faster with computers than with typewriters. In Prague, there are 15 dailies, not all of which may survive. Although media diversity has been established, various problems remain because of economic collapse, legislative confusion, and nationalist awakening. Much concern exists over the future of television, as always, a powerful political instrument. Despite efforts to end state television monopolies and open the way for private networks, governments hesitate to act.

In Moscow, the public has access to a wide range of print and electronic news sources. Through radio and television, Muscovites can listen to BBC World News, CNN (Cable News Network), Dan Rather on CBS (Columbia Broadcasting System), and ITN (Independent Television News) World News, as well as their own uncensored stations. In late 1994, Russians had their first chance to watch a real war within Russia as it happened on uncensored Russian television. The images of Russian soldiers fighting (and losing) battles with insurgents in Chechnya had a major impact on public opinion and created a real rift between Boris Yeltsin and the press.[16] Although many Russian media are free from government control, the lines between information and business interests are becoming increasingly obscure. Today, Russia's largest television stations and newspapers are owned by energy companies, large banks, and entrepreneurs with close ties to Boris Yeltsin. The concentration of power in the hands of a relative few, along with the ties of big money, big media, and government power, have raised questions about a possible threat to Russia's democracy.[17]

Revolutionary Concept

Lenin provided both some of the ideology and rationale for another and more ephemeral view: the Revolutionary. Simply stated, this is a concept of illegal and subversive communication using the press and broadcasting to overthrow a government or wrest control from alien or otherwise rejected rulers.

Lenin in his famous work *What Is to Be Done?* (written in exile before the 1917 Revolution) proposed that the revolutionaries establish a nationwide, legal newspaper inside czarist Russia. Such a paper could obviously not advocate revolutionary goals, but its distribution system could be an excellent mechanism for a political machine. The newspaper, Lenin postulated, would be a cover for a far-flung revolutionary organization and a means of communication among followers, a way to keep them in touch.

The early *Pravda,* although it was not a legal newspaper (and was edited by Stalin at one time), was published outside czarist Russia, and smuggled copies were widely distributed—a fine example of the Revolutionary concept.

The revolutionary press is a press of people who believe strongly that the government they live under does not serve their interests and should be overthrown. They believe they owe such a government no loyalty whatsoever. Pure examples are difficult to find, but one surely was the underground press in Nazi-occupied France during World War II. The editors and journalists of the *Editions Minuit* literally risked their lives to put out their papers and pamphlets. Many other publications called "underground newspapers," such as those that flourished in America during the antiwar protests in the late 1960s, were not truly revolutionary because they were generally tolerated by authorities and the risks of publishing were not great; some editors were harassed by local authorities, but none faced firing squads.

Better contemporary examples of the Revolutionary concept were the samizdat, the clandestinely typed and mimeographed copies of books, political tracts, and the like, that were passed at great risk from hand to hand among dissidents inside the Soviet Union. Often such publications are merely expressing grievances or petitioning for civil rights, but to authoritarian regimes such expression is clearly revolutionary and subversive.

The history of anticolonialist movements in what used to be called the Third World is replete with examples of the Revolutionary press concept. Throughout the British Empire, especially in West Africa, political dissidents published small newspapers, often handwritten, that first expressed grievances against the British rulers, then encouraged nationalism, and finally advocated political independence. Aspiring political leaders such as Azikiwe, Awolowo, Nkrumah, Kaunda, and Kenyatta were editors of these small political newspapers that informed and helped organize the budding political parties and nationalist movements.[18] British authorities were surprisingly tolerant, even though they disapproved of and sometimes acted against the publications and their editors.

Much in the Anglo-American tradition supported these newspapers, and the editors claimed the rights of British journalists. Had not Thomas Paine used political pamphlets to help run the British out of the American Colonies? Had not Thomas Jefferson (and his words were echoed later by Supreme Court Justice William O. Douglas) said the people have a right to revolution, including the right to subsequent revolutions if that proved necessary?

In the postindependence years, radio broadcasting has become a valuable tool of revolutionary groups seeking to overthrow the fragile governments of developing nations. Black Africa has been plagued with numerous coups d'état, and during times of acute political crisis, radio broadcasting has often played a significant role as the primary medium of mass communication in most nations. Rebels have recognized the importance of controlling information at the political center of power. Hence, insurgents often seize the radio station before heading for the presidential palace. Military struggles during a coup attempt frequently occur outside the broadcast station, because if rebels can announce over the nation's only radio station that a coup has been accomplished (even while the issue is still in doubt), it helps accomplish the desired end.[19]

More recently, two other communication devices—the photocopying machine and the audiocassette—have proved quite useful in revolutionary efforts. In Iran, the revolution of the Ayatollah Khomeini has been called the first cassette revolution. Thousands of cassette recordings of the Ayatollah's speeches propagating his revolutionary ideas were played in the mosques, which were not kept under surveillance by the Shah's secret police. These small, portable instruments were able to reach millions while circumventing the government-controlled press, radio, and television. At the same time, when revolutionary "night letters" and pamphlets arrived mysteriously at offices in Tehran, sympathetic secretaries made many photocopies, quickly and more secretly than possible with a printing press.

Anthony Sampson said that "the period of television and radio monopolies may prove a passing phase, as we find ourselves in a much more open field of communications, with cassettes and copied documents taking the place of the books and pamphlets that undermined 18th century governments." He suggested an epitaph for the Shah's regime: "He forgot the cassette."[20]

Even though television and radio stations—more controllable than the printing press—can give autocratic governments a monopoly of news and propaganda, the Revolutionary concept still can be fostered in divided societies by innovations in more personal and decentralized communication methods. The videocassette recorder (VCR), despite its cost, is spreading rapidly in societies with controlled media systems because it enables individual viewers to select their own television programs and not be passive recipients of officially sanctioned fare. This has created a worldwide market for illegally smuggled videocassettes, usually of movies and popular music from the West.

Personalized media, with their interactive capabilities, all present challenges to centralized autocracies trying to control news and information. These personalized media undoubtedly played a role in the overthrow of Communist regimes in Poland, Romania, and East Germany, as they did in the failed Chinese student uprising in Tiananmen Square in 1989.

The continuing struggle of Chinese dissidents for civil rights provides perhaps the best current example of the Revolutionary concept in action. That contest goes on with dissidents now using the Internet as well as other new media to advocate democratic change in China. (See Chapter 5, "Global Impact of Western News and Pop Culture," for more details.)

Developmental Concept

By its very nature, the Revolutionary concept is a short-term affair: the successful subversive use of mass communication to topple a despised regime is self-limiting. Once goals are achieved, the gains must be consolidated and then another concept takes over. In recent decades, a variation on the Authoritarian concept—the Developmental concept—has been emerging in the wake of political independence in impoverished nations throughout the developing world.

The Developmental concept is an amorphous and curious mixture of ideas, rhetoric, influences, and grievances. As yet, the concept is not clearly defined. Some aspects are straight from Lenin and the Communist concept of the press. Perhaps of greater importance are the influences of Western social scientists who have posited a major role for mass communication in the process of nation building in newly independent countries. American academics such as Wilbur Schramm, Daniel Lerner, and others, all libertarians at heart, have argued that the communication process is central to the achievement of national integration and economic development. In so doing, they may have unintentionally provided a rationale for autocratic press controls.

Other more radical academics, mostly Europeans, have echoed Marxist views and added a strong touch of anti-Americanism to the concept, for the concept is to some extent a critique of and reaction against the West and its transnational media. It also reflects the frustrations and anger of poor and media-deficient nations.

The Developmental concept is an approach to mass communication in nations that are clearly lacking in newspapers, broadcasting, and video facilities—the world's "have-nots" in media resources.

In general, the concept holds that

• All the instruments of mass communication—newspapers, radio, television, motion pictures, national news services—must be mobilized by the central government to aid in the great tasks of nation building: fighting illiteracy and poverty, building a political consciousness, assisting in economic development. Implicit here is the social responsibility view that the government must step in and provide adequate media service when the private sector is unable to do so, as is the case in many poor nations.

• The media therefore should support authority, not challenge it. Dissent or criticism has no place, in part because the alternative to the ruling government would be chaos, it is argued. Freedom of the press, then, can be restricted according to the development needs of the society.

• Information (or truth) thus becomes the property of the state: the flow of power (and truth) between the governors and the governed works from the top down as in traditional authoritarianism. Information or news is a scarce national resource; it must be utilized to further the national goals.

• Implied but not often articulated is the view that individual rights of expression and other civil liberties are somewhat irrelevant in the face of the overwhelming problems of poverty, disease, illiteracy, and ethnicity that face a majority of these nations. (Critics argue that the concept provides a palatable rationale for old-fashioned authoritarianism.)

• This concept of a guided press further implies that in international news each nation has a sovereign right to control both foreign journalists and the flow of news back and forth across its borders.

Some critics say that central to the Developmental concept is the rejection of the Western view. As British journalist Rosemary Righter wrote, there is a growing feeling that the Western model of the press is undesirable in itself. Instead of backing diversity and free flow, the mass media must adopt a didactic, even ideological, role of explaining to the people their part in forging a new social order.[21]

Western news media are attacked on several scores. To begin with, some critics say the Western international media are too monopolistic and powerful; they penetrate too widely and effectively. The world news organizations—AP (Associated Press), CNN, Reuters, BBC, and AFP (Agence France-Presse)—are particular targets, charged with creating a clear imbalance, a one-way flow, and a near monopoly of news that favors the affluent North.

Furthermore, Western media represent an alien viewpoint, which they impose on nations trying to build independent modern identities. Traditional cultures, it is charged, have been threatened by the inundation of news and mass culture—television programs, pop music, movies, videocassettes, and audiocassettes—principally from America and Britain. Such domination, it is argued, amounts to cultural aggression.

Finally, a few proponents of the Developmental concept charge that the Western media are part of an international conspiracy by which the economic and political interests of the capitalist nations are using global mass communication to dominate, even subjugate, the developing nations. Some advocates of this concept argue that the world needs a "new international information order" to redress these imbalances.

The Developmental concept is a view of mass communication from the many nations of the former Third World where most people are colored, poor, ill-nourished, and illiterate, and it reflects resentments against the West where people are mainly Caucasians (except in Japan), affluent, and literate. The concept is related as well to what some feel is the major problem facing the world today: the widening gap between the rich and the poor debt-ridden nations. The same nations that decry the trade and GNP (gross national product) imbalances between North and South also excoriate the Western news media.

In the continuing frictions between the Western and Developmental concepts, several qualifications are in order. Advocacy of a guided media system comes mainly from political leaders and government representatives. Some journalists support this, but many other journalists throughout the developing world—in India, Nigeria, the Philippines, Kenya, Pakistan, and other countries—advocate and try to practice, often under great difficulty, journalism that is independent of state control.

Some perceive the Developmental concept as only a temporary and transitional condition pending achievement of a more developed and participant society. In numerous countries where government-controlled media are advocated by unelected leaders, there are journalists, lawyers, and academics who support the values of independent journalism and the free flow of information. And, curiously, government spokespeople in many countries with government-controlled media insist their newspapers and broadcasting are much freer and open than they actually are.

By the mid-1990s, the Developmental concept appeared to be losing momentum among developing nations. Much of South America, including Brazil, Argentina, and Chile, moved from dictatorships to democracies during the 1980s. The same trend, with mixed results, occurred in Pakistan, the Philippines, South Korea, and Taiwan. In Africa, a clear trend toward multiparty government and privatization of state-run enterprises augured well for democracy for a time, but persistent poverty, political instability, and other problems seemed to blunt the trend.

The current global trends toward more democracy and market economies appear to have boosted the Western press concept, but the odds that many of the new democracies will succeed are not good.

At the same time, the Communist press concept appears to have disappeared as a viable press theory. Communist regimes persist in North Korea, Cuba, and the People's Republic of China, but the ideological fervor and justification seems to have waned; only police states remain.

China has jettisoned Marxist economic theory while holding onto centralized, totalitarian controls over its people. The resulting mix has been called *market Leninism,* which has produced a rapidly growing economy and seems to have something in common with the *corporate capitalism* or neo-authoritarianism of its Asian neighbors, South Korea, Taiwan, Singapore, and Malaysia.

By 1998, however, the economies of Indonesia, Thailand, South Korea, and Malaysia were in deep trouble due in part to government corruption, cronyism, and the lack of legal and fiscal controls. Government leaders in Malaysia and Indonesia blamed the foreign press for reporting the Asian nations' problems to the world and thus scaring off investors.

The controversies engendered by these conflicting concepts of mass communication have long been marked by rancor, but this, too, has shown some signs of abating. By the late-1990s, ideological conflict between press systems seems to have clearly subsided, if only temporarily.

Some would argue that in today's world only two viable concepts of the press remain: the Authoritarian concept that insists on its right to control news and information and restrict its circulation, and the Western concept that argues that news and information, like knowledge itself, belong to all people and that journalists have the right to pursue and report news wherever it can be found.

Yet there remain valid arguments on all sides of these political and ideological confrontations, each reflecting differing social, political, and cultural traditions that are difficult to reconcile. But, as the international news system becomes more integrated and interdependent, the conflicts over how news and information are to be controlled may become reconciled.

Although few if any nations fit neatly into any of these five normative concepts of the press, the concepts are still useful in illustrating some of the divergent perceptions of the nature of news and how it should be disseminated. But the problems surrounding the gathering and delivery of international news are more complex and varied than can be neatly categorized to fit into set classifications.

And, despite the variety of news and views refracted through the world news prism, the great bulk of foreign news is gathered and disseminated by Western news media. Since 1989 and the fall of communism, two clear trends have emerged: the triumph of the Western concept of the press and the reality that many, many more millions of people, mostly in the Eurasian landmass, have joined the vast world audience of international communication.

CHAPTER 3

International News System

What we are building now is the nervous system of mankind, which will link together the whole human race, for better or worse, in a unity which no earlier age could have imagined.

—Arthur C. Clarke

Millions of Americans were sitting down on January 16, 1991, to watch the evening news on television. The official time was 6:30 p.m. EST, but for television it was "real time" as the anchors interrupted the prepared newscast to announce that correspondents in Baghdad were reporting that an aerial bombardment was occurring. Soon eyewitness reports of antiaircraft fire and bomb explosions were coming in as network reporters in Baghdad described the beginning of the Gulf War—as it was happening. The "prime time" opening of the war attracted the largest television audience in American history—78.8 percent of the people in homes with televisions were watching what one critic later called the "most exciting television evening ever." CNN had the best coverage and so was the center of much of the viewing as it moved up with ABC (American Broadcasting Co.), CBS, and NBC (National Broadcasting Co.) as a major player in television news. (Although only received on cable in the United States, CNN had a bigger audience that evening than CBS, and CNN abroad was received in over 100 countries.)

Thus, television's first "real time" war had dramatically begun, and soon reports on every aspect of the conflict flooded newsrooms and broadcast stations around the world. (See Chapter 9, "Reporting Today's Wars," for more details.)

This story, like most major news stories, was essentially reported by journalists working for the news organizations of Western nations for, to Americans, Western Europeans, the Japanese, and some others, news—like electricity, water, and gas—has become an essential service that is taken for granted. By merely turning on a radio or television set or picking up a newspaper at the door, we expect to find the latest news, whether it be from the Middle East, Europe, Africa, or wherever. (Such is not the case, however, in most nonindustrialized nations.)

Indeed, most people cannot remember when important breaking news was not available immediately (like any other public utility) at the flick of a switch; the technicalities of news delivery are of little public concern and at best only dimly understood. The fact is, however, that global news communication is of fairly recent origin. The far-flung apparatus or "system" through which news flows around the world has evolved and expanded greatly since World War II, along with our modern information society. We learned, for example, about the important battles of World War II many hours or often several days *after* the events—and then through radio or newspapers; about 30 years later, the day's clashes in Vietnam were brought to us in full color on our home television screens at dinnertime, sometimes on the same day they occurred.

Naturally, the public's perceptions of a war have always been colored by the way journalists have reported them, but color television pictures of Vietnam, including U.S. dead and wounded, had an unusually strong impact on public attitudes. And today, as with a terrorist incident, a national election, or a regional conflict in Bosnia or Kosovo, the public follows many dramatic news events *while* they are taking place.

In this century, and particularly since 1945, an intricate web of international communications has been spun about the planet, greatly expanding the capability for news and political interaction at a time when the need for information has become so much more urgent. This rapid growth of what Colin Cherry termed an "explosion" in mass communication around the world has had widespread significance—for international relations and world politics; for the flow of news and information; for the cultural impact abroad of motion pictures, television, and video from the West; and for the institutions of international communication: news agencies, broadcast networks, and international newspapers, magazines, and other publications. Further, today the world reacts politically much more quickly and perhaps emotionally to events than ever before.

As we become, in various ways, a more interdependent world community with common problems, if not common values and goals, the world's ability to communicate effectively with all its parts has been greatly expanded. We now have a global economy, and we are trying to develop institutions to deal with it. That requires reliable news and adequate communications.

This communication explosion has three broad dimensions: *geographically,* vast areas of Africa, South and East Asia, and Latin America have been drawn into the global communication network for the first time; the *amount* of traffic and the *number* of messages carried in the system have multiplied geometrically; and the *technical complexity* of both the new hardware and the skills and specialized knowledge to maintain and run the network has become increasingly sophisticated.

"For two thousand years and more the means of distant communications were various postal services, derived from the Roman *cursus publicus,* working at the speed of the horse (up to and including the Pony Express); and then the explosion hit us, not immediately upon the invention of the telegraph, but nearly a century later," Cherry wrote. "It is the sheer suddenness of the explosion which is of such profound social importance, principally following the Second World War."[1]

From crystal sets in 1920 to a television service in 1937, as Cherry pointed out, was only 17 years. The first transistor appeared in 1948, and electronic memory chips, the silicon brains of microcomputers, came soon after that. The first *Sputnik* went up in 1957, and only nine years later *Early Bird,* the first generation of the global INTELSAT system of communication satellites went into operation in 1965 and brought television pictures from Europe. Just 25 years later, INTELSAT VI was in the heavens and, compared with *Early Bird,* had 55 times more power and a total communications capacity that had increased 170 times. Comparing the communications capacity of *Early Bird* INTELSAT I to INTELSAT VI, a major carrier of international news, is like comparing the height of a toolshed with the World Trade Center in New York City.[2]

International News System

The expanded international news system is largely an outgrowth of Western news media, especially those of Britain, the United States, and, to a lesser degree, France and Germany. A world news system exists today because the peoples of Western democracies wanted world news, and the great independent newspapers, newsmagazines, news agencies, and, later, broadcast organizations have cooperated and competed to satisfy those wants and needs. Editors and correspondents, working for independent (that is to say, nongovernmental) and profit-making news organizations, have developed the traditions and patterns of providing the almost instantaneous world news upon which people everywhere have come to rely. The credibility and legitimacy that such news generally enjoys rests on its usually unofficial and independently gathered nature as well as its informational or generally objective content. The enduring ethic of Western journalism was summed up over 100 years ago by an editor of the *Times* of London:

> The first duty of the press is to obtain the earliest and most correct intelligence of the events of the time, and instantly, by disclosing them, to make them the common property of the nation. The duty of the journalist is to present to his readers not such things as statecraft would wish them to know but the truth as near as he can attain it.

That nineteenth-century statement represents a journalistic ideal; actual practice is often much different. Some transnational media have close, compromising ties to their governments, and all independent media are subject to varying kinds of controls and influences from the corporate interests that own them. Nonetheless, the news media of Western nations have more freedom and independence to report world news, and hence more credibility, than media of other nations. And because of greater financial resources and technology, Western media have greater *capability* to report world news.

Some newspaper and broadcasting organizations use their own correspondents to report foreign news, but the global workhorses and the linchpins of the world news system have long been the so-called world news services—AP, UPI (United Press International), Reuters, AFP, and TASS, which are in effect "newspapers for newspapers." It is no coincidence that they come from the United States, Britain, France, and the former Soviet Union. [With the breakup of the USSR, TASS, now Information Telegraph Agency of Russia (ITAR)-TASS, has slipped considerably in importance.] In a general sense, great powers have been great news powers. Today, however, the continued importance of France and Britain in world news may be due more to relationships developed during their imperial pasts than their geopolitical importance today.

What made these five organizations *world* agencies is their capability to report news from almost anywhere to almost anywhere else. Although they are sometimes perceived as dominating world news flow, the Western agencies are definitely not in an economic class with such powerful multinational corporations as Mitsubishi, Exxon, or Shell. UPI, for example, has been in a shaky financial condition for two decades and has been teetering on the edge of collapse, its operations drastically cut back. AFP has been losing money for years and depends on subsidies from the French government. Reuters is a major news service yet is only a part of a successful larger organization that specializes in business and financial information. The Associated Press, with over 15,000 subscribers in 112 countries, was in a sound and dominant position. Yet, with an annual budget of around $300 million, AP was small potatoes indeed compared with the scope of the giant oil companies such as Exxon, which reported $4 billion in profits for a single year.

News organizations in two great economic powers, Deutsche Press Agentur (dpa) in Germany and Kyodo News Service in Japan are approaching world-agency status. Other second-tier agencies are ANSA in Italy, efe in Spain, Tanjug in the former Yugoslavia, and Mena in Egypt.

Several news services attempt to compete with, or at least supplement, the world agencies. Inter Press Service (IPS) has a near global capacity and emphasizes news about the developing world, as do Depthnews, Gemini, and South-North News. Pan African News Agency (PANA) serves Africa; in addition are Caribbean News Agency (CANA) and the pool of News Agencies of Non-Aligned Countries. These alternative services are useful in themselves and form part of the international network of support for the world news system that is provided by the estimated 120 regional and national news agencies that have emerged since World War II, especially in the former Third World. The United Nations Educational, Scientific, and Cultural Organization (UNESCO) reports that national agencies in 90 sovereign countries provide their nations' newspapers and radio and television stations with domestic and foreign news. In 50 countries, the state directly controls or operates these agencies; in the 40 others, one or more of the organizations are cooperatively financed and operated by newspapers or public corporations. The quality and professionalism of these news agencies differ greatly. Many are merely government information offices and do little real news gathering. Most subscribe to or have exchange agreements with one or more of the world agencies and are often the only channels within their countries that receive foreign news from the world agencies and which, in turn, distribute that national agency's domestic news abroad. Thus, by exchanging their news with world services, the small national agencies help extend the reach of the world news system.

The national agencies become a vital link then, especially in the developing nations, between the major world agencies and the "retail" newspapers, broadcast stations, and other recipients of the reports of AP, Reuters, and AFP. The world services sell their reports to the national agencies, which in turn distribute the news reports to local media that otherwise might not receive them. Finally, the national agencies stand as key gatekeepers (and potential censors) deciding which news can and cannot be distributed to the local media within their own nations.

The dominant institution in the world news system is Associated Press, a cooperative owned mainly by American newspapers. Reuters competes with AP, often effectively, in certain areas such as Africa or the Middle East, but does not match its comprehensiveness and financial resources.

Some of the great newspapers of the world—the *Times, Daily Telegraph, Financial Times,* the *Independent,* and the *Guardian* of London; *Le Monde* of France; *Frankfurter Allgemeine* of Germany; *Neue Zürcher Zeitung* of Switzerland; *Asahi* of Japan; *New York Times, Washington Post, Los Angeles Times, Wall Street Journal,* and others in the United States—maintain their own correspondents abroad, as do the extensive broadcasting systems—BBC, CBS, NBC, ABC, CNN, and others—and the leading newsmagazines—*Time, Newsweek,* the *Economist, L'Express,* and *Der Spiegel,* among others.

Several newspapers, such as the *New York Times, Washington Post,* and *Los Angeles Times,* and the *Guardian* of London, syndicate their news and sell it to other newspapers at home and abroad. As a result, their news stories and features supplement as well as compete with the world news agencies. It is well to remember that once a news event is reported—the death of a king or a major earthquake—it becomes the common property of journalism and can be repeated anywhere; only the precise wording of a news story can be copyrighted, and this rarely becomes a factor in news flow.

With the growing importance of broadcast media, people receive more and more of their news from electronic sources, especially television. As a result, two television news services, Reuters TV (formerly Visnews) and Worldwide Television News (WTN), as well as the great Western networks, have been playing an increasingly important role in the international news system. Live feeds from another continent are usually identifiable as the work of the network involved, but the source of the news on tape or film is not as evident. Most viewers are unaware that much of the foreign news viewed on television is supplied by two television news agencies dominated by American and British interests.

Reuters TV, the biggest and best known, is the world's leading supplier of international news actuality material for television, servicing more than 409 customers in 83 countries, and is distributed by both satellites and airmailed videocassettes. Reuters TV says it reaches 1.5 billion people daily. In 1992, Reuters bought out its co-owners, NBC and BBC, and changed its name from Visnews. Reuters TV staffs 38 bureaus and works with contract crews in about 70 countries.[3]

The Avis of these services is WTN, also located in London, which remains a center and clearinghouse for international news exchanges. WTN is 80 percent owned by ABC and cooperates with ABC and CNN in distributing video news. WTN has 15 overseas bureaus and contracts with film crews in about 70 countries.

Both services also have exchange agreements with the U.S. networks, ABC, CBS, NBC, and CNN, all of which maintain several bureaus overseas. The U.S. networks sell some of their news products abroad and thus contribute to the interchange that makes the international news system work.[4]

Eurovision, the regional television exchange system in Western Europe, gets about 40 to 50 percent of its material from Reuters Television and WTN. The majority of television systems around the world depend on these two services for all of their world news on television. In numerous small African nations, often a lone television service depends on a five-minute package of world news from Reuters TV for its evening news show.

The broadcasting services are tied in to the world news agencies and, there, AP's major role is undisputed. By the agency's count, more than a billion people have daily access to AP news. To collect foreign news abroad, AP maintains bureaus in 67 countries manned by 617 full-time foreign correspondents.[5] Like other world agencies, AP uses an extensive network of leased satellite circuits, submarine cables, and radio transmissions to supply newspapers and broadcasters with up-to-the-minute information on developments around the world 24 hours a day. AP Broadcast Services are used by 6,000 radio and television stations. As a result, newspapers and broadcasters, whether in Singapore, Buenos Aires, Johannesburg, or New Delhi, can receive news bulletins simultaneously, regardless of how distant the news being reported. Three key centers—New York City, London, and Tokyo—channel the millions of words and pictures transmitted daily to its many foreign subscribers. On a given day in AP's New York bureau, some 182,000 words flow in—stories, financial reports and tables, messages, other traffic—to the foreign desk, which produces 50,000 words for U.S. newspapers and other subscribers. About 87,000 words emanate from Europe, the Mideast, and Africa; another 59,000 come from Asia, and 36,000 words are filed from Latin America.[6] Without its full and free access to the news and photos of all members of the cooperative, AP would have to expend much more than the $300 million it spent in 1989 for news gathering, which was far more than any competitor.

It has been said with some but not much exaggeration that an American's right to know is the world's right to know. For any news story that gets into the American news media can and often does flow rapidly around the world and can appear in local media anywhere if it gets by the various gatekeepers that select and reject the news of the day. Stories about civil war in Chechnya, riots in Algeria, a summit meeting in Geneva, a hurricane in Florida, or any other report prepared for the U.S. news media can and often will be read or viewed or listened to in Africa, Asia, or Latin America. The same, of course, can be said for a story appearing first in London, Paris, or Bonn.

The domination of international news by AP and other Western news organizations is often resented in other nations. The poorer nations particularly are dependent on the Western agencies and media to find out about themselves and their neighbors, and they criticize what they consider a one-way news flow from North to South, from the rich to the poor. They resent the fact that Western journalists with Western values set the agenda for the world's news.

Without question, there is a basis to some complaints about this Western-dominated system. But the West does not enjoy a closed monopoly of world news; any news organization is free to report world news, but few have the capability and credibility for so doing. Moreover, far-ranging and technically sophisticated as it is, the world's present news system is not as pervasive and efficient as it might be, considering the world's diversity and its need for information. Western journalists do an imperfect job, and most operate under a variety of constraints, which are discussed later. But it is the only operational news system the world has, as Martin Woollacott, the *Guardian*'s chief correspondent in Asia, pointed out:

> For all its defects, the Western foreign press corps is all that the world has got in the way of an efficient international news gathering organization. Even in Western terms, it is a curiously unrepresentative affair, dominated as it is by the big American and British news agencies, newspapers, magazines, and broadcasting organizations. The French are in it, but are a poor second. After them trail the other Western European countries, with the Japanese foreign press, in spite of the manpower it deploys, on the periphery. This organization, whose oddities are a product of history, is, however, the only existing means of maintaining a flow of reasonably reliable information between countries. The news establishments of the Communist countries hardly offer a feasible alternative. And the occasional efforts of Asian and African countries to set up their own systems of international news gathering have all been failures. Their papers cannot afford foreign correspondents, and the few projects for Asian and

African news agencies have collapsed for lack of money, expertise, and customers.[7]

Though written in 1976, Wollacott's words regrettably are still largely true today.

Brief History of News Distribution

The history of today's international system of news distribution is essentially the story of the world news agencies and their utilization of technological innovations. As the telegraph, cable, teletype, wireless (later radio), and communication satellites became operational, the news agencies or "wire services" (as they were once called) employed each new device to transmit more and more news ever more quickly from capital to capital.

Modern transnational information exchange probably had its beginnings with manuscript newsletters containing political and economic information that were circulated in the late Middle Ages between the various branches of large trading companies. The sixteenth-century newsletters of the house of Fugger of Augsburg, Germany, were particularly well known and were read by selected outsiders involved in trade, shipping, or commerce.

The contemporary news agencies, however, evolved in nineteenth-century Europe and America. In 1835, Charles Havas, a young Frenchman of Portuguese birth, organized a service with correspondents around Europe to collect news of interest to businessmen, financiers, and diplomats. Employing semaphore signals and carrier pigeons, Havas got the news to his clients more rapidly than the usual post or special courier. Several years later, newspapers began taking advantage of the faster Havas service.

Competitors soon followed. In 1848, Bernard Wolff, a former Havas man, set up a joint news service between German and northern European papers; this later became the Wolff News Agency. Still another former Havas employee, Paul Julius Reuter, a German, established a pigeon post system to deliver the final stock prices between Brussels and Aachen, then the only gap in a telegraph system uniting the commercial centers of Berlin and Paris. After the completed telegraph link rendered this pigeon communication system obsolete, Reuter recognized that he had to be at one terminus of a cable or telegraph in order to survive. Since the Germans already controlled one end and the French the other, Reuter moved to London; when the cross-channel cable link reached the British capital in 1851, he was there to exploit it. Reuter's Telegraph Company became known as Reuters.

Reuters' slogan directive to "follow the cable," which was the practice of other news agencies as well, epitomized the utilization of the world's increasing capacity in telecommunications. Reuters grew with and survived the British Empire, which controlled the underseas cables.

Reuters today is a serious competitor to the Associated Press and is the only strictly international news agency since it covers Britain like any other country and most London papers rely on the domestic Press Association for British news. Reuters maintains 968 correspondents in 74 countries and serves 29,310 subscribers in 131 countries. It says it produces 1.5 million words a day. In addition, Reuters is the largest supplier of financial information anywhere.[8]

Agence Havas of France became the dominant news service outside the British Empire—in France, Switzerland, Italy, Spain, Portugal, Egypt (with Reuters), and Central and South America. Following the fall of France in 1940, Agence Havas was dissolved. It was reborn in 1944 as Agence France-Presse but required subsidies from the French government to survive financially. In 1957, AFP became autonomous under a controlling board that included eight directors from French newspapers, although its ties with the French government have remained close. Currently, AFP has about 550 full-time correspondents in 150 countries, distributing news in French, English, Spanish, German, Arabic, and Portuguese.[9] Although the French government has a minority say in the running of the company, it plays a major role in its financing as the customer for some 55 percent of the agency's subscriptions, for use in various embassies and government offices in France and other francophone nations, mostly in Africa. For years the agency has been losing money and falling behind the other "Anglo-Saxon" agencies in opening new markets.[10]

The three nineteenth-century European services were all profit-making organizations, selling their news to any newspaper willing to buy. American newspapers, finding foreign news expensive to collect, decided to cooperate rather than compete. In 1848, the leading New York papers formed the New York Associated Press to share the costs of obtaining foreign news transmitted on the newly perfected telegraph from Boston. During the remainder of the century, other regional cooperatives were formed (and some dissolved) until 1900, when the system was reorganized and incorporated in New York as the Associated Press.

Because AP members denied their service to competing papers, rival agencies were established. In 1907, newspaper publisher E.W. Scripps organized the United Press Association to compete with AP, and William Randolph Hearst formed International News Service in 1909 to supply his own newspapers. UP bought out INS in 1958 and, in the mid-1980s, United Press International claimed 6,972 customers in 100 countries. Since 1986, UPI has been through three owners, two bankruptcies, and one court-ordered liquidation. In March 1997, the latest owner, the Middle East Broadcasting Co., based in London and with ties to the Saudi royal family, was then concentrating on clients wanting short articles and news summaries. UPI is still far from profitable and no longer effectively competes with AP or Reuters.

Atypical among the big five global agencies was TASS, long an integral part of the Soviet Union's government. With the breakup of the Communist media in 1989, however, it had the chance to be more independent and competitive and, in 1992, announced that it would change its name to Information Telegraph Agency of Russia, sending stories carrying the logo of ITAR-TASS. Established in 1918 under the name ROSTA, TASS actively supported official Soviet policies, but operated on a worldwide basis, often supplying its service at little or no cost to media in some countries. In 1989, it claimed 4,000 subscribers in the Soviet Union and more than 1,000 in 115 countries abroad. Few papers outside the Communist orbit relied on it completely, though TASS provided useful information and maintained exchange agreements with Western agencies. With the breakup of the USSR, ITAR-TASS is unlikely to play a significant role as a world agency. In addition, it must now compete with Interfax, an unofficial news agency in Russia.

Historically, these five agencies flowered because of an extensive root system of telegraph lines and submarine cables. Reuters' early dominance grew out of its accessibility to the cables linking the British Empire. The cable press rate was established at about a penny a word between points in the empire, and this markedly affected what news flowed where around the world. Wireless and shortwave radio started to weaken the importance of the cable, a process that was completed with the development of the INTELSAT communication satellite system, which can deliver the news (as well as telephone calls, television pictures, financial data, airline reservations, etc.) anywhere in the world. As noted, carrying capacity of the INTELSAT system has increased exponentially since then.

News, whether by communication satellite or carrier pigeon, is highly perishable and often only of local concern, but if interest in a particular story is wide enough, the story will move at incredible speed to numerous points in the world, providing there are no political or technological barriers to its transmission and reception. And it is the communication satellites (Comsats) that have made the same-day or at times instantaneous reporting of international events on the evening television news show so compelling and yet so commonplace.

CNN and Global Television News

The successful establishment of the 24-hour Cable News Network has been a major innovation in international news. Ted Turner, the Atlanta, Georgia, broadcaster, started the around-the-clock news service to attract viewers to cable television and to compete in news with the three major U.S. networks. Started in 1980, its growth and success have been impressive. CNN is seen in more than 140 countries and has viewers in more than 200. It has two 24-hour-daily news channels, a Spanish-language service (two 30-minute newscasts daily), as well as CNN International, the worldwide channel put together from the two domestic services plus other programming. CNN and its companion cable service, Headline News, have an estimated value of $1.5 billion. CNN employs 1,800 staffers in nine domestic and 19 overseas bureaus, all feeding their reports through Atlanta to CNN's widening global audience.[11]

While CBS, NBC, and ABC were cutting back on overseas operations, CNN was opening new bureaus in such places as Nairobi, New Delhi, Frankfurt, Paris, and Beijing—at a cost of about $600,000 to open and staff each additional office overseas.[12] But it has been in international news, especially during times of crisis, that CNN has found its global niche. When a major crisis breaks out overseas, ABC, CBS, and NBC will issue news bulletins and then go back to scheduled programming and perhaps do a late-evening wrap-up, but CNN stays on the air for long stretches of time, continually updating the story. The networks' version of the story will be seen in the United States; CNN's version will be seen all over the world.

Overseas, travelers often can watch CNN in their hotel rooms, foreign television services pick up the whole service or some news programs from CNN, and individual television viewers get it off their satellite dishes or subscribe to the service locally.

During prolonged crises, such as the Gulf War and its aftermath, CNN played a key role with its extensive coverage of all facets of the story. Indeed, CNN's international position often makes it a player in diplomacy as well as a reporter of major events. With its reports available in all world capitals, political leaders and diplomats watch closely and are willingly interviewed on CNN in order to get their views widely known. (CNN recognizes its near-diplomatic status, and reporters are aware of the danger of being manipulated by their interviewees, whether they be Saddam Hussein or Bill Clinton.)

Recently, CNN has not been without its problems and its critics. When there is not an international crisis, viewership of CNN drops off sharply and recently revenues from advertising have declined as well.

As the Gulf War ended, nearly 11 million of CNN viewers had switched back to the big three networks and CNN's audience was reportedly down to about normal, which is 600,000 households.[13] During the O.J. Simpson trial, CNN audiences soared when it provided gavel-to-gavel coverage, often to the neglect of foreign news coverage.

By July 1997, CNN's coverage of Senate hearings on campaign financing abuses attracted fewer than 300,000 viewers. Ten years earlier, CNN drew triple that audience for Oliver North's testimony to the Senate.

It can be argued that CNN is primarily a technological innovation in international news by reason of its ability to interconnect so many video sources, newsrooms, and foreign ministries to so many television sets in so many remote places in the world. In this regard, CNN has undoubtedly had a major impact on diplomacy. But as journalism, CNN leaves much to be desired. Tom Rosenstiel said, "In certain respects, it has had a pernicious effect on the rest of journalism: it has accelerated the loss of control news organizations have over content, which in turn has bred a rush to sensationalism and an emphasis on punditry and interpretation at the expense of old fashioned reporting."[14]

Nonetheless, a television news channel of true global reach was an innovation whose time had come and, as proof of that, CNN now has international competition. In 1991, the BBC began its own World Service Television (WST) and has been expanding it rapidly. In 1994, BBC announced plans to create news and entertainment channels in Europe, Asia, and the United States. With a British partner, Pearson P.L.C., BBC will invest $45 million in two satellite-delivered channels in Europe.

CNN, as an around-the-clock cable news channel, was also feeling more competition from NBC's MSNBC channel, owned jointly with Bill Gates' Microsoft, and from Murdoch's Fox News Channel. CBS was also reportedly trying to get into cable news but has lagged behind. Both in the domestic as well as international areas, there were questions about how many 24-hour TV news channels could survive.

Both Rupert Murdoch and NBC's Jack Welch have had their sights on global networks similar to CNN International and BBC World. Some experts argue that in normal times the overwhelming interests of audiences everywhere are not about global news per se but, in a more focused way, about their own region and locality. Yet when the next major world crisis erupts, as one surely will, global television news will take center stage once again by reporting, explaining, and influencing the world's response to great events.

The success of CNN and the establishment of WST illustrates the ways that media technology can shape the contours and impact of international news—and will continue to do so. Further, with the merger of Turner Broadcasting with Time Warner in September 1995, the future financial support of CNN seems assured.

With the greatly enhanced technological reach of international communication, the location of a sender or receiver is no longer as important as it once was. The key gatekeepers of the world news system are still concentrated in New York City, London, Paris, and similar metropolitan centers, but it is not necessary to be in those cities to follow the news of the world. A shortwave radio or a satellite dish and now a computer with Internet connections can keep a person almost anywhere in touch with the day's principal events. Furthermore, distance has become increasingly less a factor in the cost of long-distance news communication, whether it be private telephone, computer or fax messages, television reception, or news reports bounced off satellites. Essentially the same technological process (and at the same cost) is required to send a news flash via satellite from London to Paris as from London to Tokyo. And the greater the traffic on the system, the less is the unit cost of messages sent. International communication is tied to computer technology, and in that explosive field the costs of computers are dropping as rapidly as their efficiency is increasing. In addition, the capacity of communication satellites to carry information is expanding.

Note of Caution: Cracks in Conduits

If technology is the good news, then performance in recent years is the bad news. In earlier years, the American "national media"—particularly the *New York Times, Washington Post, Los Angeles Times, Wall Street Journal,* CBS, NBC, ABC, *Time,* and *Newsweek*—which set the news agenda for other media, did much of the gathering of news from abroad with the help of news agencies.

But that situation has changed. The television networks and the news-magazines give much less attention to serious foreign news than during the Cold War years. One indicator: in its heyday, CBS maintained 24 foreign bureaus; by 1995, it had reporters in only four capitals—London, Moscow, Tel Aviv, and Tokyo. Dan Rather admitted to Harvard students, "Don't kid yourself, the trend line in American journalism is away from, not toward, increased foreign coverage."[15]

Max Frankel, former editor of the *New York Times,* wrote, "A great shroud has been drawn across the mind of America to make it forget that there is a world beyond its borders. The three main television networks obsessively focus their cameras on domestic tales and dramas as if the end of the Cold War rendered the rest of the planet irrelevant. Their news staffs occasionally visit some massacre, famine or shipwreck and their anchors may parachute into Haiti or Kuwait for a photo op, but these spasms of interest only emphasize the networks' apparent belief that on most evenings the five billion folks out there don't matter one whit."[16]

Foreign news is expensive to gather and often not of interest unless American lives—as soldiers or terrorism victims—are at stake. Instead, network television and the newsmagazines throw their resources and considerable talents into high-profile stories of scandal, celebrity, and sensation, such as stories of White House sex scandals, the violent death of Princess Diana, and the O.J. Simpson trial.

The covers of *Time, Newsweek,* and *U.S. News and World Report* reflect the declining interest in global news. By late September 1996, *Time* had run five covers that year on international topics, versus 11 in 1995. *Newsweek* featured four international covers by September, compared with 11 in 1995. *U.S. News* published no international covers by late 1996, but ran six in 1995.

The trend is a continuing one. Throughout 1995, *Time* devoted 385 pages, or 14 percent of the magazine, to international news. *Newsweek* used 388 pages, or 12 percent of its coverage, and *U.S. News* had 386 pages of foreign news, or 14 percent. For all three magazines, this was a significant decline from 10 years earlier. In 1985, *Time* had run 670 pages, or 24 percent, of foreign news; *Newsweek* had 590 pages, or 22 percent; and *U.S. News* 588 pages, or 22 percent.[17]

However, a few major daily papers still report the world. The best and most comprehensive foreign reporting, some of very high quality, comes from just seven daily newspaper groups, those owning the *New York Times, Washington Post, Los Angeles Times, Wall Street Journal, Chicago Tribune, Christian Science Monitor,* and *Baltimore Sun,* all of which maintain overseas news bureaus. These papers, whose total daily circulation is about 11 million, represent only about 20 percent of newspaper circulation of all U.S. dailies. This small group plus AP and Reuters are the prime sources for foreign news.

It should be noted that a good deal of serious foreign news is available to radio listeners of National Public Radio's two daily programs, "All Things Considered" and "Morning Report."

Despite shortcomings in recent years, the elaborate international news system is still in place and fully capable of handling any major news that breaks anywhere in the world.

CHAPTER 4

Comsats, Internet, and New Media

> We are laying the foundations for an international information highway system. In telecommunications we are moving to a single worldwide information network, just as economically we are becoming one global marketplace. We are moving toward the capability to communicate anything to anyone, anywhere, by any form—voice, data, text, or image—at the speed of light.
>
> —John Naisbitt

The presidential election of 1920 holds a place in communications history as the first in which election results were broadcast on radio. A crackling KDKA in Pittsburgh kept a small number of devotees of the newfangled wireless in a small area of the country up to date on the tabulations as they slowly were counted.

But for large numbers of interested voters in remote rural regions of America far from telegraph lines, without telephones, and beyond large population centers with daily newspapers, it was two weeks before the news reached them that Warren K. Harding had defeated James M. Cox for the presidency.

Eighty years later, there is not a place in the United States—nor in much of the world—where one cannot follow a presidential election tabulation instantaneously and, indeed, be told the winner's name even before the polls close.

The drastic differences between then and now dramatize the fact that the mechanics of delivering the news to an interested public is a significant factor in the communication process. New technologies have been shaping and changing editorial content in the news media. News, particularly international news, has over the years been directly affected by each new invention in communications. The postal service, telegraph, cable, telephone, and radio in turn have greatly extended the reach of foreign correspondents and world news agencies and the speed with which they can deliver news—each innovation supplementing rather than replacing earlier methods of communication.

The pattern continues today with communication satellites (Comsats), miniature videotape cameras, fiber optics, and computers. Like many other institutions and organizations, the news media—newspapers, news services, radio stations, television, cable channels and networks, and newsmagazines—are being strikingly altered by the information revolution. News communication is being dramatically affected by ongoing revolutionary changes in communication satellites, computers, digitalization, miniaturization, and the Internet.

Stuart Loory pointed out that information was once transferred from one power center to another in Washington, D.C., by newspapers but that recently, television news, mainly CNN, has been doing the job: "The executive and legislative branches increasingly exchange news and views via live, ubiquitous coverage."[1] Now new technologies make it possible for international journalists to do for the entire world what domestic television and, to a lesser extent, print media do in Washington. "The corollary," Loory said, "is that television will have increasing significance for foreign policy making. Programs like ABC's 'Nightline' and 'Capital to Capital' and events like the 'spacebridge' [two-way live conversations between nations] have demonstrated the possibilities."[2] Here again we see the steadily increasing importance of CNN, MSNBC, BBC World Service television, and global news media.

To these media must now be added the Internet, which has been playing a facilitating and supplementary role in the rapid dissemination of a fast-breaking story such as the death of Princess Diana or the Washington sex scandals of 1998 involving President Clinton and Monica Lewinsky. On-line news junkies not only have quick access to more news but also to a heady mix of unconfirmed rumor, conjecture, commentary, discussion, and conspiracy theories. Some critics felt that news reporting of the Lewinsky story was badly compromised by rumors and baseless charges that originated on the Internet and later found their way into the serious news media. Further, the Internet and 24-hour cable news greatly accelerated the story, often to the detriment of traditional journalistic practices such as verifying sources.

More and more Americans are getting their news from cable and the Internet. A June 1998 survey by the Pew Research Center for the People and the Press found that people now watch news programs on cable television networks about as regularly as those on broadcast networks.

They also found the number of Americans who get their news from the Internet is rising rapidly, and they estimated almost as many people use the Internet on a typical weekday as spend time reading a magazine. About 20 percent of U.S. adults, or about 36 million people, get news from the Internet at least once a week, compared with 6 percent, or about 11 million, two years before.

Key Role of Communication Satellites

In our immediate concern with how international news moves about the globe, the significant changes launched by communication satellites, a major by-product of the space age, must be recognized. Recently there has been a quantum jump in the ability of people to talk to and see one another.

Marshall McLuhan once wrote that we were experiencing a "global electronic village" being created by television. John Naisbitt countered that it is in fact the communication satellite that is "creating a super tribal community unlike any environment previously known to mankind since the Tower of Babel."[3]

In the past 30 years, global telecommunications by satellite has achieved remarkable results. Joseph Pelton pointed out that "trillions of dollars of electronic funds transfers and hundreds of millions of dollars of airline reservations flow through global networks each year. Billions of conversations carry on international business, diplomacy, finance, culture, and recreation as a matter of routine."[4] Included in these vast communication flows are, of course, the world's news in pictures, sounds, data, and words.

As computer technology revolutionizes the commonplace telephone network, telecommunications is becoming the world's biggest business. The U.S. Commerce Department predicted the industry would soon generate worldwide sales worth more than $500 billion *annually*. Sales of equipment and services for circulating the world's messages and pictures (including those relating to transnational news) have in a recent year amounted to $325 billion.[5]

Each Western nation is trying to get its share of this new expanding world of global communications. Michel Poniatowski, a French official, predicted that "the nations that develop the new planetary communications will command economic and even political power in the next century as surely as the railroad building countries have dominated the last century of history."[6]

Our concern here is with the impact of telecommunications on international news flow. And the most immediate short-term effect of Comsats is a reduction in the cost of long-distance communications and a corresponding increase in the amount of words, data, and images exchanged. In other words, more news is flowing at less expense. We have seen dramatic changes in long-distance telephone calls which form the bulk of traffic on the INTELSAT system, which is operated by a multinational consortium controlling long-distance point-to-point Comsat communications.

Arthur Clarke dismissed the notion that Comsats are merely an extension of existing communication devices and will not engender much change. He placed Comsats in the same class as the atomic bomb and automobile, "which represent a kind of quantum jump which causes a major restructuring of society." Clarke recalled a parliamentary commission in England a hundred years ago when the chief engineer of the post office was asked to comment on the need for the latest American invention, the telephone. The engineer made this remarkable reply: "No Sir. The Americans may have need of the telephone—but we do not. We have plenty of messenger boys."[7]

That telephone, in time, came to have its own revolutionary impact on modern life, and now the personal letter has been replaced by the long-distance call as well as by fax. And telephone services, as has been noted, constitute the primary activity today of communication satellites and are the major source of revenue for INTELSAT. (The telephone, it should be remembered, is a major tool as well in news gathering, formerly mainly for local use, now for global utilization as well.)

At the same time, the old-fashioned conduit for international telephone calls, the underseas cable system, has been resuscitated by fiber optics. In December 1988, the first fiber optic cable, capable of carrying 40,000 calls simultaneously across the Atlantic Ocean, went into service. This new cable tripled the volume of the three existing copper cables, plus satellites, which together can carry 20,000 calls. A fiber optic cable across the Pacific went into service in April 1989. A single fiber optic cable can carry more than 8,000 calls, compared with 48 calls at once for a copper wire.

At the end of the 1970s, the traffic of INTELSAT was still mostly people talking to people, but since the mid-1980s, at least half the information volume has been machines communicating with other machines. The mind-boggling information-carrying capacity of INTELSAT VI is driving this trend and INTELSAT VII, launched in 1993, and INTELSAT VII-A, in 1995, have continued it. Pelton developed a term to show the relationship between human capabilities of processing information and the speed of the information machines—present and future. One term he used is "TIUPIL," which represents the Typical Information Use Per Individual Lifetime. He defined a TIUPIL as 20 billion bits of information—the total information received by a person who lives 70 years and processes some 27,000 written or spoken words a day. A TIUPIL can be transmitted on INTELSAT VII in a matter of just *seven seconds,* or about nine times a minute. "Soon we will have networks of satellites capable of sending up to 100 billion bits of information in a second. This means we will have machines capable of processing information thousands or even millions of times faster than the human brain," Pelton wrote. "If one asks why we need such high-speed machines, the answer is clearly for machine-to-machine communication. Once we have communication satellites and fiber optic cables capable of handling super high-definition, 3-D television, the meeting of telephone or human data requirements will be small potatoes indeed."[8]

Although they have been called microwave relay towers in the sky, Comsats do have broader, unique properties. They do not link just two points, but many. They can receive from many places at the same time and transmit to many more, sending a panoply of message forms at once—television, telephone, telex, photo facsimile, fax, and high-speed computer data. For example, an increased mobility of money is a result of the computer revolution.

Computers and Comsats have created a global financial marketplace, and it has been estimated that during each business day, nearly $1 trillion—more than the entire money supply of the United States—moves through the machines of the Clearing House Interbank Payments System of 11 big New York banks. Were the flow to stop unexpectedly, financial empires would teeter and governments tremble.[9]

Further, with Comsats, distance is not a factor in the cost. Communications between Tokyo and Seattle, about 5,000 miles, and communications between Seattle and Portland, 175 miles, require identical facilities: two earth stations and a satellite. Irrelevant as well are the historic patterns of the world's telecommunications, which were once channeled through the capital cities of the former colonial powers, all in the Northern Hemisphere. As late as the 1960s, a telephone call from one African country to another had first to go through London or Paris or both. In Latin America, a call between countries often had to go through New York or even London.

International journalism as well as sports events and pop music have benefited greatly from the developments that have made satellites an inte-

gral part of the telecommunications industry. An estimated 2 billion people watched the 1988 Olympics in Seoul, South Korea, but the biggest
Comsat media event to date has been the Live Aid Concert of 1985. Organized by Bob Geldorf to feed the starving in Africa and broadcast from
both England and the United States, the new technology created a "live"
16-hour worldwide network that had not been seen before and has not
been seen since. It raised over U.S. $127 million. The Live Aid event used
satellite communications in their entirely for the first time. Thirteen satellites and 22 transponders brought in an estimated 2 billion television viewers plus a billion more radio listeners. The music event took place at two
locales: the U.S. Philadelphia remote, which had 17 cameras, at least 500
technical and production personnel, and 34 remote vans for broadcast, and
the BBC remote at Wembly, near London, which was just as extensive.
Other nations provided a technical and production pickup for five other
musical inserts, or "injects."[10] Hal Uplinger concluded, "The Live Aid
event showed that global or near global, live television hookups are now
feasible. They may not yet be routine, but considerable expertise exists.
Whether politicians will allow us to demonstrate it to the full extent possible is another question."[11]

Today, satellite systems are operational at the international (intercon-
tinental) level, the regional (continental) level, and the domestic (national)
level.

Satellites extend the range of over-the-air broadcasting systems, but
they have a much greater impact on satellite-cable networks. CNN and
various other cable services, such as Home Box Office and other pay services, extend their reach dramatically by being tied in with cable services.
In addition, numerous specialized satellite systems are functioning, such as
those designed for military, data relay, and maritime and aeronautical purposes.[12] As a result of the endeavors of dozens of laboratories and hundreds
of scientists and engineers, some 3,300 satellites had been launched by
1990.[13] And the numbers are steadily increasing.

INTELSAT is the largest and oldest system, with 15 satellites (plus
backups) over the Pacific, Atlantic, and Indian Oceans. Some 120 nations,
each with its own earth segment, belong to the consortium, and any two
member countries can communicate directly without going through former colonial capitals.[14] User countries, territories, and possessions total
about 170, operating internationally on almost 1,500 preassigned path-
ways. INTELSAT also functions as the carrier for national domestic services in about 30 countries.

In acquiring regional Comsat systems, the developed nations (North

America, Western Europe, and Japan) were moving at a much faster rate than those of the developing world. Still, there has been significant progress among the poorer nations, which lack terrestrial telecommunications systems and so stand to gain much from regional Comsats. Far-flung Indonesia with its thousands of islands has been moving ahead with its PALAPA satellites.

The U.S. space shuttle *Challenger* launched the *Insat 1-B* (Indian National Satellite) in 1983. Built by Indian scientists at a cost of $130 million, the Comsat has the capability of land-based telecommunications that would have cost a trillion dollars to construct. *Insat 1-B* places 70 percent of the Indian population within range of television signals and is being used primarily for telephone services, weather forecasting, nationwide linking of computer services such as transport and tourism, and, interestingly, providing community television services to thousands of Indian villages.[15]

China, which has been enjoying unprecedented economic growth, announced in 1994 that it will launch 30 foreign-owned satellites in the next seven years.[16] China has been sending its own satellites into space since 1970, although ironically it has officially forbade the use of satellite television dishes on private homes. China and its neighbors are currently a major locale of Comsat competition, with Star TV of Hong Kong, Home Box Office Asia, MTV Asia, BBC's World Service TV, CNN, ESPN, and Tele Communications, Inc., all vying for a share of the giant market.

Television transmissions via Comsats were accelerating at a fast clip in the United States and have become commonplace. In 1985, a total of 60,000 were sold each month. By 1990, nearly 3 million satellite dishes were operating, and 400,000 were expected to be purchased the same year at an average of $2,500 per dish.[17]

An important breakthrough came in April 1994 when American consumers were offered a new choice: satellite television beamed to an 18-inch receiver. Two huge satellites launched by the Hughes Corporation made it possible to beam 150 channels to any home in the United States. Using powerful transmitters, the system does away with 10-foot backyard dishes and offers the first digital television service. Choices include 35 cable networks and dozens of pay-per-play movies. On the downside, customers will have to pay for reception equipment.[18]

Dishes can intercept a range of programming far exceeding even the offerings of the most complete cable systems, catching signals from as many as 150 broadcasters. Myriad economic, technical, and legal problems involving, for example, copyright, invasion of privacy, and pirating have resulted and are yet to be resolved.

Pay TV services and superstations now scramble their signals, requiring dish owners to pay the services or stations for unscrambling devices. Nevertheless, these dish antennas mean that remote areas, from the hills of Appalachia to the Arctic wastes of northern Canada, can now receive a variety of television services previously available only in population-dense areas.

Competition is fierce among the new media, so, for example, the future success of television reception by dish satellite receivers is by no means assured. The home dishes may yet lose out to cable reception, the Internet, or some other digital technology still to be developed.

International News by Comsats

Comsats have greatly expanded the capacity of the news media to move international news around the globe, but the ability of the satellites to relay color television signals, giving that medium a global impact, is what has made Comsat technology such a significant mass communication development. This is true even though television use accounts for a comparatively small proportion of the monthly revenue of INTELSAT.

When *Early Bird,* the first commercial Comsat, was launched in 1965, the principal television use was expected to be for occasional live events such as sports, state funerals, space missions, and the coverage of disasters and wars. While reportage of such major events still accounts for much television traffic on INTELSAT, the most extensive and consistent use of the global system is for daily television news "packages" sent from one country to another.

The U.S. networks—NBC, CBS, and ABC—plus CNN daily incorporate satellite news feeds from their correspondents in various parts of the world or, for special coverage, sporadically purchased from foreign broadcast news services, such as Reuters Television or Worldwide Television News.

New Technology and News Gathering

Innovations in communication technology are both changing the ways that global news is gathered and disseminated and the ways that individuals receive the news. The speed and scope of foreign news reporting is constantly expanding as the use of portable VDTs (video display terminals) is

increasing. Foreign correspondents have long said that their worst problems are not censorship or other authoritarian restraints, but communications—getting to the remote news scene, such as an earthquake in Peru or
a civil war in Congo, and then getting the story out. The technology to
solve part of that problem has been developed and increasingly utilized: especially small portable computers that can transmit stories over phone lines
directly to newsroom systems. Initially, these portables were used to cover
golf matches, auto races, football and basketball games, and court trials,
but now journalists covering the whole range of news carry them.

A major technological advance for television reporting was the development of new highly portable "satellite uplinks," which can be disassem-
bled, checked as baggage, and flown to the site of a breaking story in order
to feed back live reports. A "flyaway" dish can become a temporary CNN
or ABC bureau in just the time it takes to get one on the scene.[19]

Another communication innovation that promises to be useful to foreign reporters in the field (as well as to individual citizens) is the portable
wireless telephone. Brenda Maddox predicted that of the estimated $640
billion that the world spends annually on telecommunications equipment,
a good share will go for mobile radio, including satellite-borne maritime
communications, air-to-ground services, and a limitless variety of automobile and carry-along telephones. The growth of mobile communication
will be aided by the increasing sophistication of cellular radio, which opens
the possibility of a telephone on every wrist and a personal telephone number. Such communication technology has obvious advantages for the reporter in the field.[20]

In June 1990, Motorola became the first company to announce plans
for a small, portable phone that can be used anywhere on earth. A 25-
ounce handset costing $3,500 would fit into a coat pocket and enable the
user to send and receive calls from the North Pole to Antarctica. That
phone system was expected to be operational in six years and it was.[21]

In May 1998, Motorola announced that with a 66-satellite "constella-
tion" now orbiting 421 miles above the earth, people will now be able to
send and receive telephone calls or electronic messages from any point on
earth by using handheld phones and pocket-sized pagers. Applications for
global news were obvious.

This means an editor could telephone a foreign correspondent,
whether he or she was covering a conference in Geneva or a civil war in
Africa. And that correspondent could, if necessary, send in the story by his
or her cordless telephone. During the Gulf War while he was the only
Western correspondent in Baghdad, Peter Arnett of CNN used a $50,000

cordless phone to send out his stories by satellite.

Another significant aid for reporters today are databases, which are collections of text or numbers that are stored in computers. On-line databases, of which there are now thousands, are mainly for the retrieval of information by researchers who tap into a data bank through telephone lines attached to a computer terminal. Increasingly, newspapers and broadcasters have used such sources for investigative and general reporting. Distance is not a factor, for in a matter of minutes a U.S. reporter can gain access to anything printed in the *Financial Times* of Britain or distributed by ITAR-TASS. Closer to home, the reporter can call up and scan the full text of about 75 dailies offered by various newspaper databases such as the Nexis database, which carries more than 140 international newspapers, magazines, news services, and newsletters.

A further utilization of Comsats that is changing the structure of daily journalism is facsimile production and distribution of national and international newspapers, pioneered by the *Wall Street Journal.* Daily, a fax of each page of the paper is sent from its production plant in Chicopee, Massachusetts, to 12 or 13 various printing plants around the country. The page-size fax pages are processed onto offset pages. The *Wall Street Journal* has extended this expertise to Asia for its subsidiary, the *Asian Wall Street Journal,* and further expansion of the entire Dow Jones network (which includes the *Wall Street Journal*) is under way. This kind of technological innovation, plus an informative, well-written news product, has moved the *Wall Street Journal* into first place in circulation among U.S. dailies.

Another national daily newspaper, the Gannett Company's *USA Today,* has employed the same facsimile production methods, circulating 1,168,222 copies from 30 U.S. printing sites. In 1985, *USA Today* began beaming facsimile pages of its international edition to Singapore for printing and distribution in the Far East. Other publications routinely utilize facsimile transmission technology, including *International Herald Tribune* in Paris, *Die Zeit* of Hamburg, *China Daily,* the *Economist, Time,* and *Newsweek.* The national edition of the *New York Times* is printed in several regions of the United States to facilitate its same-day delivery across the nation.

Personalized Media: Empowering the Individual

Innovations in information media—personal computers with Internet connections, photocopiers, printers, fax, modems, videocassettes, cordless and mobile telephones, interactive television, databases, cable, and satellite connections—are often considered "personalized media" and are having profound effects on the audience or recipients of international news communication. In fact, the term "audience" itself is becoming obsolete because it implies a mass of passive receivers of communication. Increasingly, personalized media are supplementing traditional media in the affluent West, but less so in nonindustrialized countries, where the print and broadcast model has little competition.

In today's information societies, an individual is no longer a passive recipient of news or entertainment but now is an "information seeker" who can select or choose his or her news or information from a widening variety of sources, many of which governments are unable or unwilling to control. Further, individuals themselves, such as those involved in computer networking, become *sources* of information, that is, communicators. Autocratic governments find it difficult to control personalized communications.

With a personal computer and a modem connecting to a telephone, a Westerner can tap into the fast-growing Internet system, providing access to thousands of databases, including news publications and other current information from home and abroad. Further, that receiver can become a *sender* by freely communicating with other computers through the Internet, e-mail, and various networks and bulletin boards.

The printed word has changed as well. Fax, the same technology that sends the *International Herald Tribune* from Paris to Hong Kong, sends millions of documents, letters, and messages across continents and oceans. Facsimile transmissions have played a role in challenging or even toppling unpopular regimes from Iran to Panama to China to the collapsing Soviet Union. Not only does fax foster immediate human interaction across great distances, it also facilitates the vital flow of information into and out of repressive regimes.

Cassette recorders, both video and audio, have greatly enhanced the ability of individuals to choose what they will hear or see and, as a result, have expanded rapidly in recent years even to remote corners of the Southern Hemisphere. (Because they are mainly conveyors of popular culture and entertainment, VCRs are discussed in Chapter 5, "Global Impact of Western News and Pop Culture.")

With the development of microcomputerization, the personal computer, and the television set, either together or separately, can become a kind of home encyclopedia, spewing out an almost limitless amount of written information, including the day's news. Much of the talk of a "Superhighway of Information" involves the idea of a merging of computers, telephones, and televisions (video, text, and sound) to provide new delivery systems and content options. Two models for the so-called *infobahn* are offered: broadcast and the Internet. In the broadcast model, entertainment would be the driving force, leading to the 500-channel future, with features such as video on demand, interactive home shopping, entertainment and advertising. The latter model is on the lines of the Internet, the vast computer/communications network begun in 1969 that now connects millions worldwide. On the Net, anyone with a computer and a modem can send and receive information to anyone else anywhere.[22]

Internet and International News Flow

The potential of the Internet for international news communication is beginning to become realized. Daily, the Internet carries more news than 1,600 daily newspapers to a *worldwide audience* of 40 to 50 million Internet users. More and more Internet users are getting their news on-line and from media in far-off places.

An Internet user in Pakistan, Paris, or Pretoria can read either the online edition of the *New York Times,* the *Times* of London, or *Die Zeit* of Hamburg. Major newspapers and other news media, magazines, radio and TV broadcasters, and cablecasters, from a variety of mostly Western nations—what was called the "foreign press"—are available in ways never before possible for those with the means and inclination to log on.

The Associated Press has adopted the World Wide Web to distribute its articles and photographs over the global Internet. And, in so doing, it followed other mainline news organizations into uncharted journalistic territory.

Even the lowly and widely criticized on-line Drudge Report provides links for such foreign news media as the *Jerusalem Post;* from London the *Times, Daily Telegraph,* and *Daily Mirror;* BBC, BBC radio, and Skynews from Britain; and Agence France-Presse and North Korean News, among other news purveyors.

Much news or information in the Net is of dubious value and may be deliberately wrong or misleading. But the discriminating and critical viewer can still find solid, reliable information because the world's best news organizations—newspapers, newsmagazines, television, and radio—are reporting the real news daily. (An important role for interactive news media is to act as a check on unreliable reports such as wild conspiracy theories which proliferate on the Internet.)

The Internet has certain unique advantages. For example, CNN Interactive, which is one of the world's busiest news websites with some 3.5 million "page views" a day, features extensive original coverage of environmental and ecological issues. Although Internet users are still comparatively small in numbers, many interactive news media go into depth on all kinds of stories that receive only a minute or two on television or a few paragraphs in a newspaper story. Cyberspace is not limited by the time restraints of broadcast news or the space limitations of the printed media.

Cybernews so far is complementing the traditional news media but may soon become a new kind of journalism. John V. Pavlik wrote, "Since networked news can be interactive, on-demand, and customizable; since it can incorporate new combinations of text, images, moving images, and sound; since it can build new communities based on shared interests and concerns; since it has the almost unlimited space to offer levels of reportorial depth, texture, and context that are impossible in any other medium—new media can transform journalism."[23]

Perhaps the single most significant characteristic of the Internet is that it is a communication device that lets people share ideas (including news and information) on a global network. That suggests that international news communication has made tremendous strides in the last 25 years. Twenty-five years because that is the age of the personal computer, and a PC with a modem hooked up to a telephone line means the world—literally the world—is more available than ever before. Not only individuals but professional news media now can reach and hold not just audiences or readers but communities of shared concerns literally anywhere in the world.

Thoughtful persons in mainstream journalism or the "news business" are well aware of the potential as well as the many pitfalls for journalism on the Internet. Publishers, broadcasters, and journalists believe the news media must be involved with the Net, but neither they, nor anyone else, seems to know where this brave, new world of communication is headed. Just a few years ago, no one had foreseen even the technology much less the potential of the Internet.

Probably every news medium worth its salt now has its web site and is working (and innovating) to keep up with this fast-moving medium. As most know, a newspaper's web site can be simply a screen or two of information, or it can be an extensive and complex number of offerings with short news items, long complex stories, photos and illustrations, documents, and background stories rarely included in a printed edition.

As of April 1998, MSNBC, which is both on cable and on-line, was named the number one general news site on the World Wide Web. The site had an audience of about four million and drew about 4.8 percent of Internet users the previous month. CNN Interactive and *USA Today*'s on-line sites were close behind with 3.3 percent each of Internet users.

For the news media, two basic uncertainties cloud the future of on-line journalism. First, will the public pay for news on a medium which, after a basic fee is paid, has been free? Second, will advertising displayed on the web make money on a medium that lacks a way to track advertising response or to ascertain the demographics of users—information that advertisers deem essential? Definitive answers are not yet in, but most media managers are betting that news on the Internet will in time attract great audiences and become profitable.

International Concerns About Cybernews

The rapid spread of interactive journalism has raised some nagging questions. For example, who will benefit and who will not? Globally, the information revolution has been flourishing mainly in America, Japan, Western Europe, and other highly industrialized countries. The poor nations want the new media but lack the economic and social infrastructure to utilize and sustain them. Only 12 of Africa's 54 countries are linked to the Internet, and experts warn that unless Africa gets on-line quickly, what is already the world's poorest continent risks ever-greater marginalization. Without network connectivity, large areas of Africa will be prevented from participating in many evolving aspects of life on this planet. As in all nations, the younger, better educated, and more affluent are using the Internet; the poor, undereducated, and outcast have no way to access the information highway.

Among Western democracies, there are unresolved questions about how much freedom of expression (including press freedom) can be legally permitted on what is being recognized as the most participatory marketplace of ideas the world has yet seen. In the United States, the U.S. Supreme Court in 1997 resoundingly supported free expression when it declared as unconstitutional the Communications Decency Act, which made it a crime to send or display "indecent" material on-line in a way available to minors. The court held that speech on the Internet is entitled to the highest level of First Amendment protection, similar to that given to newspapers and books. The decision was not the final word—new challenges are still ahead—but the decision bodes well for the Internet as a purveyor of serious news and information.

Other democracies are not as tolerant. In Germany, for example, a prosecutor decided that certain material carried on CompuServe was offensive and threatened legal action. As a result, CompuServe voluntarily denied its four million subscribers access to over 200 newsgroups. More such legal challenges are ahead.

The Internet faces more draconian censorship from authoritarian regimes or despotic rulers. The small, affluent, and authoritarian nation of Singapore thinks it can control the technologies of freedom that threaten its one-party rule. To control television, satellite dishes have been banned, and the country has been wired for cable television, thus enabling the government to screen out objectionable material. Controlling cyberspace is more difficult, but Singapore is trying. Schools are equipped with computers and Singaporeans are urged to link up with the Internet by dialing a local telephone number. Thus, the government can monitor Internet usage through the local servers. Local officials concede that some users can bypass this system by dialing into the Internet through foreign phone systems. Singapore is not expected to be able to sustain such controls over the flow of electronic information so essential for the global economy.

Another authoritarian regime, China, has made greater efforts than any nation to regulate and censor the Internet. In early 1998, China adopted new rules spelling out in detail the government's definition of computer crimes. These included use of the Internet to defame government agencies, to promote separatist movements, to divulge state secrets, or to transmit pornography, as well as the prowling of hackers. Particular targets were the rapidly increasing use of electronic mail and web sites by dissidents to spread their messages.

Use of the Internet to retrieve information and send e-mail has soared since China first allowed global connections in 1994. In late 1997, a total of 620,000 Internet subscriptions had been established. Many accounts were shared by 10 to 20 people. E-mail is particularly difficult to control. For example, an electronic magazine, *Tunnel,* a weekly forum for political discussion, is mainly written inside China. The contents are then sent by e-mail to a Silicon Valley address where it is electronically mailed back into China to thousands of addresses. Some 20 issues have appeared since it began in June 1997.

China's efforts to control the Internet reflect a central quandary for the government: how to foster economic growth and freedom while keeping tight controls on politics.[24]

For now in the West, electronic newspapers and the Internet do not pose any serious threat as yet to the newspapers dropped on millions of front porches daily. Most people apparently would rather browse through a newspaper over a cup of coffee at breakfast than call up information on a computer. But in the long run the electronic delivery of news and information will only increase and proliferate.

In November 1995, the Associated Press announced it would utilize the World Wide Web to distribute its articles and photos over the global Internet.

Implications of Rapid Change

To summarize, innovations in communication technology suggest certain broad trends for transnational journalism:

1. The unit cost of international communication of news will continue to drop as usage of the world news systems increases and efficiency, speed, and reach of the hardware become greater.

2. Technology is making it possible to send and receive news and other essential information from almost anywhere in the world and with increasing speed. The continuing integration of computers with telecommunication means much more *interactive,* or two-way, communication.

3. The two-way capability of cablevision, tied in with Comsats and personal computers on the Internet, means that information users can seek out or request specific kinds of information or news and not remain a passive mass audience. The two-way capability of telecommunications means that there will be more two-way flows of information, with consumers having more choice about what they receive. The trend toward such interactive communications systems is clear.

4. Because of technical improvements, the potential number of channels and sources of information is virtually unlimited, and the possible varieties and kinds of future communication stagger the imagination.

5. A gradual merger of the science and technology of computers and electronic communications has been taking place. In fact, a new term, *compunications,* has been coined to reflect this reality. In 1998, five leading high-tech companies introduced a technology that promises to accelerate the convergence of mobile communications and computing by enabling the wireless transfer of voice and data among mobile phones, laptop computers, and other portable devices.

6. These personalized communications, typified by the Internet, fax, videocassettes, and cablevision, present a challenge to authoritarian gov-

ernments, which traditionally control their newspapers and broadcasting. How does Big Brother stop someone from watching a pirated videocassette, or from calling up distant information on the Internet, or picking up Dan Rather off a satellite, or receiving e-mail from a dissident group overseas?

7. So far, this communications (or compunications) revolution is essentially taking place principally in the United States, Japan, and Western Europe. These and other information societies, mostly in the rich, industrialized North, are widening the already broad information gap between themselves and less-developed nations. A highly industrialized nation like Japan can utilize any new technology much faster than, say, Kenya or Pakistan and, as a result, the resentments of the former Third World over information inequities are exacerbated. The poorer nations want the new communications technology but lack the social and economic bases needed to utilize it. For many of the poor, debt-ridden nations of the Southern Hemisphere, sophisticated and expensive electronic systems are still out of reach. Such factors only add to the deep rift between the haves and have-nots of the world, a condition many consider the greatest of global problems.

8. In the brave new world of international communication, the main players—corporate media giants such as Murdoch, Time Warner, NBC, Sony, Bertelsmann in Germany, Fininvest in Italy, Disney, Microsoft, and others—are getting richer and more powerful and fewer in number due to recent mergers (see Chapter 6, "Internationalizing the World's Media"). In the United States, the ownership of major media corporations has consolidated into fewer and fewer hands, from about 50 companies in 1983 to 20 as of 1994. However, technological innovation is moving so fast that some of the these media powerhouses may fall by the wayside in the global scramble to dominate world markets for the by-products of mass communication.

9. Finally, concern is growing about the effects of all this greatly expanded communication flow on its audiences. Most people spend no more than an hour a day reading newspapers and/or getting the news from television or radio, but the news volume cascades on. David Shenk wrote that in the middle of the century, "We began to produce information much faster than we could process it. We have moved from a state of information scarcity to a state of information surplus—from drought to flood in the geological blink of an eye." In his recent book, *Data Smog: Surviving the Information Glut,* Shenk argues that information overload is bad for your health, promoting stress, memory overload, compulsive behavior, and at-

tention-deficit disorder. Shenk argues that the well-known global village, created by mass communication, is at the same time growing increasingly fragmented and fractionalized as people, despairing of being able to master a grand overview, retreat into their own special interests. He argues that cyberspace, including the Internet, promotes a highly decentralized, deregulated society with little common discourse and minimal public infrastructure.[25]

Concerned persons here and abroad are pondering the implications of all this. Society, in short, faces the danger of computer/communications technologies advancing faster than our ability to develop methods of controlling and using them for the general welfare of humankind. This has always been true of technologies, but today that gap is becoming ominously wide.

Nonetheless, innovations in media technology will continue to shape international news. Julius Barnathan of ABC News sees the development of multilanguage broadcasts as a next important innovation. One video will be accompanied by as many as eight narrations.

Stuart Loory predicted that "by the year 2000 cameras and transmission equipment will be so small and sophisticated that within minutes of the event, live reports from anywhere in the world will be available. ... Technology will give future journalists even greater power than they have now. Those journalists must not allow technology to overtake substance if they are to continue to be honest brokers of political ideas and ideals."[26]

Finally, Pelton of INTELSAT saw much more to come. New and perhaps totally different architectures for space communications are likely to evolve in the 21st century and the long-term growth and development of space communication seem relatively well-assured, despite the rapid evolution of fibre optic cable technology. In short, the 21st century should see the beginning of the true long-term road to space communications, making it truly the beginning of the 'golden age' of space communications."[27]

CHAPTER 5

Global Impact of Western News and Pop Culture

The tumultous throng that poured westward through the rents in the Berlin Wall last November [1989] emptied the supermarkets and the video shops. Within hours there was neither fast food nor deodorant left. West Berlin emporiums were stripped of their ample supplies of soft and sometimes hard-core video cassettes. T-shirts and jeans, a currency across the Wall in the days of the two Germanies, flew off the shelves. Wide-eyed and knowing, moving to the beat of heavy metal and rock, which, clandestine or overt, had been the odes to freedom throughout Eastern Europe, the young and not so young, enacted the first TV revolution.

—George Steiner

Great world events of our times have given us a glimpse of the role that global news communication plays in assisting and accelerating political change. Intense television coverage of such an event as the crisis over Iraq or the agonizing civil war in Bosnia obviously does not determine the political outcome of such events, but such reporting (or nonreporting) has a clear impact on public opinion, which in turn will influence decisions made by diplomats and political leaders of great nations.

In the post–Cold War world, fast-moving political and social changes are being shaped and accelerated by transnational communication. Not only have speed and volume increased along with greater geographical dispersal of international news flow, but the nature and effects of the content have changed and diversified as well. Instead of the mere words and numbers of yesteryear's news, vivid color television coverage of great events is now delivered to the world's news publics, greatly increasing the impact of the message. As a result, a new and significant kind of audience involvement and participation in world events has emerged. The propaganda truism that the report of the event is as important as the event itself has greater impact than ever in the age of media events.

In East and Central Europe, the personalized media—videocassette

71

and audiocassette players and shortwave radio receivers—were key weapons in the peoples' revolutions because they broke their governments' communication monopolies and piped in the siren songs of the West. Just a few years later, Peter Lewis of the *New York Times* wrote, "Today, political dissidents of all nationalities are discovering a homeland in the worldwide web of communication known as cyberspace. ... Today, many human rights advocates are exploring an even more powerful medium, (than fax) the computer web called Internet, as a way of defying censorship."[1]

On the other hand, the fact that the Western media were largely barred from reporting, say, the prolonged war in Afghanistan between Soviet forces and Afghan guerrillas greatly minimized the impact of that struggle on the world's awareness. Again, if the world is mostly unaware of an event, then for many millions the event has not occurred. In past years, numerous small wars in Africa—Western Sahara, Angola, Sudan, and recently Algeria—have passed largely unnoticed because the world's new media could not, or would not, report them.

Electronic Execution of Communism

The collapse of communism in Central and Eastern Europe in 1989, along with the end of the Cold War, were two of the most significant political events since World War II (some said since 1848) and all the more dramatic because they were so unexpected. Certainly Western mass communication—going over, under, and around the Iron Curtain—played a role in raising expectations and in breaking the Communists' monopoly on information and popular culture.

Critic George Steiner added these to his above-quoted words,

> Once "Dallas" had come their way [it could be picked up several hundred kilometers east of Checkpoint Charlie], once tapes of Western soap operas and rock jamborees could be multiplied and sold beyond the "Dallas line," the cataclysm and saturnalia were inevitable. Television sparked the great wild surge toward a consumer economy, and television packaged (brilliantly) the actual rush. Why live by bread alone when there is peanut butter? Why endure as a Soviet satellite when the word "satellite" means cable television?[2]

The dramatic and sudden collapse of communism in Eastern Europe came after a generation of communication interactions between the Western nations and the socialist nations of Eastern Europe, the USSR, and the Third World—all set in the context of the Cold War. Recent economic successes of the West along with the failures of socialist political economies helped explain the media changes. Further, the sheer pervasiveness of Western communications accelerated modifications of and, in time, the abandonment of communism and its press theory.

Western journalism rode the crest of the technetronic revolution that reshaped global mass communication during the past generation and created the information societies of the West. In the past generation, this technetronic revolution swept over the globe with amazing pervasiveness. (One Russian general said the USSR lost the Cold War because it was hopelessly behind the West in computer technology.) Communication satellites, computerization, global television, high-speed data transfers, and especially new media products such as videocassette and audiocassette players, all spurred by profit-making opportunities, have led to a vast flood of Western television programs, movies, videocassettes, and CD (compact disk) and taped music recordings, moving inexorably from West to East Europe.

Grist for this vast mill has not only been Western pop culture (movies, TV shows, music videos, and rock and other popular music) but also newspapers, magazines, and books. Western versions of the news, along with Western methods of news reporting and presentation, became widely accepted and emulated. AP, Reuters, CNN, BBC and Radio Free Europe, Radio Liberty, and the *International Herald Tribune,* among other media, added diversity to the monolithic news structure of the Communist regimes. Whatever their shortcomings, Western media had a crucial advantage over Communist media: they were *not* government controlled and hence achieved a wide credibility. Consequently, centralized Communist governments lost control of information.

Western news media acted as catalysts for political change in Communist nations in several ways: people in Eastern Europe did listen to Western broadcasts, which carried both world news and news about the satellite nations themselves.

Much of this news went by shortwave radio, some by AM and FM broadcasting and, for East Germany, via television from West Berlin and the Federal Republic. German-language television was received all over the GDR (German Democratic Republic) except in low-lying Dresden, which was dubbed the "Valley of the Ignorant" because of the poor reception there.

Some observers believe the beginnings of the breakup of the Communist empire in East Europe began with the successes of the Solidarity trade union in Poland. Certainly the Polish Communist regime's monopoly on news was broken in two ways: by the rise of alternative newspapers that challenged the government and supported Solidarity goals and, second, by a triangular communication flow between the alternative papers, foreign reporters, and international broadcasters. It worked this way: foreign journalists reported news of Solidarity to their Western media; these stories were beamed back to Poland via international shortwave radio, particularly by BBC, Deutsche Welle, and Radio Free Europe; then the stories were also picked up by the alternative papers in Poland.

This communication model was followed again and again. Michael T. Kaufman, who covered Poland for the *New York Times,* wrote,

> It turned out that a few dissidents using non-violent means, and exploiting the freedom of the press and airwaves beyond their borders, could in this increasingly interconnected world bring down autocrat after autocrat. Foreign correspondents wrote for their own papers, but their reports were translated and beamed back to countries where such information as they were writing was banned. The spread of portable radios and videos make such information much more accessible. The official press was forced to offer more information, more truth, as it was forced to compete for credibility with the outsiders. ... Once informed, the people were mobilized. In most places, they marched and chanted and drew placards and with the world press watching such means proved sufficient to expose previous forbidden truths and to make revolutionary changes that had so recently seemed impossible.[3]

In the revolutionary events of 1989, the media played a variety of roles. One was to report that such things happen and that times are changing. Another was to show that the world was indeed watching and that the Berlin Wall could be turned into a sieve. A third purpose was to show potential demonstrators in other countries that the unthinkable was perfectly possible. So events in East Berlin, Budapest, Prague, and Bucharest all reinforced one another.[4]

For William E. Henry of *Time,* the triumphs owed something to journalism but little to journalists:

> The function of news people was not sage or analyst but conduit, carrying the raw facts of an amazing reality to the startled citizenry in each revolutionary nation and to a waiting world beyond. ... The thrills of

1989 and early 1990 came as useful reminders that the most interesting part of the news business is, in fact, the news. For broadcast journalists, events proved anew that the chief element of their much discussed power is the simple capacity to reach many people quickly—and in cases of true turmoil, with a verisimilitude no other medium offers. TV's basic function was as the great legitimizer.[5]

Failed Coup in Moscow

Communications was one of the major reasons the right-wing coup d'état failed to topple the Soviet government in August 1991. The nine coup leaders arrested Mikhail Gorbachev, closed down all but a handful of Communist Party media, and held a television press conference proclaiming the new government. They assumed the nation would passively accept the changeover. However, the coup masterminds failed to understand how much the Soviet Union had changed in the six years of glasnost. With a more open communication system and a new taste for democracy and free expression, the resistance in Moscow rallied around Boris Yeltsin. They used fax, photocopying machines, and cellular phones to let fellow citizens know it was not too late to resist the coup. Inexplicably, the plotters failed to shut down international telephone calls and the satellite relay station and did not jam shortwave radio. No actions were taken against the large foreign media in Moscow, which sent out a flood of words and pictures to a disapproving world. CNN was even received in some Soviet republics. It was as if the coup leaders became immobilized like deer before car headlights by television camera lights recording and transmitting the events within the parliament and the street barricades outside.

Soviet journalists, emboldened by glasnost, refused to accept the coup restrictions. Blocked at the printing plants, dozens of independent publications ran off photocopies and passed them out on street corners. Moscow's subway was quickly papered with handbills. Interfax, the independent news agency, distributed underground reports along with its own stories, and the independent radio station, Echo Moscow, played games with the police and went on the air five times during the crisis.

The impact of Western radio was even more impressive. The BBC doubled its Russian-language program to 18 hours, its largest increase ever. It also relayed the banned broadcasts of a Moscow station. Radio Liberty's 24-hour broadcasts in Russian and 11 other Soviet languages reached an estimated audience of 50 million. Gorbachev later said he gratefully listened to BBC, RL, and Voice of America while under house arrest at his dacha in the Crimea.

As *Newsweek* commented, "The coup leaders apparently relied on popular indifference and fear of authority. But those are not the attributes of people in the know. And last week Russians proved that they have entered the information age."[6]

Ironically, the new communications openness that propelled Yeltsin to political power after the failed coup also caused him severe political damage in the winter of 1994–95 when he sent the Russian army into Chechnya to put down a rebellion. In Moscow and throughout the nation, millions of Russians watched television pictures of the brutal suppression of the revolt and the killing of thousands of civilians. And many Russians did not like what they saw.

World Media at Tiananmen Square

Another great anti-Communist uprising occurred in mid-May of 1989 when thousands of Chinese students and others marched in Tiananmen Square in Beijing in support of the prodemocracy movement. After a brief flowering, the movement failed, and protesters were crushed by Chinese soldiers. For one brief week, however, the Chinese people had a glimpse of what a free press would be like. Chinese newspapers and broadcasters themselves suddenly began to give colorful and candid coverage of the sit-in protest at the Square; students were shown as equals asking Premier Li Peng pointed questions and pressing demands.

All the while, global television networks—CNN, ABC, NBC, CBS, and BBC—were transmitting words and pictures around the world while many thousands of sympathetic Chinese outside of China demonstrated in Hong Kong, Taiwan, Australia, and all across America. Many signs carried by protesters in Beijing were in English, intended for foreign television viewers: "We Shall Overcome" was sung, and the adapted words of Patrick Henry, "Give me democracy or give me death," were heard on American television. Pictures of the papier-mâché Goddess of Liberty, modeled on the Statue of Liberty, and of the lone Chinese youth standing before a line of tanks became instant and lasting icons of the failed revolt.

Still, the Tiananmen uprising was more than a television event. Before and especially after the Chinese government shut down the foreign television cameras, Chinese students at home and abroad used personal computers, long-distance telephone, and fax machines to communicate back and forth with sympathizers. At Harvard, a Chinese student set up a Beijing-to-Boston hot line, which was a round-the-clock open telephone line that carried news from Tiananmen Square to his Cambridge home. From there, news went by fax, telephone, and computer to Chinese students all over the United States. Chinese students at Berkeley and Stanford created a "news lift" by using fax machines to send back to striking students the latest news from the U.S. media.[7] The student movement in China also printed an underground newspaper, utilized wall posters, and made public speeches in many cities.

Perhaps the major role was played by shortwave radio—Voice of America (VOA) and BBC World Service reached many millions through their Mandarin services. One scholarly study found that the VOA was the most important of all international media involved in the event; its Mandarin broadcasts made it the most widely used alternative news medium in China, informing millions in the countryside who could not otherwise obtain the information VOA provided. Conservatively, VOA reached 100 million Chinese people, possible 200 to 300 million.[8] (See Chapter 7, "Public Diplomacy and Propaganda," for more on the continued importance of an "old" communication medium—shortwave radio—in international news.)

After the 1989 crackdown and all Chinese media were brought back under Party control, shortwave radio still managed to report what had happened, illustrating again that despite draconian efforts to control information, news can still get through. The Tiananmen Square conflict showed the potentialities of personalized media to be a catalyst for political change. It also showed its limitations: communication does not always win out over raw military power.

The authoritarian Chinese government may have won the battle of Tiananmen Square. However, currently it is facing a quieter but far more serious challenge in the form of the "hundreds of thousands of satellite dishes that are sprouting, as the Chinese say, like bamboo shoots after a spring rain. Already, millions of Chinese can hook in via satellite to the 'global village' bypassing the Communist Party commissars and leaving them feuding over how to respond."[9] Nicholas Kristof reported that the information revolution threatens to supplant the Communist Revolution, which long has been sustained by the Party's monopoly on news and propaganda that is now crumbling. The information revolution that began in the 1980s with shortwave radio has spread rapidly. Fax machines are widely available in private homes, and direct-dial international phones and computers are multiplying as well, with many Chinese able to use the Internet, including e-mail and electronic bulletin boards.[10]

The media proliferation in China is fueled by the fact that the country is modernizing and growing economically. One of the great dramas of modern history is taking place in China: several hundred million people have risen out of abject poverty and are enjoying unprecedented higher standards of living—including access through telecommunications to the world outside their remote villages. Politically, China is still rigidly Communist, but economically it has opted for free enterprise and trade in emulation of its prosperous Asian neighbors. But the resulting "market Leninism" has created severe tensions that may lead to either continued prosperity or, to avoid chaos, an abrupt return to rigid autocracy.

In October 1993, China banned the purchase or possession of satellite dishes by ordinary Chinese, but so far Chinese authorities have been unable to enforce the order effectively. Some feel it is too late—the information genie has been out of the bottle for too long. In 1993, satellite dishes had sprouted on an estimated 500,000 roofs in the country, but because of cable hookups on apartment buildings, the government estimates there are 15 million subscribers to multichannel systems. In a village near Beijing, even the apartment buildings housing the dreaded public security bureau are wired for satellite programming from the United States, Great Britain, and Hong Kong.[11]

In China and throughout Asia, Comsat-delivered television programs have been pouring in—from Star TV in Hong Kong, HBO (Home Box Office) Asia, CNN, ESPN, MTV (Music Television) Asia, and BBC World Service Television—bringing in entertainment and news and information.

Some Asian countries welcome satellite television, but others see it as a threat to their cultural identity and political stability. The power of Comsat television was shown again in 1992 in Thailand when street riots in Bangkok between Thai soldiers and prodemocracy crowds helped overthrow a military government. Although local television was barred from showing scenes of unarmed civilians being killed in the street, satellite-dish owners taped the scenes of violence shown on BBC and CNN. Within hours the tapes were shown around Thailand, angering the public and speeding the downfall of the military rulers.[12] Singapore and Malaysia restrict the public from owning satellite dishes. Viewers can see satellite channel programs only as rebroadcast over local television, which is tightly controlled by the government. Singapore cable service carries CNN and HBO Asia but not Star TV, which is owned by Rupert Murdoch.

In 1994, in an effort to curry favor with the Deng regime in China,

Murdoch summarily dropped the BBC's World Service Television from Star's offerings. Chinese authorities had objected to the BBC's coverage of allegations of human rights violations in China.

Then, in February 1998, Murdoch's HarperCollins, the book publisher, abruptly canceled its contract to publish a book by Chris Patten, the last British governor of Hong Kong, because Murdoch thought the Patten book took too negative a view of China. Murdoch has extensive holdings in China and ambitious plans to expand them. Further, Patten had criticized Murdoch's 1994 move against the BBC, calling it "the most seedy of betrayals" for those who champion freedom of speech in one country "to curtail it elsewhere for reasons of inevitably short-term commercial expediency."[13]

However, governments are finding it nearly impossible to stop people from grabbing their entertainment and news from the skies. In 1994, Saudi Arabia banned satellite dishes as "un-Islamic" and ordered more than 150,000 dishes to be taken down; Kuwait was planning to do the same. In India, Hindu fundamentalists, outraged at the racy videos on MTV Asia, demanded that the dishes be banned. In Iran, where people are bored by official television, Iranian-made satellite dishes, costing $700, dot the apartment roofs of Tehran, beaming in BBC news and soft-porn movies from Turkey. But governments that try to shut down satellite TV find themselves outwitted by stubborn viewers. Dishes are easily put together from imported kits, and they are growing smaller, cheaper, and more powerful. Bowing to what seems to be the inevitable, some repressive governments are allowing the dishes to stay. Myanmar places few restrictions on them, and Indonesia seems to welcome satellites as a more efficient way to beam its own programs to its 13,000 far-flung islands.[14]

Terrorism and Television

The very nature of global television and telecommunications that can bring people closer together while sharing the mutual grief of tragic events, such as the assassination of John F. Kennedy or the slaughter at Tiananmen Square, also can be manipulated to capture the world's attention. Unquestionably, certain acts of international terrorism, such as jet hijackings, political kidnappings, and civilian bombings as in Oklahoma City, are perpetrated primarily to capture time and space in the world's media. Terrorism has been called "propaganda of the deed": violent criminal acts (usually against innocent people) performed by desperate people seeking a worldwide forum for their grievances.

Terrorism, of course, is not new. But the flare-ups of the phenomenon—especially in the Middle East, Northern Ireland, Latin America, Turkey, Italy, West Germany, and the United States—have been caused in part, some charge, by global television coverage that beams images of terrorist violence into millions of television sets around the world. Many terrorist groups have mastered a basic lesson of this media age: television news organizations can be manipulated into becoming the final link between the terrorists and their audiences, and as with all sensational crimes, the more outrageous and heinous the terrorist act, the greater attention it will receive in the world's news media. Walter Laqueur said, "The media are a terrorist's best friend. ... Terrorists are the super-entertainers of our time."[15]

Be that as it may, terrorism *is* news, and as such it poses worrisome questions for broadcast journalists: Does television coverage really encourage and aid the terrorists' cause? Is censorship of such dramatic events ever desirable? Raymond Tanter wrote, "Since terror is aimed at the media and not at the victim, success is defined in terms of media coverage. And there is no way in the West that you could not have media coverage, because you're dealing in a free society."[16]

Terrorism coverage is a journalistic problem of international scope, just as international terrorism itself is a transnational problem that individual nations cannot solve without international cooperation. Broadcast journalists argue about whether the violence would recede if television ignored or downplayed an act of terrorism. Most doubt that self-censorship by news organizations is a good idea or even possible in such a highly competitive field; however, television organizations have established guidelines for reporting terrorism incidents in a more restrained and rational way.

Hostages in Iran

The seizure of the U.S. embassy in Iran in November 1979, with more than 50 American citizens (virtually all diplomatic personnel) held hostage, added a new and deepening dimension to the history of terrorism and the media's increasingly blurred role as both reporter and participant.

For the first time, a sovereign government became an overt party to the terrorism by supporting, instead of ousting, the young militants who took over an embassy compound and imprisoned its personnel. Their stated purpose was to dramatize the grievances of Iranians against the deposed Shah Mohammad Reza Pahlavi and force the U.S. government to return him to Iran for trial. Most observers agree that the militants and Iran's rulers expected that heavy coverage of the outpouring of support for the terrorists by the huge demonstrating crowds around the embassy gates in Tehran would convince American and world public opinion of the justice of their cause.

The saturation coverage of that year's biggest story quickly engulfed the U.S. news media, especially television, in controversy and brought charges that they were being used and controlled by Iranian militants. Particularly controversial was an interview by NBC News with an American hostage under conditions dictated by the Iranian captors, conditions that both CBS and ABC had found unacceptable.

For the more than 300 foreign journalists working in Tehran in the first months of the crisis, there was indeed a thin line between being manipulated by the Iranian militants and responding to legitimate demands for the latest information from their own highly competitive news organizations and their publics at home. Indisputably, the Western journalists in Tehran were part of the story and, inevitably, part of the controversy.

Replay in Beirut

In June 1985, TWA (Trans-World Airlines) Flight 847 out of Athens was hijacked and its crew and passengers held captive in Beirut. For more than two weeks, the three U.S. networks devoted more than half of their evening news shows to the story. One study found that CBS, NBC, and ABC broadcast a total of 491 hostage stories over the 17-day crisis period, comprising about 12 hours of news time.[17] In most newspapers, the story was on page 1 from June 15 to July 7. Indeed, the event looked like a replay of the Iranian hostage story and one that the news business could not ignore.

As before, television was accused of aiding and abetting the terrorists by sympathetically publicizing their cause. Prime Minister Margaret Thatcher of Britain proposed a voluntary media code of self-censorship during terrorist incidents. The idea was seconded by U.S. Attorney General Edwin Meese. Fred Friendly, a former president of CBS News, said the worst errors in coverage had been caused by a "haphazard frenzy of competition" and the compulsion to obtain "exclusives": "We have to learn that they (the terrorists) watch TV. We need to get across that you can't shoot your way onto our air," Friendly said.[18]

This time, however, a measure of restraint and responsibility by television news was evident in some quarters. Despite the many specific criticisms of television's coverage of this highly emotional story, there was general agreement that such stories must be covered but with restraint and good judgment. After it was over, the *Columbia Journalism Review* commented, "One of the tasks of journalism is to provide an assessment independent of that of the government and to stand apart from, rather than incite, the jingoism and xenophobia that spread so rapidly in situations involving the seizure of American citizens. In the Beirut hostage-taking, as in Iran, such detachment was hard to find."[19]

Tom Wicker of the *New York Times* summed it up well:

> But the real reason that television was properly present in Beirut, even at those bizarre "press conferences," is just that television exists; it has become a condition of being. It may on occasion be inconvenient, intrusive, and even harmful; but if because of government censorship or network self-censorship the hostage crisis had not been visible, *real,* on American screens, the outrage and outcry would have been a thousand times louder than what's now being heard, and rightly so; for we depend on television for perception as we depend on air for breath. And that's the way it is.[20]

Different Results in Iraq

When Iraq overran Kuwait in August 1990, thousands of foreigners, including many Americans, were stranded in those two countries as the military buildup began in Saudi Arabia. When Saddam Hussein announced that his foreign "guests" were not free to leave and some were sent to strategic sites as "human shields," many felt that a major hostage crisis was forming and would dominate the news. This didn't really happen, and Saddam, after selectively releasing various groups of hostages in a fanfare of publicity over a period of several months, finally permitted all foreigners to leave Iraq before Christmas.

Why such a different result from the Iran hostage crisis of 10 years earlier? Some said that the most remarkable thing about the Iraqi hostage crisis was that it was never referred to in those terms. Unlike the Iran episode, the U.S. government and media, as well as public opinion, decided to see the event as part of a broader crisis. President George Bush avoided the topic in press conferences and was never photographed with hostage families. As a result, American foreign policy was not paralyzed, and the hostages were released.[21] Also, Saddam obviously believed that hostage holding had become counterproductive.

It was widely held that the U.S. government and people had learned from the Iran experience, but there were differences between the two crises. In Iraq, the hostages were a sideshow; the main event was possible war. In Iran, for the Jimmy Carter White House, as well as the media, the hostages were the whole story. Another explanation was that by the time of the Iraq crisis the American public had become bored with any "hostage story" in general. Among industrialized nations, Americans are the most prone to personalize foreign policy and, at least this time, the public and media showed more concern for the military personnel sent to Saudi Arabia than for those who had voluntarily gone into that unstable area and became hostages. The extent to which television, in particular, has a responsibility for the effects of its coverage of such stories is a problem still to be resolved.

Communication and Organization

A less obvious and more benign impact of improved international communication is its capacity to *organize*. As Daniel Lerner pointed out, communication is the neural system of organization:

> Wherever people must act together (an informal definition of organization), there they must exchange information (an informal definition of communication). Communication, in the sense of shared information, is the organizing mechanism of social actions. ... The proposition—that communication shapes organization—is applicable to all varieties of collective behavior in social institutions: large and small, formal and informal, hierarchal and egalitarian.[22]

The ability to communicate, in other words, determines the effectiveness and the boundaries of any organization. The growth in the nineteenth century of a continental nation such as the United States would have been impossible without the telegraph and the railroad—two aspects of communication that "organized" an expansive hinterland. Similarly, in the last part of the twentieth century, long-distance communication—including jet air travel and some surface transport, communication satellites, and high-speed telecommunications—is coalescing areas of the emerging nations previously isolated and splintered.

Although generally poor and deficient in modern communications, the nations of Africa, for example, have been transformed in recent decades by their increased ability to communicate with one another. Because of greatly expanded air travel and long-distance communication between capitals (but still not much between a capital city and the adjacent hinterland), Africa is *organizing* itself. African leaders may often decry European influences on their continent, but it was precisely such "neocolonialist" influences as the BBC, INTELSAT, Air France, Reuters, *Le Monde,* AFP, *Newsweek,* British Airways, and others that have made possible the interaction and cooperation among Africans possible.

The shared policies and activities of black Africa directed at ending white rule in South Africa would have been impossible without long-distance communication and jets. Comparable political changes throughout the world have been spawned by such communication and transportation advances, even though, at the same time, new communication technology is contributing to the widening of the gap between rich and poor nations. Would there be, for example, the same sense of common cause within the diverse Arab world stretching from Morocco to Iraq without greatly enhanced long-distance communication and jet travel?

Diffusion of Mass Culture and Entertainment

Another major impact of the global communication system is its role in the diffusion of the mass culture of the West to all—literally all—corners of the world. Whether conveyed by printed word, electronic image, or recorded sound, Western motion pictures, television programs, popular music, books, videocassettes and audiocassettes, and magazines have had a profound impact on traditional cultures around the world that can only be described as revolutionary. To the extent that we are moving toward a rudimentary world community, it can be argued that the world is beginning to share a common mass culture based on that of the West. The traditional cultures of diverse ethnic societies and nationalities are being steadily eroded and modified by this cultural intrusion, principally from the United States and Britain. Without question, much of the wondrous diversity of the world's many cultures and languages is being lost forever. This trend is, of course, part of a long-term historical process that predates modern mass media, but in recent years the pace of change has accelerated.

For example, in 1988, U.S. sales in Europe of motion pictures and television programs amounted to $844 million, with movies accounting for two-thirds of the total—a fivefold increase over 1980. That year, American films seized more than 50 percent of the French market, 50 percent of the Italian, Dutch, and Danish markets, 60 percent of German market, and 80 percent of the British market. But the largest audience for Hollywood movies outside the United States is Japan.[23] That dominance continues: in 1993, of the world's most-attended films, 88 were American, *Variety* reported. The highest-ranking foreign competitor, France's *Visiteurs,* was ranked 27. "And that's not counting even pop music, television, novels, and the more nebulous, all pervasive imagery of American street fashion."[24]

In the news area, over 450 newspapers outside the United States subscribed to either the *New York Times* or the *Los Angeles Times/Washington Post* supplementary news services. "CBS Evening News with Dan Rather," from the night before, airs at 8 a.m. daily in Paris. The Japanese are watching Dan Rather, too, along with the "Lehrer News Hour" and "Nightline" with Ted Koppel.[25] Seventy-five percent of all imported television programs come from the United States, but most are not news. Everyone in Europe can now watch "Oprah Winfrey" subtitled or dubbed. American basketball, played in 192 countries, may become the world's most popular sport. The NBA finals in Phoenix and Chicago in June 1993 were broadcast in 109 countries in 20 languages.[26]

John Naisbitt[27] noted these random examples of American mass culture abroad: "Dallas" has been seen in 98 countries; 40 percent of television programming in New Zealand was American; Mickey Mouse and Donald Duck, dubbed in Mandarin, have been seen weekly in China; "Sesame Street" was seen in 184 countries; and the hottest game show on French television was "La Roue de la Fortune."

In *Video Night in Kathmandu,* Pico Iyer wrote perceptively about the penetration of Western mass culture and lifestyles throughout Asia:

> I had come into town the previous afternoon watching video reruns of *Dance Fever* on the local bus. As I wandered around, looking for a place to stay, I had noted down the names of a few of the stores: the Hey Shop, The Hello Shop, Easy Rider Travel Service, T.G.I. Friday restaurant. After checking into a modest guesthouse where Vivaldi was pumping out on an enormous ghetto blaster, I had gone out in search of a meal. I ran across a pizzeria, a sushi bar, a steak house, a Swiss restaurant, and a slew

of stylish Mexican cafes. ... After dinner, I had made my way to a nearby cafe for a cappuccino. Next to the cash register were enough stacks of old copies of *Cosmo, Newsweek,* and the London Sunday *Times* to fill six doctors' waiting rooms. Behind the counter was a backgammon set for customers and a homemade library of faded paperbacks—Erica Jong, Ken Follett, Alexandra Penney. From the Casablanca, the showy, two-story singles bar across the street, Bruce Springsteen was belting out "Dancing in the Dark." ... *An American Werewolf in London* was playing at the local cinema. A few Men At Work songs were poring out of cassette stores opened to the street, only to be drowned out by the roar of Suzukis erratically ridden by local boys in leopardskin shirts. ... I was, of course, in Bali, the Elysian isle famous for its otherworldly eroticism, its cultural integrity, its natural grace.[28]

Mass culture also conveys lifestyles. Like their Soviet counterparts, young Chinese prefer American jeans and T-shirts as well as rock music. Young people in Germany are using such slang terms as "break dance," "rap music," "bodybuilding," "windsurfing," and "computer hacking" and, what is more, are doing those things.[29]

Advertising research has found that the differences that divide nations are disappearing among teen-agers, thereby creating a "new world teen" almost 1 billion strong, remarkably similar across disparate cultures.[30] The study tested the hypothesis that this is the first generation uniquely tied together around the world because of media. The commonality manifested itself most clearly in jeans, T-shirts, and running shoes being a teenage uniform whether in Asia, Europe, Latin America, or the United States. But in deeper attitudes, such as a sense of mortality and worry about loved ones and yet at the same time an optimistic welcoming of the future, they showed themselves to be "mature beyond their years," the study reported.

According to Walter Truett Anderson of Pacific News Service,

The emerging global culture is not all T-shirts and fast foods, thank God. It is also a widening acceptance of principles of human rights. Such principles are becoming global norms, fragile ones to be sure, often honored in rhetoric and brutalized in practice, but nonetheless, understandable statements of what peoples all over the world can demand for themselves, and can expect to be demanded of them by others.[31]

One of the most powerful influences on that global youth culture has been MTV, which first appeared on U.S. cable television in August 1981;

since then, it has exploded into a global phenomenon reaching by 1995 into 250 million(!) homes worldwide and is still expanding—despite much criticism and unease among the older generation. The recording business, by hitching would-be music hits to television, found a marketing tool that has brought it unprecedented profits. Sumner Redstone, chairman of Viacom, owner of MTV, said, "What we have found, you see, is that kids on the streets in Tokyo have more in common with kids on the streets in London than they do with their parents. We're catching these kids at a stage in life when all kids are essentially the same, when they virtually have to rebel against their parents. By the way, that is why freedom fighters all over the world associate themselves with MTV."[32] With MTV firmly established in Europe, Australia, Japan, Brazil, Latin America, and much of Asia, current plans to expand into India, South Africa, and China could eventually increase the number of households with MTV to 500 million. Much of MTV's success is based on adapting the musical programming to the musical tastes of teenagers of the region receiving it.

Videocassette Revolution

The global dissemination of Anglo-American mass culture, especially movies and music videos, has been greatly facilitated by the rapid dissemination of videocassette recordings and the equipment, videocassette recorders (VCRs), to play them on.

Media experts use the terms "explosion" and "revolution" to describe the VCR phenomenon of recent years. "Indeed, in less than a decade, the videocassette recorder and videocassette, or tape, have penetrated areas that the printing press and other information paraphernalia have not successfully reached after centuries."[33] The spread has been explosive through the less-developed nations as well as in the affluent West. Depending on culture and political structure, VCRs can have profound effects not only on viewers but also on broadcasting and other media. Widespread use can challenge the usual system of government control of television in most of the non-Western world by providing diversity and variety in entertainment. (Audiocassettes are doing much the same thing to radio broadcasting.) VCRs circumvent the use of broadcast television for both development and political control by bringing about de facto media decentralization. People, including youth, now have a newfound freedom to view what they want to view, not what Big Brother (or even their parents) thinks is best for them. And apparently much of what they want to view are movies, pop music, and videos from the West.[34]

In Saudi Arabia, the only choice on over-the-air television is the puritanical, heavily controlled, and dull programming of government programs. (For example, religious orthodoxy requires that a Saudi woman's face not be shown on television.) As a result, VCRs have proliferated, and much of the viewing includes the forbidden fruit of Western movies, including pornographic films, most of them smuggled into the country.

In India, many people annoyed by the inadequacies of state-run broadcasting networks are to turning to private enterprise "alternative television" news on videocassettes. The producer of "Business Plus," a monthly tape on political and economic issues, said India has the only private video newsmagazines in the world. The tapes, made in English and Hindi, rent for about 60 cents a day or sell for about $8. The audience is small but middle class and cosmopolitan and dissatisfied with the vacuity of official television news and documentaries. The trend to news-oriented videotapes began two years earlier with "Newstrack," a fast-paced monthly video magazine of investigative reporting with a segmented format like that of "60 Minutes."[35]

Throughout the emerging nations, small shops renting or selling videocassettes from the West have become commonplace. In the remote nation of Bhutan, people were watching videos on television sets before the nation had over-the-air television service. To an American, the VCR is an easy way to watch a movie, a music video, or a recorded television program at a more convenient time and place, but to millions in non-Western nations, VCRs are a means of enjoying the sometimes prohibited Western mass culture—a media activity that authoritarian governments have largely failed to censor or control.

Many videocassettes as well as compact disks and computer software sold around the world are pirated copies of Western movies, music recordings, and computer programs. The pirating of such intellectual property has been particularly flagrant in China, Hong Kong, and Japan. In February 1995, the United States and China reached an agreement that apparently solves a long-running dispute over China's failure to halt the illegal practices. But, in March 1998, pirated video compact disks of Hollywood movies such as "Titanic" were selling openly in Shanghai for $2 a copy and Chinese authorities had virtually given up efforts to prevent their sale.

Another threat to authoritarian or illegal actions is the ubiquitous camcorder, a lightweight hand-held television camera with a built-in VCR. More and more thousands are now owned by private citizens, and anyone can record a newsworthy or controversial event which may appear later on television. A police scandal erupted in Los Angeles in 1991 when an individual videotaped a prolonged and vicious beating of an arrested man, Rodney King, by a group of Los Angeles policemen wielding nightsticks. Shown repeatedly on television, the tape precipitated a national debate over police brutality and in time led to widespread rioting after King's trial in Los Angeles.

VCR technology is just a part of the steady flow of Western entertainment over the globe that has resulted in a love/hate relationship between many peoples around the world and the United States, in particular. The same persons who condemn the pervasive influence of American mass culture embrace things American or Western—whether in dress, music, entertainment, or lifestyle. (The differentiation between "American" and "Western" culture has become increasingly blurred due to cross-fertilization between fads, ideas, styles, and trends that seem to originate in more and more different sources. Just as science and technology have become internationalized, so has mass culture.) The young European or African intellectual who castigates America as a crass commercial influence is likely to be a fan of U.S. popular music and movies, to wear jeans, and to follow the shifting trends of the American youth culture.

Downside of Exporting Mass Culture

The West, it has been said, not only won the Cold War but also the battle for the world's leisure time. Mass culture has become one of America's most lucrative exports (after aerospace technology), but the problem is that, instead of exporting serious art as was done during the early Cold War, we are now sending out movies of Rambo-esque violence and Disney sentimentality, as well as much cultural trash. Critics say that the worst, instead of the best, of American mass culture is flooding the world. We are said to be advertising to the world escapism, consumerism, and the ideology of having fun.

A good example is "Baywatch," an inane television show about California hunks and babes which NBC initially canceled after just one season. Yet "Baywatch" has gone on to a new life—heard in 15 different languages and seen in 144 countries, including Iran and China, drawing more people than any other entertainment show in history. And movies that fail in the United States often recoup their losses abroad. For instance, Kevin Costner's fiasco "Waterworks" made nearly $176 million in foreign sales.

Critic Michiko Kakutani commented, "Some of America's cultural exports are so awful that you suspect that we're using the rest of the world as a vast toxic waste dump, and charging for the privilege."[36]

Further, serious and important foreign news often tends to be pushed aside or de-emphasized as the news media, particularly television and newsmagazines, give greater attention to the soft news of celebrities, scandals, trivia, and titillation. A good example was the unprecedented media coverage given to the death of Princess Diana. Her violent death in a high-speed car crash while being pursued by paparazzi in Paris was, of course, a major news story—AP considered it the biggest story of 1997. But the death of a Princess went on to become much more—a major, long-running cultural phenomenon about the most widely photographed and recognized person in the world, but not someone of political power.

For weeks, the story and its aftermath of accusations, recriminations, and rumors filled the world's news media. Buckingham Palace received 500,000 letters and 580,000 e-mail letters of sympathy. In London, Ian Jack, editor of *Granta,* cited the press-clippings agency Durrants as saying that the coverage in the world's magazines and newspapers by far exceeded that generated by any other event, anywhere in the world, at any time in history. That would seem to say that, for the British, Diana's death was the biggest news story ever!

For serious journalists, the question is this: Does such a story deserve such overwhelming coverage? During the Diana saga, the American public was inundated with detailed and repetitive news about the tragedy, but for the rest of that same year, Americans had received very little other news about the United Kingdom, its politics, economy, social problems, et cetera. Most Americans did not know who Tony Blair was, but they certainly knew all about Diana's companion Dodi Al-Fayed and her sons, Princes Harry and William. The death of Diana represents a nagging problem for global news coverage—how to maintain balanced and responsible reporting standards when the news media are competing vigorously over details of a news story of very high interest but low intrinsic importance.

Related to this media-driven dissemination of mass culture are the accompanying trends toward the internationalizing of mass communication and the growth of media conglomerates such as Murdoch's News Corporation, Time Warner/CNN, and Disney/ABC, which provide and distribute much of the mass culture fare abroad.

CHAPTER 6

Internationalizing the World's Media

> Mankind has become one, but not steadfastly one as communities or even as nations used to be, nor united through years of mutual experience ... nor yet through a common native language, but surpassing all barriers, through international broadcasting and printing.
>
> —Alexander Solzhenitsyn

If Jules Verne's adventurous Phineas Fogg traveled *Around the World in Eighty Days* again today he would find that as an Englishman abroad he would have little trouble keeping up with the news and entertainment. At almost every stopover, he would be able to buy a copy of the *International Herald Tribune* or possibly the *Financial Times*, and at his hotel's newsstand he would have a choice of the *Economist, Time,* or *Newsweek,* among other English-language publications. In his hotel room, he would be able to watch the day's televised news either from CNN via cable and Comsat from Atlanta or BBC World Service Television. On the local television station, he could see a world news package of stories put together by Reuters Television outside London. And if he had a small shortwave radio, he would be reassured by listening to the BBC World Service from Bush House in London or the Voice of America. Also, on local television, he would likely find reruns of his favorite British programs, and if he sought out a local movie theater, he likely would have a choice of current Hollywood productions. And chances are that a local bookstore or airport newsstand would have a wide selection of English-language magazines and paperback books.

The increasing availability of such Western publications and electronic media fare (most of it in English, the lingua franca of international communication) are examples of the way all the major institutions of news communication—world news services, satellite services, broadcast systems, great newspapers and magazines—have become increasingly internationalized or globalized in recent years. This change is due in part to innovations

91

in media technology (facsimile printing and satellite distribution, in particular) and a growing elite cosmopolitan audience, as well as other social and political realities. Whatever the cause, the fact is that more and more of the activities of the major news media now transcend parochial or national concerns and serve broader transnational purposes.

Out of the capitalistic West have been arising several media conglomerates that some critics feel may dominate, if not unduly influence, much of international communication and entertainment in the near future. Frequently mentioned among these "media baronies" are those of Rupert Murdoch of Australia, Britain, and America; Silvio Berlusconi of Italy; Time Warner, Turner Broadcasting, General Electric (NBC), Disney Company (ABC), and Viacom of the United States; Reinhard Mohn of the Bertelsmann group of Germany; Sony and Fujisankei of Japan; and the Hachette group of France—all multimedia and multinational. The competitive gambits of these media entrepreneurs are being keenly felt in Western Europe as well as the United States, where four major Hollywood film studios have been purchased by overseas interests. (More about these media baronies and their recent mergers follows later in this chapter.)

Whether this trend toward fewer, bigger, and more like-minded media of global communication is good or bad usually depends on the critic's personal tastes and ideology. But the internationalization of mass communication is proceeding in response to the needs and economic opportunities of a shrinking world. The transnational media are doing more than seizing the chance for greater profits from new markets, albeit those factors are obviously important. Whether viewed as another example of Western "media imperialism" or as a significant contribution to global understanding and integration, the international media are becoming increasingly cosmopolitan, speaking English, and catering to an internationally minded audience concerned about world affairs.

An American in Paris

The daily, ink-on-newsprint newspaper is still a major prop of journalism, and there are more than 8,000 dailies worldwide and many thousands more weekly journals. A few of the more serious "prestige" papers attract readers far beyond their national borders. Not many Americans read foreign publications, so they are unaware of the extent to which people abroad depend on newspapers and magazines published in other countries. The intellectually demanding *Le Monde* of Paris, famous for its analyses of world affairs, is widely read in the Arab world and francophone Africa. The London-based *Financial Times* uses a plant in Frankfurt to print nearly 53,000 copies daily of an edition described as "Europe's business paper" and has a U.S. edition printed in New York City for American readers. Gannett distributes in Europe copies of *USA Today* printed in Switzerland; the only difference is that the weather maps are of Europe and Asia. Britain's *Guardian* and *Daily Telegraph* are found on many foreign newsstands, as are the *Frankfurter Allegemeine* and the *Neue Zürcher Zeitung* of Zurich.

But the newspaper that has evolved furthest toward becoming a truly international daily is the *International Herald Tribune* of Paris. The *IHT* is the sole survivor of a number of English-language papers, including the *Chicago Tribune, Daily Mail* (of London), *New York Herald Tribune,* and *New York Times,* that earlier published Paris or European editions for English-speaking travelers. Started by James Gordon Bennett in 1887 as the Paris edition of the *New York Herald,* the *IHT* has outlived its parents and today is jointly owned by Whitney Communications, the *Washington Post,* and the *New York Times.* The *IHT* is produced by an editorial staff of 40, including copyboys and clerks. Much of its copy comes from the *New York Times, Los Angeles Times, Washington Post,* and the news services. Recently, much more of the paper is staff written. Averaging about 16 pages a day, the *Herald Tribune* sold about 200,000 copies six days a week in 181 countries (in Europe alone, sales were about 135,000), and no single country accounted for more than 15 percent of the total. This marvel of distribution appears daily on some 8,500 newsstands all over Europe, supplied by editions printed in Paris, London, the Hague, Marseilles, Rome, and Zurich and more recently in Hong Kong and Singapore.[1] African and Middle Eastern subscribers are served by mail; total mail subscriptions were 47,900 in 1995. In 1986 the *International Herald Tribune* began printing in Miami to facilitate distribution in North America, Latin America, and the Caribbean. As editors and compositors complete their work in Paris each evening, an electronic image of each page is sent via INTELSAT V-A Comsat to each of the nine printing plants at a speed of about four minutes per page. The *IHT* thus became the first newspaper in history to publish the same edition simultaneously on all continents.

Although it remains an American newspaper in outlook and perspective, it has gradually acquired an important non-American readership. Nearly half its readers are an elite group of European internationalists—businesspeople, diplomats, and journalists fluent in English. Publisher Lee Huebner called this a special community: "That global community of in-

ternational people in business and politics who may have been born in
New York or Stockholm, live in Lagos, but have more in common with
someone in Tokyo than with the guy next door."[2]

International Information Elite

These non-American readers are part of what William Read and other researchers have identified as an "international information elite" who, regardless of geographic location, share a similar rich fund of common experience, ideas, ways of thinking, and approaches to dealing with
international problems. A U.S. Information Agency survey found, for example, that "on the average as many as 15 to 30 percent of selected elite
audiences in non-Communist countries read *Time*."[3]

Read noted, "So when American media play an agenda-setting role
globally, the effect can be to assign the degree to which international attention is focused on the issue."[4]

U.S. Information Agency (USIA) research concludes that the "information elites" have similar clusters of interests, principally international affairs and economics. To a lesser degree, they are concerned also about social problems but do not share a high interest in art and popular culture.
The research indicates a "preference for substantially useful information related to a two-tiered world: global interdependence in politics and economics balanced against global diversity in cultural preferences."[5] A salient
feature of the transnational elite audiences, Read wrote, is that they sit atop
indigenous societies that are, in the main, highly nationalistic.

Numerous other publications, particularly magazines, have reached
and helped shape this international information elite. Hearst Magazines
International has had much recent success in publishing magazines abroad
with 64 foreign language editions of eight magazines. In 1995, its leaders,
Cosmopolitan, Esquire, Good Housekeeping, and *Popular Mechanics,* were
distributed in 14 languages to 60 countries.[6]

Another success story of transnational magazines is, of course, *Reader's
Digest,* which established its first foreign edition in Britain in 1938. By
1995, there were 47 international editions printed in 18 languages. Almost
13 million copies a month are sold abroad. In some countries, including
nearly all Spanish-speaking countries, the *Reader's Digest* was *the* most popular magazine.[7] So successful has been its adaptation to foreign soil that
many readers are unaware that the *Digest* is not an indigenous publication.
Although studies show that *Digest* readers abroad belong to a "quality audience" of the affluent, the well educated and the well informed, it is not

that same audience of decision makers that read *Time* and *Newsweek,* which are primarily news media.

Time and *Newsweek,* besides spawning such notable imitations as *Der Spiegel* in West Germany and *L'Express* in France, have been quite successful as transnational publications, and both can claim strong appeal to that internationally minded readership.

Time, over the years, has evolved into a multinational news medium for a multinational audience. *Time's* total circulation was 5.5 million in 1998. Of that, *Time Canada's* share was about 350,000, *Time Europe's* (including Africa and the Middle East), about 500,000, the edition for the Pacific region, about 350,000, and for Latin America, 90,744.[8] Readership studies found that *Time's* readers abroad are affluent, multilingual, and cosmopolitan. Often the reader is a comparatively young business executive, who is "likely to be internationally oriented in his economic and political opinions."[9] *Time* has increasingly tailored the editorial contents of its regional editions to those readers' interests, and for advertisers abroad, the magazine has offered more than 60 different editions based on geography.

Newsweek, with a foreign readership of about one-third of its total 1998 circulation of 3.25 million and with a European circulation of 300,000, has done much the same thing overseas. *Newsweek International* has carried hundreds of exclusive stories and featured numerous covers, all different from the domestic edition. While *Time* tailored its overseas editions to regional interests, *Newsweek* tried to be more global in its approach. Only about 15 percent of its readers abroad are Americans; the rest are from 150 countries. *Newsweek* has always had signed columns, but American columnists rarely appear in the international edition. Instead, the magazine publishes another team of internationalists who include journalists from Australia, Italy, Britain, Indonesia, West Germany, France, Japan, and Sri Lanka. In addition, *Newsweek* publishes a Japanese-language edition, *Newsweek Nihon Ban,* with a circulation of about 150,000.

Another American competitor of the newsmagazines abroad is the *Wall Street Journal.* With a satellite-assisted leap across the Pacific, the highly successful *Journal* launched in 1976 an Asian edition in Hong Kong that covers a 16-country, 6,000-square-mile business beat from Manila to Karachi. Averaging 12 pages, about one-third the size of the domestic edition, the *Asian Wall Street Journal* tries for the same mix of authoritative business and political news, a risky experiment for a region with so little press freedom. And pressures have been applied, mostly by Singapore's authoritarian ruler, Lee Kuan Yew. In November 1985, the editor of the *Asian Wall Street Journal* apologized to a Singapore court for any contempt of court raised by a *Journal* editorial commenting on Singapore politics. The incident raised questions about the appropriate responses when a foreign court challenges the editorial freedom of an American newspaper published abroad.[10] By mid-1990, after three years of harassment and a lengthy legal dispute with Lee, the *Journal* announced that it was ending circulation in the island republic.[11]

Similar problems seem to be on the horizon for Hong Kong which, when it was still a British colony, was second only to Japan in enjoying the most press freedom in Asia. While under British rule, Hong Kong became the major news center in the region and home for a large contingent of foreign correspondents as well as the publishing center for the *Far Eastern Economic Review, Asiaweek, Newsweek, International Herald Tribune,* and *Asian Wall Street Journal.* However, since the Crown Colony reverted to China in 1997, this open free-press situation has come under pressure and has started to decline markedly. By mid-1998, there was concern over efforts by local politicians with links to Beijing power centers to take over some of the Hong Kong papers.

The *Wall Street Journal* also has a European edition, printed in the Netherlands, and written and edited in Brussels, Belgium. The paper, which can be purchased on the day of publication throughout Europe and Britain, is edited for the international business executive doing business in Europe.[12] The Asian *Journal* has nearly 33,000 readers, whereas the European *Journal* has attracted about 47,000 readers.[13]

Almost anywhere one travels abroad, stacks of foreign publications can be found on newsstands, including in non-Western countries. An American tourist in Paris or London has a choice of the *International Herald Tribune, Time, Newsweek, USA Today,* or *Wall Street Journal.* A traveler arriving in francophone Abidjan, the capital of Ivory Coast, is impressed to find almost all the major French magazines plus that day's editions of the major Paris dailies, all flown in by jet. Similarly, in Nairobi, Kenya, a choice of British papers, including same-day delivery of the Sunday papers, is available at hotels and newsstands. This plenitude of reading matter may represent unfair competition with the struggling local press, but these publications do provide a window on the world for that small but essential group of influentials who need to be informed about world affairs.

In economically booming Latin America, following the invasion of cable television, American newspapers and magazines have been gaining many new readers in the region. In l997 and 1998, magazine publishers started Spanish-language editions of *Newsweek, Glamour, Discover, People,*

National Geographic, and *Rolling Stone.* The *Miami Herald* has become the international English newspaper of Latin America, with ten printing plants and a circulation of about 35,000 to 40,000. In 1998, Brazilian sales of *Reader's Digest* in Portuguese jumped from 35,000 to 600,000 in two years.

Changes in World News Services

The subtle changes in the world news services as they have expanded in postwar years are further evidence of this growing internationalization of transnational media. Although they claim to "cover the world," the agencies historically have tended to serve primarily their own national clients and those in their spheres of influence; that is, Reuters serviced British media and the British Commonwealth, AFP worked mainly for the French press and overseas French territories, and UPI (when it was in its prime) in addition to its U.S. clients long had strong connections in Latin America. But these world agencies have become more international in scope, selling their services to whoever will buy wherever they may be. AP is so widely used in Germany that it is practically a German service and a strong competitor to Deutsche Press Agentur (dpa).

In addition, the personnel of world agencies have become significantly internationalized. Formerly, the AP, for example, boasted that its news from abroad was reported by American AP correspondents who had experience in running an AP bureau in the United States. The agency would not depend on foreign nationals to provide news from their own countries for AP use in the United States.

That has changed. With the increased professionalism of journalists abroad, news agencies not only find it more economical to use qualified local journalists but often get better reporting from those who know their own country, its language, and its social and political traditions. Today, of about 400 AP staffers abroad, only 100 are Americans.

Nevertheless, AP's ties to its own U.S. media clients remain strong (no overseas client can be a member of the AP cooperative), and the news values of these domestic clients are of major importance in deciding news priorities, even though it makes business sense for a world news agency to sell its services overseas as widely as possible. For example, the more customers there are in Latin America for Reuters, the easier it is for Reuters to collect Latin American news, and, in turn, the greater the incentive not only to send that news to its British clients but also to distribute it among Latin American clients.

Although the world news agencies have been accused of neocolonial domination of news flow to and from developing nations, the fact remains that these highly competitive services must *sell* their news reports, and to make them saleable or useful to editors and broadcasters abroad, a news agency must supply news that foreign editors are interested in using. Furthermore, in many non-Western nations, world news agency reports are sold directly to national or official news agencies, which redistribute them to local media.

Numerous efforts have been made in recent years to organize these national agencies into continental or regional services to compete effectively with the world agencies. (These efforts are discussed in Chapter 10, "Muted Debate Over News Flow.")

Another facet of internationalization is foreign syndication of news by major daily papers. The New York Times News Service sends over 50,000 words daily to 550 clients, of which over 130 are newspapers abroad. The Times Syndicate also transmits 25,000 words weekly from major Spanish papers, 30,000 words from Italian papers, 10,000 words from a Japanese paper, and 40,000 words from a French paper.[14] Its close competitor is the Los Angeles Times/Washington Post News Service, which transmits about 60,000 words daily to 50 nations or about 600 newspapers, half of which are outside the United States. This total includes papers in West Germany and elsewhere that receive the dpa with which the service is affiliated.

As noted previously, there is syndication as well of television news film and videotapes, especially those of America's NBC, CNN, CBS, and ABC and Britain's BBC and ITN, most of it distributed by two Anglo-American firms—Reuters Television and World Television News—via videotape and satellite (and sometimes by airmail) to almost every television service in the world. There is probably more international cooperation than competition in the transnational video news business because most nations have only one government-controlled television service.

Unlike the print media, which usually carry a credit line on agency reports or syndicated material, syndicated television news is usually presented anonymously. Whether watching news from Cairo or Nairobi, the viewer is rarely told who supplied or who took the foreign video. Therefore, most viewers around the world are unaware that Reuters Television and WTN dominate the distribution of news film from many nations of widely differing standards of professionalism.

Advertising Goes Worldwide

Advertising, too, has followed the global trend. Recent "megamergers" among advertising and marketing services companies point up how internationalized Madison Avenue, the symbolic home of American advertising, has become.

In 1986, the biggest merger in advertising history took place when Saatchi & Saatchi of London agreed to buy Ted Bates Worldwide for $450 million. Saatchi & Saatchi thus became the world's biggest agency, with U.S. billings for 1985 of $4.6 billion and world billings of $7.6 billion. (Saatchi changed its name in 1995 to Cordiant after founders Maurice and Charles Saatchi left the firm in a bitter departure.) The second largest advertising empire was created with the amalgamation of three other major concerns—Doyle Dane Bernbach Group, BBDO International, and Needham Harper Worldwide—which combined had world billings of $5 billion and U.S. billings of $3.7 billion.[15] Later, England's WPP agency bought out two American giants: J. Walter Thompson and Olgilvy and Mather.

Agency executives involved in these mergers cited the industry's understanding of the need to offer clients worldwide service as a primary motivation. As an executive of Young & Rubicam pointed out, "There is a trend toward global assignment of agencies. If you don't have a complete set of worldwide resources, you're in danger of being left out in terms of getting the best clients."[16] Implied in all of this is the view that transnational advertising agencies would be in a position to channel standardized advertising from transnational corporations into transnational media with minimum effort. The same commercial—whether for Coke or McDonald's—could just be translated into many languages and placed in media anywhere in the world.

However, this "global sell" theory has not worked out, according to Alvin Toffler, who wrote, "What's wrong with the global sell theory is that it makes little distinction between the world's regions and markets. Some are still in a pre-mass-market condition; others are still at the mass-market stage; and some are already experiencing the de-massification characteristic of an advanced economy."[17] Due to cultural preferences, widespread consumer differences about products persist as do attitudes toward food, beauty, work, play, love, and politics. Toffler concluded that "globalization is not the same as homogeneity. Instead of a single global village, as forecast by Marshall McLuhan, we are likely to see a multiplicity of quite different global villages—all wired into the new media system, but all straining to retain or enhance their cultural, ethnic, national, and political individuality."[18]

Increased communication, as was stressed earlier, leads to increased organization and consequently some concentration of control in the international news media. Fewer and fewer editors and broadcast executives are making editorial decisions for more and more people. The need to cooperate and join together in ever-larger organizations seems at times stronger than the demands of independence and competition. Regional and continental media organizations are playing increasingly crucial roles in international news communication.

A good example of such supranational cooperation is the European Broadcasting Union (EBU), which has developed some highly regarded news exchanges on Eurovision. (London is a major television news center in part because it has the advantage of membership in the Eurovision News Exchange.)

Media Change in Europe, West and East

The increasing economic integration of the European Community plus the demassification and deregulation of broadcast media are rapidly *internationalizing* much of mass communication in Western Europe. Although Europeans, like people everywhere, prefer to read, view, and listen to communications in their home or native languages, the push toward transnational communication is still strong. This is due to the rapid expansion of cable and satellite options for viewers as well as increased numbers of private or commercial television and radio channels and the increasing popularity of VCRs and the Internet.

As already mentioned, major American and British print and broadcasting organizations are each trying to increase their readers and audiences in European nations. And other media conglomerates in France, Germany, Italy, and Japan are buying up media properties abroad. Deregulation of and privatization of radio and television and the expansion of cable and pay television, assisted by satellite distribution, also have added potentially important new daily news outlets in English as well as many more entertainment options for Europeans. Major players, including Ted Turner's Cable News Network, Rupert Murdoch's Sky Channel, Société Européenne des Satellites (SES) in Luxembourg, and various other consortia, including Anglovision and the BBC's World Service Television, a 24-hour news channel to rival CNN, are trying to break into the expanding electronic news and entertainment market in Europe.

Europe's broadcasting systems, formerly run by governments or by public corporations (paid for by special taxes or fees), have heretofore generally offered high-quality programming but with limited choices. But West Europe is now following the deregulated American models, with greatly increased choices. As a result, there has been a big rush for the huge profits to be made. Adherents of Europe's tradition of public service broadcasting feel that much programming quality will be sacrificed by deregulation and commercialization.[19] Today Europe has more than 50 satellite television services and most, of course, cross national boundaries. When the 1980s began, there were only 28 major commercial television channels in all of Europe. By 1989, that had doubled to 56. As satellite and cable services mature in the 1990s, the growth is expected to be spectacular: 120 major channels, by one estimate, filling an additional 200,000 hours of air time each year.[20] The money to be made from advertising, viewer fees, and revenues from movies and video programs is expected to run into the billions.

Western Europe nations, particularly France, concerned about the influence and popularity of American movies and television shows on European audiences, have established quotas on imports and subsidized their own productions. However, another quieter invasion has taken place—American companies have infiltrated nearly every corner of the European television business. Time Warner, Viacom, Disney/ABC, Cox Cable, NBC, US West, and others are getting involved in European-based television programming, in broadcast stations, in cable and satellite networks, and in the coming convergence of telecommunications and entertainment. And they see a huge market—350 million in 12 major Western European nations and 650 million overall west of Russia, many of them hungry for televised news and entertainment.[21]

In Eastern Europe, the media and their audiences are changing as well. As Jane Perlez reported,

> Poland, a country of some 10 million television sets, all dutifully tuned to propaganda during the 40 plus years of Communist rule, is being wired for almost anything these days. Foreign channels, beamed in from London, Frankfurt, and Paris, offer news, sports, soft porn, movies, exercise sessions and the most popular foreign programming, MTV. Hundreds of local cable channels, many of them "mom and pop" businesses that wire single apartment buildings, deliver pirated American B movies

with Polish voice-overs. The fare on the two state channels is more staid, although "Murphy Brown" has been a hit on Channel 1, where tooth paste and car commercials now generate revenue.[22]

The fact that Poles are watching what they want to watch, whether it is CNN, the Simpsons, MTV, or Polish news stations, is certainly changing life in Poland.

New Media Baronies

Many of the innovative changes in European media, as elsewhere, are being made by the transnational media barons, themselves a by-product of rapid changes in international communication. There is growing concern as well about the economic, and potentially political, power wielded by these powerful forces in global communication.

The prototype of the new media barons and very much a key player is Rupert Murdoch. With the 150 media properties he owns in Australia, Britain, and the United States, Murdoch has been carefully putting together a vertically integrated global media empire.[23] In the United States, he owns the Fox television network as well as *TV Guide*. In addition, he has a significant share of 20th Century Fox broadcasting, which owns the rights to thousands of hours of films and television programs. In Europe, he has pioneered in satellite broadcasting and owns 90 percent of Sky Channel (a satellite television system), a new sports network, and a 24-hour news channel that draws from his two London papers, the *Times* and the *Sunday Times*. Other properties include STAR TV, a regional satellite service based in Hong Kong, two-thirds of daily newspaper circulation in Australia, HarperCollins Publishers, *New York* and *Seventeen* magazines, and other British papers, including the *Sun* and *News of the World*. Total assets of the News Corporation, Ltd., Murdoch's holding company, have an estimated value of over U.S. $12 billion. Constantly juggling his properties (and his considerable debts), his News Corporation, which had revenues of less than $1 billion in 1980, had expanded its revenues to $9.7 billion in 1996. Murdoch's biggest recent gamble has been Sky Channel, his four-channel direct satellite service in Britain, which he recently merged with British Satellite Broadcasting, his main rival for that lucrative market. In the United States, he has been aggressively expanding his Fox television network.[24]

Murdoch's current strategy apparently is to own every major form of programming—news, sports, films, and children's shows—and beam them via satellites or the television stations he owns or controls to homes in America, Europe, Asia, and South America. He recently said, "We want to put our programming everywhere and distribute everybody's product around the world."[25]

Murdoch's media acquisitions apparently influenced three major U.S. media mergers in 1995—all of which had implications for the future of international communications. In August 1995, the Walt Disney Company announced its purchase of Capital Cities/ABC in a deal valued at $19 billion. The merger brought together ABC—then the most profitable television network, including its highly regarded news organization (Peter Jennings as anchor)—and its ESPN sports cable service, with an entertainment giant: Disney's Hollywood film and television studios, cartoon characters, theme parks, etc., *and* the merchandise they generate. (In 1995, the Disney Company sold more than $15 billion worth of Disney merchandise worldwide, a total more than seven times the global box-office receipts for Disney movies.)

A month later, Time Warner and Turner Broadcasting Co. announced they would merge their sprawling operations, reinforcing Time Warner as the world's largest communications giant. Both companies had major news-related media with overseas involvements. Warner had *Time* and other major magazines as well as HBO, Cinemax, Hollywood studios, and 50 record labels. Turner Company had CNN, CNN International, and Headline News in addition to film and television production.

The third big merger of that year was Westinghouse's takeover of CBS Inc., creating the nation's largest broadcast station group, with 39 radio and 16 television stations reaching 32 percent of the nation.

These megamergers positioned the resulting giants—Disney/ABC, Time Warner/Turner, and Murdoch—to better penetrate and dominate the growing international markets for television, movies, news, sports, records, and other media programs. At the time of the merger with ABC, Disney president Michael Eisner spoke glowingly of India's middle class of 250 million as a great potential audience for Disney movies, cartoons, news, and sports programs. NBC and NFL games have been gaining large audiences overseas; hence the importance of the ESPN networks. Critics noted that news organizations, such as Time or CNN, were just a small part of these entertainment giants.

The keen competition among CNN, MSNBC, and Murdoch's Fox network for a 24-hour cable news channel in America (see Chapter 3, "International News System") has strong international potential as well.

Broadcast networks have been looking to international markets as a way of gaining hundreds of millions of new viewers. NBC's international holdings currently are about 20 percent of the network's worth of $10 to $20 billion; in the next 10 years, half of the network's value is expected to come from international holdings. Asia is predicted to be the main area of global audience growth because about 25 percent of the continent's 400 million households are expected to receive cable by the year 2000. By contrast, the U.S. market, with cable in 65 million of its 97 million households, is nearing saturation. Numbers of cable viewers are expected to rise abroad in time for the startup of NBC Europe as well as related NBC services in Latin America. Other competitors in the global broadcasting race after CNN and NBC are Disney/ABC, BBC, and NHK of Japan.

Other European Baronies

Among European media groups with far-reaching holdings is Bertelsmann A.G. of Germany, headed by the little-known Reinhard Mohn, who was a German prisoner of war in Kansas during World War II and was impressed by U.S. democracy and the Book of the Month Club.[26] Returning to Germany, he took over the family's Bible-publishing house and went on to build the Bertelsmann group into a media giant with book and record clubs in Germany, Spain, Brazil, United States, and 18 other countries. Bertelsmann owns Bantam, Doubleday, Dell publishing in the United States, and Plaza y Janes book publishers in Spain, in addition to 37 magazines in five countries, record labels like RCA/Ariola, and a number of radio and television properties.

In March 1998, Bertelsmann shocked U.S. book publishing by announcing it was buying Random House for an estimated $1.4 billion, consolidating its claim as the world's largest English-language publisher of trade books. Considered the crown jewel of American book publishers, Random House had $1.1 billion in sales in 1996. With the sale, half of the top 20 U.S. publishing firms, with a 28 percent share of the total U.S. market, were in foreign hands. The deal heightened the power of Bertelsmann, which had $12.86 billion in revenues in 1997 and ranked as the world's third largest media conglomerate, behind Time Warner and Disney companies.[27]

Possibly the most swashbuckling of the new barons is Italy's Silvio Berlusconi, who has built a multibillion dollar media television and newspaper empire, Fininvest, of unusual power and influence. With 42 percent of Italy's advertising market and 16 percent of daily newspaper circulation, he has concentrated his power more into a single market than any of the aforementioned barons. Fininvest had earnings of $9 billion in 1991. He owns Italy's three main private television channels, Rete 4, Canale 4, and Italia 1, as well as *Il Giornale,* a leading Milan paper, two leading news weeklies, 13 regional dailies, and a large book publisher. He has reached over into France, where he was part owner of Le Cinq, which went bankrupt, and also to Germany, where he is part owner of Tele-5.[28] Using his extensive media power, he became prime minister of Italy in April 1994 after forming a coalition with members of an ex-fascist party. The media baron-turned-politician promised a revolution of prosperity and clean dealing. However, he was soon in political hot water. By November of 1994, the 58-year-old billionaire was forced to resign when charged with corruption. In 1998, he was convicted on corruption charges.

Aside from Murdoch, few of these barons are well known in America. Some Americans, however, have been distressed at the way that Hollywood's assets have been sold off to foreigners, particularly to the Japanese. In November 1990, MCA, one of the nation's largest entertainment companies, was acquired by Matsushita Electric Industrial Company of Japan for $6.13 billion. MCA owned, among other entities, Universal Studios, Universal Pictures, MCA Records, theme parks, and Putnam's publishing firm.

Another Japanese giant, Sony, Matsushita's arch-rival and owner of CBS Records, Columbia Pictures, and Tristar Pictures, had earnings of $3.5 to $4.5 billion in 1991. Sony and Matsushita between them controlled more than a quarter of the American movie market. However, in 1994, the Sony Corporation announced it was taking $3.2 billion in losses on the value of the Hollywood studios it had acquired only five years earlier.

As mentioned, Murdoch owns 20th Century Fox, and MGM-Pathé of Italy has acquired the former MGM/United Artists studios. Only Warner, Paramount, and Disney motion picture studios are still owned by American companies.[29] Such transnational acquisitive media activities are a natural and expected result of the globalization of mass communications.

But the United States and other democracies may need to update their own communication policies formulated before news, entertainment, magazines, and other mass communication moved so freely and pervasively across borders. What, for example, are the effects on U.S. communication law regarding monopoly, competition, and diversity of views, as well as freedom of expression? The U.S. Commerce Department said it would look at how widespread the globalization of mass communication had become and study the economic and competitive factors underlying it. In particular, the study would examine the impact of global media on social, cultural, and political developments worldwide.[30]

English as the Media Language

Finally, a word about a basic fact of the globalization of mass communication: the widespread role of the English language. Effective communication across national borders, regardless of other cultural and political differences, certainly requires that sender and receiver communicate in a mutually understandable language. More and more, that language is English, which is clearly the leading tongue of international communication today.

Among the "Big Ten" of world languages, English ranked second with 415 million native speakers in 12 countries after Mandarin Chinese with about 800 million, and is ahead of Russian with 282 million speakers, Spanish with 285 million, Arabic with 171 million, and German with 118 million. Furthermore, English is the most widely used geographically, and for about 400 million educated persons around the world, English is their second language. Several hundred million more people have some knowledge of English, which has official or semiofficial status in some 60 countries, which thus can be reached through English. What is more, this number includes most of the world's leaders. In all, there are about 1 billion English speakers in the world, and by the year 2000 that number is expected to reach 1.5 billion.

Unquestionably, English has become *the* global language of science and technology.[31] More than 80 percent of all information stored in 100 million computers around the world is in English, and 80 percent of all scientific papers are published first in English. English is the language of the information age: computers talk to each other in English. English is the most-taught language in the world; it is not really replacing other languages but supplementing them.

In many developing nations, English is the language of education, providing an entrée to knowledge and information. (But one unfortunate result is that many native English speakers, especially Americans, have much less incentive than, say, Israelis, Dutch, or Swedes to learn other peoples' languages. Few Americans even learn to speak Spanish, although it is widely spoken here and is the first language of over 90 percent of our over

20 million Hispanic population.)

For these and other reasons, English has also become the leading media language in international communication. Most of the world's news—whether by cable, shortwave radio, telex, telegraph, the Internet, or communication satellites—is carried in English. Not only AP, Reuters, and WTN but also AFP, dpa, and even ITAR-TASS transmit some of their news in English, as do many national news agencies. Six of the world's biggest broadcasters—BBC, CBS, NBC, ABC, CNN, and CBC—reach a potential audience of about 300 million people through English-language broadcasting. English is also the dominant language of satellite television.[32]

Moreover, English is the leading linguistic medium in a major field of world communications: shortwave radio broadcasting targeted to audiences in foreign countries.[33] A total of 100 broadcasting outlets with central studios in 84 countries use English as a means of reaching listeners beyond their national frontiers. Russia, China, Japan, the Philippines, and Sri Lanka use English in some of their foreign broadcasts.

The imperialism of nineteenth-century Britain was a major reason, of course, why so many people from Singapore to India to Kenya to Nigeria to Bermuda converse today in English. Not unrelated is the phenomenon of the many English-language daily newspapers still flourishing today in countries where English is neither the official nor even the most widely used language. Beginning with the *Chronicle of Gibraltar* in 1801, English-language dailies, catering to expatriates, the foreign community, and local educated elites, have long survived, if not always flourished, in such diverse metropolises as Mexico City, Caracas, Paris, Jerusalem, Taipei, Rome, Athens, Cairo, Beirut, Manila, Bangkok, Singapore, and Tokyo, as well as throughout India and Pakistan and the former British territories of Africa, such as Nigeria, Ghana, Sierra Leone, South Africa, Uganda, Kenya, Tanzania, Zimbabwe, and Zambia. In parts of polyglot Africa, English has almost evolved into another African language because of the role it plays in education, commerce, and mass communication.

Most of the artifacts of mass culture that move across national borders are in English. Jeremy Tunstall said that English is the language best suited for "comic strips, headlines, riveting first sentences, photo captions, dubbing, subtitling, pop songs, billboards, disc-jockey banter, news flashes, and sung commercials."[34] A great appeal of English as an international language is that it is easy to speak badly.

English, the most widely spoken language of Western Europe, has gained wide currency in Central and Eastern Europe in part because much of Western pop culture is in English. In Poland and Czech Republics, words like "trip," "smoke," "car," "dance," "gag," and dozens of others are part of young people's vocabulary.

This thrust of English as a world media language has become self-generating, and any educated person of whatever nationality who wishes to participate in this shrinking and interdependent world finds it useful to know English. In fact, since English is now spoken as a second language by more people around the globe than by the British and the Americans combined, it must now be considered as belonging to the world, as indeed it does. For when two persons of differing linguistic backgrounds are able to converse, the chances are they will be speaking English.

The sharing of language and journalistic traditions has resulted in a good deal of intermixing of journalists of Britain, Canada, and the United States. Recently, an influx of Brits has had an impact on American magazines. Tina Brown, editor of the *Tatler* in London, came to New York City as editor at *Vanity Fair* and became editor of the *New Yorker*. (In 1998, she was succeeded by David Remnick.) Her husband, Harold Evans, former editor of the *Sunday Times* of London, was founding editor of *Condé Nast Traveler* and later became president of Random House. He is now a supervisory editor of *U.S. News* and the *New York Daily News*. British editors have taken over the helms of the *National Review, Details,* the *New Republic, TV Guide,* and *Harper's Bazaar.*[35] The *Economist,* the British financial magazine, has gone from a mere 20,000 U.S. circulation in America in 1978 to nearly 221,000 just 15 years later, accounting for 45 percent of its global circulation.

So many Canadians are among us in television news and entertainment and seem so Americanized that we are hardly aware of their backgrounds. Canadian-born television journalists include Peter Jennings (ABC), Morley Safer (CBS), Robert MacNeil (PBS), Arthur Kent (NBC), Bob McKeown (CBS), Doug James, (CNN), Barrie Dunsmore (ABC), and Sheila MacVicar (ABC). Many more are prominent in entertainment.

The English language has also been described as the greatest neocolonialist force in the world today. Perhaps in some contexts it is, but, more importantly, English is the principal language in which the world communicates with itself. As a result, the English language is the cement that holds together much of international mass communication.

CHAPTER 7

Public Diplomacy and Propaganda

> When it came to radio waves the iron curtain was helpless. Nothing could stop the news from coming through—neither sputniks nor minefields, high walls, nor barbed wire. The frontiers could be closed, words could not.
>
> —Lech Walensa

There was a time not so long ago when a shortwave listener could tune into Albania's then-powerful Radio Tirana and hear in Balkan-accent English, "First, the news: The revisionist Titoist clique of imperialist lackeys has attempted again to violate the true teachings of Marxism-Leninism." Such harangues have receded into a quaint past since the end of the Cold War, reported David Binder.[1]

Broadcasting over shortwave, however, has not receded in volume. On any given evening, an Arab sitting at a cafe in Algiers, a Peruvian llama herder in a shelter in the Andes, or a Chinese dissident in Beijing can share a common communication experience. By merely flicking on a shortwave radio receiver and twisting the dials, each will hear the same polyglot cacophony of sounds detailing the news, unfolding diverse feature programs, and playing all sorts of music. The variety of languages spoken is immense, but each listener can, with little difficulty, find a program he or she understands. Nowhere is the prism of international communication more apparent. In shortwave radio broadcasting, one person's "truth" or news is another person's "propaganda," and vice versa. And again, one person's music is another's "noise." Transnational radio is also a major conveyor of what is sometimes called public diplomacy.

For over 40 years, public diplomacy (a government's overt efforts to influence other governments) and shortwave radio were dominated by the great East-West struggle called the Cold War, which in effect ended in 1990 with the reunification of Germany and the withdrawal of Soviet troops from Central Europe. But public diplomacy and its propaganda wars continued on other polemical battlefield—in the Persian Gulf after Iraq invaded Kuwait; in the tragic and prolonged struggle between the Serbs, Croats, and Bosnian Muslims in the former Yugoslavia; and over human rights in China. With the globalization of the economy, international frictions are now more concerned with economic competition and business contentions between nations, rather than political and ideological differences. Concerns about incipient war on, say, the Korean peninsula or in Kashmir are partially replaced by worries about the collapsing economies in Indonesia, Japan, or Thailand, and how these trends may undermine stable economies in the West. Political espionage has been replaced by economic espionage and concerns about the global pirating of videos, movies, CDs, and computer software. For example, 90 percent of software used on China's computers is reported to have been pirated.

Much of the flood of messages constantly washing over the globe is not neutral or "disinterested" information but "purposive" communication—words, sounds, and images intended to influence perceptions and opinions. A great deal of what refracts through the prism of international radio is purposive and is often called "propaganda," that is, the systematic use of words or symbols to influence the attitudes or behaviors of others. "Propaganda" is a loaded term, a pejorative epithet subjectively defined as a "persuasive statement I don't like." No one—journalist, broadcaster, writer, or educator—wants to be called a propagandist. Transnational communicators put on their ideological blinkers when they insist, "*We* deal in information or truth. *They* deal in propaganda."

International political communication (IPC), cumbersome term though it is, is a useful and neutral expression encompassing such terms as public diplomacy, overseas information programs, cultural exchanges, and even propaganda activities and political warfare. A useful definition for IPC is: The political effects that newspapers, broadcasting, film, exchanges of persons, cultural exchanges, and other means of international communication can achieve.

However, a distinction should be made between official and private communications and between international communications designed to have a political effect and those that are not. Here, then, are four broad categories of IPC:[2]

1. Official communications *intended* to influence foreign audiences (i.e., public diplomacy), such as those by the U.S. Information Agency, Voice of America, Radio Moscow, British Information Service, Deutsche Welle, Radio Havana, and BBC's World Service. Most international short-

wave broadcasting falls into this category, and almost every nation with the capability will sponsor some broadcasting efforts across its borders.

2. Official communications *not intended* to influence foreign audiences, a small category indeed. One example has been the U.S. Armed Forces Radio and Television Network. At its peak, AFN operated some 200 radio and 30 television transmitters serving American forces overseas and in the process acquired a huge "eavesdropping" audience. Many young Europeans developed a taste for American music and learned to speak American English by listening to AFN.

3. Private communications *intended* to influence foreign audiences politically. This is another small category including various organizations and groups working to promote international understanding, for example, peace groups advocating a freeze on nuclear weapons. "Crossroads Africa," a private group operating with U.S. funds, possibly qualifies.

4. Private communications *without a political purpose.* Among these would be Western news agencies, media enterprises overseas such as advertising agencies, and distributors of motion pictures, television programs, videocassettes and audiocassettes. Activities of church groups and relief organizations, important in poor countries, belong in this classification as well. The vast flood of American mass culture (much of it movies, music videos, pop recordings, and television programs, most of it produced within a five-square-mile area of Hollywood, has both negative and positive effects on international political communication.

Without doubt, the overseas impact of private U.S. communications is far greater than that of U.S. public diplomacy through USIA and VOA, but the actual impact is difficult to assess. As we have seen, Western pop culture certainly contributed to political change in Eastern Europe in recent years. Unintended effects sometimes can be more profound than those intended to bring change.

Lines between these four categories often become blurred. I was puzzled, for instance, to find U.S. paperback books selling far below U.S. prices in African bookstores. Later, I learned the U.S. government covertly subsidized the sale of these paperbacks. Whether or not this is "propaganda," even if the books are of clear educational value, is an arguable point. Often newsreels and short features were shown in African movie theaters without being identified as a free service of the French or British governments. Much of the popular music heard on private radio stations in Latin America was provided by the Voice of America.

Official IPC efforts are usually a supplement to diplomacy—ways by which governments try to extend their influence abroad and pursue their foreign-policy objectives. The Western approach to public diplomacy, as conducted by governments of the United States, Britain, France, Germany, and the like, has been quite different from that of former Communist nations.

The international news media of all nations play a significant role in international political communication. The privately owned media organizations of the West serve their own commercial purposes by distributing and selling news and entertainment around the globe without intentional political aims. Yet, at the same time, the news media transmit a good deal of purposive official information, that is, propaganda, because all governments work hard at getting *their* versions of news and events into the world's news media. Much of the news from official sources in national capitals is intended to serve foreign-policy goals. News and propaganda are not mutually exclusive categories. The media serve the purposes of public diplomacy whether they carry a story of President Clinton's views on Boris Yeltsin or Iraq's complaints about arms inspections by the United Nations. A continuing problem for professional journalists is that of separating legitimate news from self-serving official "interpretations" of the news— whatever the source. Nevertheless, the two are often identical.

Authoritarian as well as Communist news media, much less independent of official controls, often serve as unquestioning conduits of political communication from their own governments. Editors in Beijing or Baghdad usually face no professional dilemmas over whether to carry stories supporting their governments' foreign policies.

Less-developed nations are mostly on the receiving end of public diplomacy because most lack the communication capability to compete effectively globally. A partial exception has been the extensive radio broadcasting at times by a few developing nations—currently, Egypt and North Korea send out more hours of foreign broadcasting than France, India, or Japan.[3] On the other hand, many poor nations and their elites have benefited from the development aid, cultural exchanges, and educational assistance they have received from developed nations—all aspects of international political communication.

International Radio Broadcasting

In this day of direct-broadcast satellites, global television, and the Internet, the powerful and pervasive medium of international radio broadcasting, long capable of carrying messages around the world almost instantaneously, is easily underestimated or ignored. According to audience surveys, listening on shortwave radio continues to increase. A BBC study found that 200 million people daily tune in and, according to sales figures, there are about 600 million shortwave radios around the globe—half in Asia and Africa.[4] That is mass communication.

In the 1930s, political leaders such as Nazi Germany's Josef Goebbels talked of international radio as a "limitless medium" and saw it as a powerful instrument of international diplomacy, persuasion, and even coercion. For over half a century, transnational radio has been just that—a key instrument of international political communication as well as many other things.[5] The medium enjoyed a rapid and diverse expansion and by the late 1930s was being used by national governments, religious organizations, commercial advertisers, domestic broadcasters, and educators to carry their messages across national borders.

In the last 25 years, the total number of national broadcasters has risen to over 125, and the number of hours broadcast has almost doubled that of the 1960s.[6] Shortwave radio messages are sent from transmitters directly throughout the world to receiving sets, but international radio's growth and diversity continue today with the utilization by national broadcasters of local AM and FM with signals sent down by satellites. BBC does this with 800 stations around the world, 200 of them in the United States. But most Americans, unlike many other nationalities, do not listen much to international radio and so are unaware of how pervasive it is.

Anyone interested in making contact with the vast world of international shortwave radio can buy a small shortwave radio (for less than $100) and a copy of either *Passport to World Band Radio,* an annual U.S. publication, or the latest issue of *World Radio TV Handbook,* published annually in Denmark, which gives the program schedules and information on how to listen in on any of 1,600 shortwave stations emanating from 160 countries. They offer from two or three to 60 or more language services broadcasting for 10 to 100 hours a day or more. The formats are equally diverse: newscasts, talks, interviews, editorial comments, press reviews, documentaries, and a good deal of music. News on-the-hour every hour about domestic and foreign events is a common feature, but other informational programs try to reflect the broader cultural, social, and economic aspects of particular nations through dramas, music, sports events, and religious services.[7]

Here we are concerned with the largest international broadcasting operators. Currently, in order of total hours of weekly broadcasting abroad, they are the United States, the People's Republic of China, Russia, Great Britain, Germany, Egypt, North Korea, France, India, and Japan.

The loudest voices in world broadcasting—Radio Moscow, Radio Beijing, Voice of America, Deutsche Welle and Deutschland Funk, BBC World Service, Radio France Internationale, and Radio Cairo—rely mainly on the following languages, in descending order of use: English, Russian, Mandarin Chinese, Arabic, Spanish, French, Japanese, Indonesian, Portuguese, German, Italian, Persian (Farsi), Swahili, Hindi, Hausa, and Korean.[8]

A significant portion of international political rivalries and frictions are refracted through the prism of international broadcasting—the nationalistic and ethnic animosities in the post–Cold War world, the Arab-versus-Israeli tensions as well as those between moderate and radical Arab regimes, the North-South disputes between rich and poor nations, plus dozens of smaller regional controversies and disagreements between neighboring nations. Any major global crisis will be widely reported, analyzed, and commented upon.

As the Cold War was winding down, Radio Moscow and its related Soviet broadcasters were on the air 2,257 hours weekly during 1988.[9] The United States countered with 16 hours daily of Russian-language VOA broadcasts into the Soviet Union, while U.S.-backed Radio Free Europe broadcast into Eastern Europe and Radio Liberty broadcast in non-Russian languages to various parts of the Soviet Union. In 1988, the United States was broadcasting globally 2,360 hours weekly; China, 1,517 hours weekly; United Kingdom, 756 hours; and India, 444 hours.[10] By June 1994, after the demise of the Cold War, the United States had dropped to 2,000 hours weekly, Russia to 1,400 hours, China steady at 1,600 hours, Britain up to about 1,800 hours, and India steady at 500 hours.[11]

Amid the cacophony of sometimes strident and pejorative voices clashing over the international airwaves, it is important to remember that international radio is also a substantial news source for many millions, but nowhere is the truism that one person's news is another person's propaganda more apparent. Listeners can twist the dials to find a version of world events that suits their own needs and worldviews; this is especially true for people living under dictatorships that lack popular support. News on international radio may often be acrimonious and self-serving, but without question it provides a *diversity* of news and views for many millions.

The importance of shortwave news is demonstrated, for example, when a political crisis or attempted coup occurs in an African nation. In such situations, local broadcasters usually go off the air and local residents out of habit tune to BBC World Service or VOA to determine what is really happening in their own country.

The first days after the Chernobyl nuclear accident incident during April/May 1986 illustrated the important role that international broadcasting can, on occasion, play. As mentioned in Chapter 2 ("Changing Ideologies"), with the Soviet government providing scant information, Western broadcasters became a credible source of news to Soviet bloc listeners. Their programs also stressed practical advice for survival. The Polish-language service of Radio Free Europe was on the air two hours ahead of Polish radio stations with the news that high radiation levels had been detected in Scandinavia and with the subsequent Soviet announcement that the accident had indeed occurred. RFE repeatedly broadcast an interview with a Polish-speaking hematologist in New York City who gave survival advice, including how to wash possibly contaminated vegetables. "Whenever there is a crisis, there is a craving for information and people go out of the cities and into rural areas where there is no jamming to get information," said one RFE official about Soviet radio listeners.[12]

With so much of what fills the night air (when reception is best) perceived by many as propaganda, the credibility of an international station's news and commentaries is crucial for its reputation among foreign listeners. The international broadcaster that has long enjoyed the best reputation for believability and objectivity is the World Service of the BBC. As a public corporation, the domestic BBC is financed by license fees paid by each British household with a radio or television set.

The BBC World Service is not funded by license fees; instead it receives about $160 million annually in parliamentary grants-in-aid. The government, in consultation with the service, has the final decision over which languages are broadcast, but editorial control of the programs rests entirely with the BBC. The World Service broadcasts in English and 44 other languages and, according to its research, reaches 143 million regular listeners in a week. Of those, 122 million listen directly, whereas about 27 million, with some overlap, listen to rebroadcasts on local stations. Of the total audience, 35 million listen in English. The World Service receives about half a million letters a year; the total in 1996 was 671,002. Languages used in most letters were English, 119,897; Hindi, 107,602; Burmese, 103,602; Tamil, 86,102; and Arabic, 38,303.

The BBC says that its key aims are to deliver objective information to help meet the need for education and English-language teaching and to provide access to the best of world culture and entertainment.

BBC's high credibility abroad has developed in part because the World Service broadcasts news and programming is originally prepared for the domestic services of the BBC. The highly professional reporters and stringers, at home and abroad, are essentially reporting to British radio listeners and from this input are selected (without intervention of the Foreign Office) the news and features for the World Service. This approach ensures that the World Service reflects the diversity of British public opinion and BBC professionalism and not necessarily the views of the current government.

During Britain's war with Argentina over the Falkland Islands, Prime Minister Margaret Thatcher bitterly criticized the BBC for not sufficiently supporting the British war effort. Some saw this as evidence of BBC's independence—the independence that draws so many listeners to BBC during times of crisis.

Shortly after the BBC World Service announced the start of the Gulf War in January 1991, it expanded its Arabic-language broadcasts to 14 hours a day, 5 hours longer than before the crisis. An estimated 10 million Arabs from North Africa to the Persian Gulf listened in—a far larger number than listened to either Voice of America or Radio Moscow. Although Britain was a participant in the war, BBC regularly reported what Radio Baghdad was saying as well as news about the British antiwar movements. Also, its Hausa-language service, which goes to Muslim West Africa, dutifully reported that its listeners had elected Saddam Hussein of Iraq as the winner of its man-of-the-year contest.[13]

Two other separate organizations—the British Information Services and the British Council, which deals with cultural affairs and exchanges—supplement the broadcasting service in Britain's efforts at public diplomacy overseas.

U.S. Activities in Public Diplomacy

U.S. activities in public diplomacy share many similarities with those of Britain, but with some important differences. The United States Information Agency has been the key organization, working closely with but separately from the Department of State. The Voice of America began broadcasting in 1942 and is largely under the aegis of the USIA. (Projected reorganization plans call for the USIA to be incorporated into the Department of State; see below.)

During the Cold War, VOA's efforts were supplemented by Radio Free

Europe, which broadcast 555 hours weekly in European languages to Eastern Europe, and by Radio Liberty, which broadcast 462 hours weekly in Russian and 14 other languages (but not English) to the Soviet Union.[14]

The USIA, usually operating with a budget of about $900 million, employed about 12,000 people between Washington and some 275 U.S. Information Service (USIS) posts in 110 countries. Typically, a USIS post works under a U.S. ambassador and includes a public library. USIS personnel cooperate with local media by providing news and related material, holding exhibits, running language courses, giving seminars of various kinds, and arranging visits and cultural exchanges of both Americans and local people.

The USIA and VOA have long had an identity crisis: are they objective news and cultural organizations reflecting the diversity of American life and culture or are they arms of the State Department, vigorously pushing U.S. foreign-policy objectives?

Past managerial participation of such well-known journalists as Edward R. Murrow, Carl Rowan, and John Chancellor suggests the former. At other times, as during the Vietnam War and the Reagan and Bush administrations, the latter role has been stressed. The original charge of the USIA in 1952 was to "help achieve the U.S. foreign policy objectives by a) influencing public attitudes in other nations, b) advising the President, his representatives abroad, and various agencies and departments on the implications of foreign opinion for present and contemplated U.S. policies, programs and official statements." One critic charged that during the Reagan administration, the VOA repeatedly compromised its integrity by broadcasting misleading and biased reports.[15]

The long-running dispute over VOA as government mouthpiece or VOA as public radio continually tests what VOA staffers know as the "charter"—Public Law 94-350—signed by President Ford in 1976, which was the result of years of feuding between VOA news editors, who wanted journalistic autonomy, and foreign-service officers, who wanted VOA controlled and censored.[16] It laid down three principles: (1) "VOA news will be accurate, objective, and comprehensive"; (2) VOA will "present a balanced and comprehensive projection of significant American thought and institutions"; and (3) "VOA will present the policies of the United States clearly and effectively."

Some at VOA believe that its news credibility was diminished when, during the Cold War, the VOA took a stridently anti-Communist stance countering the "lies" and "distortions" of U.S. adversaries. But others ask, why engage in public diplomacy unless you vigorously pursue foreign-pol-

icy goals? The schizophrenic nature of U.S. public diplomacy activity is reflected in the various slogans that have appeared at times in USIA policy
statements: "Tell the Truth about America"; "Win the propaganda war";
"Reflect the diversity and pluralism of American life"; and "Win the hearts
and minds of the Third World masses."

Another policy issue debated within the USIA is audience targeting,
revolving on the question of who are we trying to influence? If it is the ruling elites of the world's nations, then the person-to-person efforts of USIS
posts and various cultural and educational exchanges seem called for; if it
is the mass publics, then expanded and more aggressive radio broadcasting
seems appropriate.

Policy matters aside, there is no question that under President Reagan's appointee, Charles Wick, as USIA director, the agency reflected a
tougher anti-Communist approach, especially in commentaries following
VOA newscasts. After 1981, the agency underwent a transformation as
thorough as any in its history. The agency undertook the development of
a government television network, called Worldnet, with the potential of
linking 60 overseas television systems to USIA headquarters in Washington.

In addition to producing cultural and public affairs programs for local overseas networks, Worldnet has employed satellite links for two-way
televised news conferences between foreign journalists and American public figures. Part of the programming in its first years included a two-hour
program of news and features to Europe five days a week.[17] During the Persian Gulf crisis, President Bush used Worldnet to address foreign publics.

Another Reagan project was Radio Marti, a VOA-linked facility pat-
terned after Radio Free Europe, to broadcast news and commentary specifically to Cuba. Named for a Cuban independence hero and poet, the radio
station went on the air in May 1985 broadcasting news, entertainment,
and sports in Spanish for 14½ hours daily from studios in Washington and
a 50,000-watt AM transmitter in the Florida Keys. A Television Marti service was later added that has been controversial. Opponents had argued
that since Cubans regularly listen to nonjammed U.S. radio and television
stations from Miami, the new service was unnecessary. At a cost of $60,000
a day, this Spanish-language TV station broadcast news and entertainment
to Cuba—from 3:30 a.m. to 6 a.m. to avoid violating global signal agreements. Although controversial, it was a project popular with Cuban émi-
grés in Miami.[18]

President Bush's choice as director of the USIA, Bruce Gelb, maintained a much lower profile for the USIA than did the flamboyant Wick

and, as the Cold War receded, the agency faced stringent budget cuts, stifling its projected expansion.

When President Clinton appointed Joseph D. Duffey, president of American University, to head the USIA in 1993, the 8,900-person agency's $1 billion budget began facing serious downsizing.

The public diplomacy efforts of Western nations such as the United States, Great Britain, France, and Germany have much in common: similar broadcasting services stressing news, cultural exchanges, and the use in foreign capitals of local information/cultural posts (usually including a library) as a part of their diplomatic missions.

Communist Model of Public Diplomacy

During the long Cold War, Communist nations followed a somewhat different model, one more consistent with their ideology and political organization. Some observers believed that the Soviet Union spent more money and tried harder than the United States in public diplomacy. (As with comparative estimates of military strength, the unadorned truth was hard to come by.) The Central Intelligence Agency (CIA) estimated in 1981 that the Soviet Union spent as much as $3.3 billion annually on various propaganda activities. This included such overt efforts as Radio Moscow and its related stations that broadcast in 82 languages over 2,000 hours weekly at a cost of some $700 million, and also $150 million for the Communist Party's international activities.[19] The $550 million spent on TASS's indirect propaganda efforts of spreading Moscow's version of world events is also added to the estimated total. (The U.S. government does not subsidize AP and UPI, but these services obviously serve U.S. information efforts.)

TASS provided most of the material for Radio Moscow, which has become over the years much more sophisticated in its efforts. Broadcasts recently include Soviet-made jazz and rock music, and the broadcasts in English are particularly subtle, using announcers who apparently are hired for their ability to sound like VOA or BBC broadcasters. Before breaking ties with Moscow in 1989–90, other Communist countries in Eastern Europe delivered more than 5,000 hours a week of pro-Soviet (and mostly anti-U.S.) broadcasting a week, more than twice the output of Radio Moscow.

The Soviet state had traditionally made use of vigorous international communications; after all, the original movement under Marx and Lenin was an international one. Top Communist leaders had always taken an active part in public diplomacy efforts; it seemed to go with the job. This top-level concern, plus the totalitarian nature of the state, facilitated the adjustment of propaganda themes as national policies changed or the international situation evolved. During the Cold War, the USSR successfully identified itself with the decolonization movements that created the Third World, making the world forget that the Soviet Union was itself the last great empire of disparate peoples on earth.

Soviet propaganda efforts were furthered by three groups in foreign lands. Foremost were the Moscow-aligned local Communist Parties, which were organized to cooperate with Moscow; their influence, however, has declined in recent years as communism lost its appeal in many nations. In addition, in 126 countries there were various Soviet "friendship societies," coordinating cultural exchanges, visits, and exhibitions. In 1979, a total of 53,300 students from the Third World were studying in the Soviet Union. In 1981, the Soviets offered 4,500 college scholarships in Latin America, while the United States offered only 4 percent of that number.

Heavy reliance was also placed on front groups and controlled organizations in other countries to help win influence. A good example was the International Organization of Journalists (IOJ) headquartered in Prague.

Another difference from the Western approach was the heavy use of direct mail as a way of delivering all over the world vast numbers of books, pamphlets, and magazines, printed in many languages.

The Soviet Cold Warrior, like his counterpart in the West, tried to use the local news media wherever possible. One often-used technique was to plant a specially prepared article in a foreign newspaper or magazine, and then quote it back to the Soviet Union or other countries as a viewpoint current in the country of the article's publication.

The former Soviet Union and the United States are not the only nations, of course, that participate in various forms of international political communication. Almost every nation that is able to maintain diplomatic representation abroad plays the game to some extent.

IPC after the Cold War

The dramatic and unexpected ending of the Cold War during 1989–90 and the accompanying demise of Communist regimes in Eastern Europe profoundly altered public diplomacy because East-West rivalries had so long dominated the propaganda wars. Most agreed that the West had "won" the Cold War. However, there was not the same certitude about many aspects of the victory.

First, almost everyone in the West was surprised by the suddenness of the collapse. Despite all the news reporting, intelligence gathering, and scholarly research conducted about the Communist bloc, almost no one had seen the events coming. Had we in the West been so mesmerized and conditioned by the Cold War rhetoric that we couldn't concede such a possibility?

Second, foreign radio broadcasting by VOA and Radio Free Europe and Radio Liberty as well as BBC and the other Western broadcasters had proved far more effective than most Western experts had supposed. In 1990, journalist Morton Kondracke commented, "If ever there was an American foreign policy success story, it's in international broadcasting. By the testimony of everyone from Václav Havel (of Czechoslovakia) to Lech Walesa (of Poland) to ordinary people in the streets of Bucharest and Beijing, democracy would not be what (and where) it is today without the two U.S. foreign broadcast networks, the Voice of America and Radio Free Europe/Radio Liberty."[20] In May of that year, *Izvestia,* the Soviet government newspaper, published a long appreciative article about Radio Liberty. After the Berlin Wall fell, it became clear that the U.S.-sponsored radio station in West Berlin, RIAS (Radio in the American Sector) had been the most popular radio station among East Berliners.

In a Reuters-sponsored conference after the Berlin Wall came down, Western journalists admitted that Western broadcasters had often been discounted by the press. As Peter Jennings commented, "When American journalists get together to talk about our effect on the rest of the world we hardly ever talk about radio. And yet the Voice of America, Radio Liberty and Radio Deutsche Welle, it's astonishing, the penetration that they have had, that we have not."[21]

A recent book by Michael Nelson, *War of the Black Heavens: The Battles of Western Broadcasting in the Cold War,* argues that the Western radio programs presented a compelling message of the good life that undermined Communist regimes and connected listeners with the cultures of Europe and North America. Nelson believes that radio, not diplomacy or the global economy, raised the iron curtain.

Yet, because of their Cold War success, U.S. planners have talked of consolidating the U.S. radio services as well as cutting back on their budgets, since they no longer seemed needed. But due to the uncertainty of economic reforms and political instability in Russia, unrest in the former Soviet Republics, and unresolved crises in the Balkans, the survival of both Radio Liberty and Radio Free Europe seemed necessary. President Václav

Havel of the Czech Republic and the new democratically elected leaders of Poland and Hungary pled that the stations be saved because they considered those broadcasts irreplaceable. The administration and Congress agreed to continue financing the stations. So, with pared-down budgets, RFE and RL moved to Prague in 1995 from Munich, where they had been since the CIA established them in 1951.[22]

The unchallenged success of RFE and RL during the Cold War led to proposals for a similar broadcaster to beam news and persuasive communications into China, still ruled by a totalitarian Communist government and beset with human-rights problems. As pointed out in Chapter 5 ("Global Impact of Western News and Pop Culture"), VOA and BBC had played a key role during the Tiananmen Square events in 1989 by providing the only Mandarin-language news reports received throughout the vast Chinese hinterland, where most Chinese live.

Congress agreed in early 1994 to establish a new radio service, Radio Free Asia, to beam news and other programming to mainland China, Burma, Cambodia, Laos, North Korea, Tibet, and Vietnam—all authoritarian nations with serious human-rights problems. The station was modeled after RFE and RL, with grants to the new station set at $30 million a year.

Radio Free Asia got off to a shaky start in September 1996. Neighboring countries loudly opposed it, and it was resented by other international broadcasters. Most Chinese who listen to radio broadcasts are devoted to the BBC, VOA, and Radio France International, all of which had bolstered their Asian broadcasting in the two previous years. Many career diplomats regarded RFA as an affront to the existing networks and as needlessly confrontational at a time when Washington sought to reduce conflict with Beijing. Further, in its first months of operation, most listeners, including American diplomats in China, had difficulty picking up RFA's signal. It will probably take several years and perhaps a political crisis before RFA proves itself.

On April 30, 1993, President Clinton signed the International Broadcasting Act establishing the International Broadcasting Bureau, which for the first time combined all U.S. government international broadcasting services under a Broadcasting Board of Governors. The board oversees the operation of VOA, Worldnet television service, and Radio and TV Marti to Cuba, as well as Radio Free Europe/Radio Liberty and Radio Free Asia.

Voice of America continues as a top competitor with the 126 similar broadcasting services in today's vast media market. VOA research indicates that about 86 million listeners tune in its 900 hours of weekly programs broadcast in 52 languages, including English, via medium-wave (AM) and shortwave transmissions. Millions more listen to VOA programs placed on local AM and FM stations around the world.

VOA's original programming, all of it produced in studios in Washington, D.C., totals almost 700 hours a week. Most programs concern news and news-related topics. Music programs from jazz to rock, classical to country, are popular. To help listeners abroad improve their language skills, VOA produces two programs, "Tuning in the USA" and "English USA," in Special English (with a limited vocabulary).

Radio Free Europe/Radio Liberty broadcasts from Prague over 500 hours weekly in 23 languages, including its Czech and Polish affiliates, to Central Europe, Russia, and the various republics of the former USSR.

In 1994, VOA began distributing via the Internet its newswire and selected newscasts and program audio files in 19 languages, along with VOA frequency and satellite information. VOA launched a web page on the Internet in May 1996. (BBC World Service offers similar information on the Internet.) Using a network of 14 relay stations worldwide, VOA transmits its programs to its global audience via satellite, shortwave, and medium wave. The connection is instantaneous, so listeners may never realize that the signal passes through several different channels before it reaches their receivers.

Current bureaucratic reorganization of the USIA and VOA may affect the impact and, indeed, the credibility of its public diplomacy efforts. In 1997, the White House announced that the USIA and the State Department will be integrated over a two-year period. The President's plan was part of Vice President Gore's "reinventing government" efforts and also involved the Agency for International Development and the Arms Control and Disarmament Agency.

In light of these changes and a declining interest in foreign news, foreign-policy experts are concerned that the United States has seriously cut back on its ability to conduct public diplomacy. On a per-capita basis, France and many other countries, including Spain, spend much more money on public diplomacy than does the United States.

Historian Walter Laqueur warned,

> No specialized expertise is needed to realize that, far from being on the verge of a new order, the world has entered a period of great disorder. This refers to all kinds of regional conflicts as well as to the proliferation of the means of mass destruction, all of which makes nuclear war in the not-too-distant future a distinct possibility. It also refers to a potential

second coming of fascism and communism and anti-Western onslaughts by other forces. ... Cultural diplomacy, in the widest sense, has increased in importance, whereas traditional diplomacy and military power (especially of the high technology variety) are of limited use in coping with most of these dangers.[23]

Public diplomacy, of course, has not ended with the Cold War (which may not be completely over). International persuasion and public diplomacy will go on as before and change and modify their forms as crises come and go and relations evolve among nations. But it is apparent that the United States, the world's only superpower, will deal with our dangerous world with a curtailed ability to conduct public diplomacy.

CHAPTER 8

Changes in Foreign Coverage

> The cause of the decline and fall of the Roman Empire lay in the fact that there were no newspapers of the day. Because there were no newspapers, there was no way by which the dwellers in the far-flung nation and the empire could find out was going on at the center.
>
> —H.G. Wells

> The press should be free to go where it wants, when it wants, to see, hear and photograph what it believes is in the public interest.
>
> —Walter Cronkite

The specialty of gathering foreign news by journalists stationed overseas has been undergoing substantial changes in recent years. Because of financial cost cutting and new technologies, less news is reported from abroad and by very different methods. The foreign correspondent—that widely traveled and glamorous specialist of American journalism—is becoming a different breed of reporter from the old days of the Cold War. The public today seems less interested in foreign news, and editors and broadcasters are giving them a lot less of it.

Serious journalists have long held that foreign news is important and should be reported thoroughly and well. Many of the best and the brightest journalists have spent part of their careers in what must be among the most demanding jobs in journalism. Without question, transnational news gathering is an exacting occupation for the professional newsmen and newswomen of Western nations who put together the various stories, reports, rumors, and educated guesses that make up the daily international news file. To them, theirs is a difficult, dangerous, and badly misunderstood enterprise. They understand its shortcomings and difficulties far better, they believe, than politically motivated critics.

In a real sense, the world's ability to learn the news about itself depends on what gets into the news flow in the 15 or 20 open societies with highly developed media systems. Once an important story appears, for example, in New York, London, Paris, Rome, or Tokyo, it immediately starts flowing through the arteries of the world's news system and will be widely reported elsewhere—but not everywhere and certainly not every story; the majority of non-Western governments act as gatekeepers, screening news in and out of their nations. These political controls, as well as poverty and illiteracy, deprive the great majority of the world's peoples from learning even the barest outline of major current events. But any major story that "breaks" in the West has at least the possibility of being reported throughout the world.

To the few thousand foreign correspondents, the world's nations are strung out on a continuum from "free" or open at one end to "not free" or closed at the other and with many variations in between. To illustrate, the Associated Press has little difficulty gathering news in open Sweden, since several newspapers there take AP services and share their own news and photos with the agency. In addition, AP correspondents can use other Swedish media as sources and can develop their own stories or easily gain access to public officials.

Sudan, like other developing nations, offers a different kind of challenge. AP has no clients in Sudan, largely because the Sudan News Agency lacks the hard currency to buy the Comsat-beamed AP world service. The local media are subject to official controls, and the AP cannot justify the expense of maintaining a full-time correspondent in Khartoum. Therefore, AP "covers" Sudan by using a local stringer (a part-timer who is paid for what news is used). Periodically, the AP may send a staff correspondent to Sudan to do background or round up stories. At other times, AP may try to report on events in Sudan from Nairobi, in neighboring Kenya.

At the "not free" end of the continuum are a few countries that for years barred all foreign journalists and news agencies. In the Cold War days, when something important happened in Tirana, Albania, for instance, AP and the world usually found out about it belatedly from a government-controlled Albanian radio broadcast monitored abroad or from travelers or diplomats leaving the country. Albania has since opened, and Western analysts were surprised that Albanian refugees knew about the collapse of communism, which they learned about by listening carefully to English broadcasts on BBC and VOA.

A foreign correspondent often defines a country as free or not free according to how much difficulty he or she has in reporting events there. This may sound narrow and self-serving, but it has validity: the freedom of access that a foreign reporter enjoys is usually directly related to the amount of independence and access enjoyed by local journalists themselves. If local journalists are harassed and/or controlled by a particular government, so very likely will be the foreign journalists.

Throughout the unstable, developing world, some nations swing back and forth between press freedom and controls. For example, under Indira Gandhi, India, the world's largest democracy, went through a not-free period when the local press was controlled and foreign correspondents were forced to leave or were subjected to censorship. Later, after an election, news access resumed, and the country regained the free press for which India had been noted.

With the availability of impressive gadgets used by today's foreign correspondents—satellite telephones, lightweight, versatile computers, reliable phone lines, and faxes—foreign reporting is now much easier. A hot item for reporters has been a $20,000 satellite telephone which few newspapers can afford.[1] Soon such phones will be much cheaper and more available. Even so, collecting news throughout the world is still an erratic and imperfect process. Some significant events are either not reported or reported long after the fact. Certain areas of the world, such as central Africa, rarely get into the world news flow.

In the dangerous and confusing post–Cold War world, foreign reporters and news organizations are going through an identity crisis over what *is* news. As John Walcott of *Newsweek* said, "The Cold War provided us with a coherent global road map, in terms of what to cover and how to cover it."[2] Don Oberdorfer of the *Washington Post* added, "Since the fall of the Berlin Wall and the elimination of the Cold-War news filter, the task of making sense of global events has become less manageable for the media." The press is not used to reacting to a world full of conflicts and violent encounters that, as George Kennan put it, offer no "great and all absorbing focal points for American policy."[3]

Central to this are disagreements between journalists and government officials over the very nature of news. To journalists, news is the first, fragmentary, and incomplete report of a significant event or happening that editors think will be of interest or importance to their readers or listeners. To many government officials, news is "positive" information that reflects favorably on their nation (and hence themselves) and serves their country's general interests and goals. Yet those same leaders want to know all that is happening elsewhere that affects their own interests and country. Keith Fuller, former head of AP, said that news is what a government official wants to read about somewhere else, whereas propaganda is what the official wants the world to read about his or her country.

Politicians and government leaders in *every* nation from north to south attempt to manage or manipulate the news so that it favors their causes, their programs, and their image.

Certainly today the news media, especially television and news-magazines, pay less attention to foreign news. It is expensive to cover, and the consensus in the news business is that you can expect international news to turn a profit only when it is really domestic news in a foreign setting, such as a U.S. military intervention when it is "our boys" who are "over there."

CBS News, long famed for its international coverage, once maintained 24 foreign bureaus. By 1995, it had reporters in only four capitals: London, Moscow, Tel Aviv, and Tokyo. Dan Rather told a group of Harvard students, "Don't kid yourself. The trend line in American journalism is away from, not toward, increased foreign coverage. Foreign coverage requires the most space and the most air time because you are dealing with complicated situations, in which you have to explain a lot. And then there's always somebody around who says people don't give a damn about this stuff anyway ... 'if you have to do something foreign, Dan, for heaven's sake, keep it short.'"[4]

The covers of the three major newsmagazines, each of which has long emphasized foreign news gathered by their own overseas correspondents, reflect the declining interest in international news. By late September 1996, *Time* had run five covers that year on foreign topics, versus 11 in 1995. *Newsweek* featured four international covers by September 1996, compared with 11 in 1995. *U.S. News* published no international covers as of late 1996 but ran six in the year before.

The same trend is found in news content. Throughout 1995, *Time* devoted 385 pages to international news, or about 14 percent of the magazine, yet ten years earlier, in 1985, *Time* published 670 pages of foreign news, or 24 percent of its news content.

Changing Correspondents

"What is commonly referred to as the world flow of information," AP correspondent Mort Rosenblum wrote, "is more a series of trickles and spurts. News is moved across borders by a surprisingly thin network of correspondents. ... The smaller countries are squeezed into rapid trips during lulls between major stories in the larger countries." Rosenblum quoted a comment from a Latin American academic that "news breaks in South America along the direct line of the international airline route."[5]

In some places, it may seem that way, and yet the total flood of daily news reports from abroad is immense. One study estimated that the big four agencies send out about 33 million words a day, with 17 million from AP, 11 million from UPI, 3.4 million for AFP, and 1.5 million from Reuters. Among the smaller agencies, dpa of Germany was set at 115,000, ANSA of Italy at 300,000, and efe of Spain at 500,000.

Considering the demand for foreign news and the difficulties of reporting from far-flung places, there are probably too few correspondents stationed overseas. Rising costs and inflation have made maintenance of a staffer overseas quite expensive. Estimates range from $125,000 to $200,000 for maintaining a newspaper bureau overseas (i.e., at least one reporter) for one year, and the costs keep going up. A television bureau can cost $1 million a year. It is not surprising, therefore, that many news media rely on the news agencies for their foreign news. In America, that means the Associated Press.

AP's foreign news corps grew from 65 full-time U.S. journalists in 1975 to about 100 in 1993, nearly half women, assigned to foreign bureaus. Hundreds more are "locals"—nationals of countries they cover.[6]

In other media as well, Western journalism is increasingly relying on foreign nationals to help report the news. Foreign journalists are not only less expensive but often have a grasp of local languages and knowledge of their own countries that American journalists cannot match. Journalist Scott Schuster sees the trend as due to a global acceptance of English as a media language and the global influence of American journalistic methods: "American influence is most profound among broadcasters, and foreign broadcast journalists need only to turn on their TV sets to receive lessons on how to do the news American-style," he said:

> American methods of news production are being adopted all across Western Europe and in many Third World countries. ... During the coming decade journalistic styles in both print and broadcast media are likely to experience continuing international homogenization. The nationality of the reporter will no longer be an issue. Brits will cover Britain. Ghanaians will cover Ghana, and a large number of American journalists will be become "foreign correspondents"—covering America for foreign media.[7]

Increasingly, to deal with rising costs and tighter budgets, news media are relying on stringers or freelancers. A recent study by Stephen Hess of the Brookings Institution of 404 foreign correspondents working for U.S.

news media found that 26 percent are freelancers. Moreover, more of these are underemployed, with 40 percent saying they do other work as well. All suffer the usual fate of freelancers: low pay, no benefits, and a precarious relationship with their employers.[8] Hess found six types of stringers: "spouses" of other correspondents; "experts," who know languages and the area; "adventurers," like Oriana Fallaci; "flingers," a person on a fling who might start a serious career; "ideologues" or "sympathizers," who are often British; and the "residents," who are often longtime residents and write occasional stories.

Although stringers and freelancers remain marginal, many prominent journalists started their careers that way, including Stanley Karnow, Elie Abel, Robert Kaiser, Elizabeth Pond, Caryle Murphy, and Daniel Shorr.

A significant change has been the increased number of women among foreign correspondents, especially as war reporters. Before 1970, their numbers were small, although there had been a few famous names: Dorothy Thompson, Martha Gellhorn, Marguerite Higgins, and Gloria Emerson. Hess found that, by the 1970s, about 16 percent of new foreign reporters were women; this doubled during the 1980s to about 33 percent. This ratio of two men for every woman was also found in Washington media as well as in U.S. journalism generally.

Some women correspondents have earned outstanding reputations, including Caryle Murphy of the *Washington Post,* Robin Wright of the *Los Angeles Times,* syndicated columnist Georgie Ann Geyer, and Elaine Sciolino and Barbara Crossette, both of the *New York Times.* Christiane Amanpour of CNN has become a kind of celebrity because of her aggressive and frankly partisan reporting of such stories as the Gulf War, civil upheaval in Africa, and civil war in Bosnia. She is still with CNN but does some stories for CBS' *60 Minutes.*

Another trend is the increasing number of married couples, both journalists, being posted abroad. Before 1970, only 8 percent of reporters abroad for the first time had journalist spouses, but by the 1980s that number had jumped to 39 percent. By 1998, it had reached 44 percent. Many of these spouses are working for competing news outlets; others share a bureau for the same news organization. Typical were Alessandra Stanley and her husband, Michael Specter, who both had worked for the *New York Times* in Moscow. Also in Moscow were another couple, Richard Threlkeld of CBS News and Betsy Aaron with CNN.

Foreign correspondents today are better educated, know more foreign languages, and have higher-status backgrounds than their predecessors. Current salaries range from about $50,000 to $90,000, with more experienced reporters earning even more.

American reporters working abroad have been steadily increasing in number. A 1969 study found 929 Americans working abroad, including broadcasting. In 1972, the number dropped to 797; by 1975, there were only 676. But in 1990, there were 1,734 and, in 1993, the total neared 2,000.[9] Some of the increase was due to more staffing abroad by business and economic publications and news services such as Reuters, Bloomberg, and Dow Jones.

Bureaus located in key capitals are a good indicator of a news medium's commitment to foreign coverage. And some papers, such as the *New York Times,* have more than one reporter per bureau, such as in Moscow. Among U.S. dailies maintaining overseas bureaus in 1994 are the *New York Times,* 22 bureaus; *Los Angeles Times,* 22; *Washington Post,* 19; *Wall Street Journal,* 13; *Christian Science Monitor,* 13; *Chicago Tribune,* 11; *Baltimore Sun,* 8; and *Boston Globe,* 5. One anomaly is that the Gannett newspaper chain, with *USA Today,* 92 local dailies, and broadcasting outlets, had no overseas bureaus at all.

Among U.S. television broadcasters in 1994, CNN led the pack with 19 bureaus, NBC had 11, ABC had 5, and CBS had 4. In radio broadcasting, ABC Radio had nine bureaus, CBS had four, National Public Radio had three, and Mutual Radio/NBC had but one bureau.[10] Among newsmagazines, *Time* started 1993 with 38 reporters in 20 overseas bureaus; *Newsweek* had 21 in 16 bureaus; and *U.S. News & World Report* had more than a dozen, with regular contributions from stringers.[11]

When a major international event such as the Gulf War occurs, broadcast media expand their coverage at considerable expense. NBC, for example, said its costs of war coverage were $44.7 million. As a result, one or more of the networks faced cuts in both budgets and regular staff. CNN, on the other hand, whose war costs were estimated at $12 to $15 million, said after the war that it planned to increase its budget and international coverage.[12]

In more tranquil times, the networks increasingly seem to be relying on news film supplied by the syndicates, Reuters Television and WTN, and other foreign broadcasters for international coverage.

These less costly ways of collecting news have undermined the credibility of some foreign news. A few years ago if you saw a foreign news story on NBC News, chances are that it was reported by an NBC reporter at the scene with film shot by an NBC crew. Now the networks are relying more on less expensive, and often less experienced, freelancers and independent contractors whose products are rarely identified on the air, leaving the impression the story was reported by network staffers.

This practice gives rise to a growing concern about quality control. "By the time the tape gets on the air, nobody has the foggiest idea who made it and whether the pictures were staged," contended Tom Wolzien, a former NBC news executive.[13]

More loss of authenticity results when U.S. network correspondents, based in London, add voice-overs to stories they did not cover. Bert Quint, former CBS correspondent said, "There's no reason to believe the person [doing the voice-over] because odds are he or she was not within 3,000 miles of where the story occurred."[14]

Not only are foreign correspondents comparatively few, they are unevenly distributed as well. One study found that over half of all American reporters abroad were stationed in 19 European countries. The vast expanse of Africa, with over 500 million people in 45 countries, is very thinly covered by a declining number of Western journalists concentrated in Johannesburg and Nairobi. However, when a major international story breaks, a herd instinct seems to stampede numerous reporters and camera crews to the foreign scene. In the 1980s, about 170 accredited foreign correspondents were based in Johannesburg, due to the continuing racial unrest in South Africa and because it was a hub for air travel and satellite transmission for southern Africa, where news was breaking not only in South Africa itself, but also in neighboring Zimbabwe, Namibia, Angola, and Mozambique. More recently the numbers have dropped.

During the height of the Iranian crisis when 53 Americans were held hostage, more than 300 Western newsmen and newswomen, some 100 of them Americans, were working in Tehran. During the crisis in the Persian Gulf and subsequent war with Iraq, more than 800 Western reporters descended on the region, but few were experts on Middle Eastern affairs. Such "parachute journalism" does not always provide informed coverage since so many of these reporters lack previous experience or understanding of the area about which they are reporting.

New York City and Washington, D.C., are major world news centers that draw reporters from over 70 countries, but principally from Britain, Germany, Japan, France, Italy, and Canada. About half of these 1,200 correspondents working in New York City cover financial news and the United Nations; another 540 are in Washington, D.C., and the rest cover entertainment news from Los Angeles.[15]

Such statistics reflect the reality that most world news originates in such northern news "hubs" as New York City; Washington, D.C.; London; Paris; Tokyo; Hong Kong; Bonn/Berlin; Rome; and Moscow; and foreign correspondents, by and large, tend to congregate in cities where news either originates or flows into.

For American readers and listeners, serious questions have been raised about the quantity and quality of the foreign news they receive. The discussion or debate tends to be circular. AP and other agencies have long maintained that their services gather ample amounts of foreign news but that their newspaper and broadcast clients do not use very much of it. The media clients, in turn, argue that their readers and viewers are not very much interested in foreign news. Yet critics say that Americans are uninformed about the world because their news media report so little about it.

Certainly the generalization that the majority of Americans, with access to the world's most-pervasive media, are ill informed about world affairs has substance. A panel at Columbia's School of Journalism in November 1994 criticized the audience:

> There is a crisis in international news reporting in the United States—and not one that should simply be blamed on the reporters, the gatekeepers, or the owners. We know there is stagnation, and even shrinkage, in the number of international stories in the media and the number of correspondents in the field for most U.S. media outlets. But the primary reason for this decline is an audience that expresses less and less interest in the international stories that do appear. What we're increasingly missing, as a culture, is connective tissue to bind us to the rest of the world.[16]

Foreigners traveling in the American heartland are uniformly impressed by the lack of world news in local media and the ignorance shown by most Americans about the outside world. By contrast, the average German, Dane, or Israeli knows more global news because his or her media carry more. Part of the problem is that Americans, like Russians and Chinese, have a continental outlook, living as they do in the midst of a vast landmass that encourages a self-centered, isolationist view of the world. With two friendly neighbors and protected by two oceans, Americans are slow to recognize their interdependence with others.

Americans' interest in foreign news has its ups and downs, depending on the perceived impact of any current crisis on their lives. During the Vietnam War, much concern was focused on happenings in Southeast Asia, but not in Latin America or Africa, where news coverage dropped off. After Vietnam, foreign concerns receded as the nation became enthralled by Watergate and its aftermath. But after the rapid increases and then decreases in the price of foreign oil, the Soviet incursion into Afghanistan, continuing Arab/Israeli conflict, and rising level of terrorism directed against Americans, the average American's interest (if not knowledge) in foreign news, especially that of the Middle East, clearly increased. Then, during the summer of 1990 after Iraq invaded Kuwait and American forces were moved into Saudi Arabia before war began in January 1991, American interest in and anxiety about the Persian Gulf soared. At that same time, U.S. concern about the economic and political turmoil of the Soviet Union and Eastern Europe seemed low considering the severity of the crises in the Gulf region. (Americans, and their media, seem to be able to concentrate on only one crisis at a time.)

In late 1994 and early 1995, interest in foreign news plummeted as the U.S. news media became mesmerized with the murder trial of O.J. Simpson and the domestic politics of the Republicans' legislative zeal in Washington, D.C., after winning control of Congress in the November 1994 elections.

In 1998, the nation's prosperity and the continuing story about President Clinton's personal problems seemed to push foreign news off the nation's news agenda—at least for a while. The continuing crises in the former Yugoslavia, Iraq, and Israel, and the teetering Asian and Russian economies did not go away; they just seemed less urgent and less visible. By mid-1998, nuclear tests by India and Pakistan and the possibility of war in South Asia brought a heightened interest in foreign news.

Some scholars believe that television is profoundly affecting Americans' news perceptions. Neil Postman believes television projects a "peek-a-boo" world, "where now this event, now that, pops into view for a moment, then vanishes again. It is a world without much sense or coherence. ... Americans know of a lot of things but about almost nothing. Someone is considered well informed who simply knows that a plane was hijacked or that there was an earthquake in Mexico City."[17]

After the U.S. hostages in Tehran were freed in 1981, Postman conducted a study to determine the extent of knowledge about Iran. One hundred people were asked simple questions about the Iranian language, religion, and government. "Because Iran was carried almost continuously on the news for a year, we expected people would not only know about Iran but would be overloaded," Postman said. "But we found that most people could not answer our questions. Almost always those who actually knew something had gotten it from print sources."[18]

Despite ignorance of the world, there is a growing recognition that perhaps the term "foreign news" is a misnomer and that in our interdependent world we are potentially affected by any event almost anywhere. Failing overseas economies threaten the U.S. stock market and prosperity. American workers who lose jobs in manufacturing due to cheap foreign imports or farmers unable to sell wheat abroad due to the overvalued dollar are becoming more knowledgeable about world economic trends. And the Iraq war and later bombings reminded Americans again of their dependence on Middle Eastern oil and the lack of a conservation policy to deal with that dependence.

Tabloidization and Infotainment

The use of foreign news in the U.S. media raises two questions: Are news media fulfilling their obligation of providing essential information so their readers can make sound judgments on foreign and national affairs? And are media contributing instead to trivializing public information and making Americans more provincial at a time when the world is getting smaller and more interdependent?

In light of current trends in major news media, especially television, the answer, according to some critics, would be *No* to the first question and *Yes* to the second. Due to competitive pressures for larger audiences and increased revenues, the so-called "national" media are neglecting serious news from abroad (and Washington as well) and instead giving much greater attention and time or space to the trivial, the sensational, the titillating, gossip, and the notorious—the kinds of stories usually found on the tabloids (such as the *Inquirer,* the *Globe,* and the *Sun*) sold in supermarkets.

Increasingly the line between news and entertainment on television as well as in print media has become blurred—hence, the current buzzword "infotainment" to characterize the new soft, gossipy, and essentially trivial news American viewers and readers are getting.

The orgy of media attention given to the O.J. Simpson trial is the most protracted and serious example of the abdication of serious journalism from its duty to report the news. For month on month from mid-1994 well into 1995, the Simpson case crowded major foreign news off the nation's television screens. Newspapers and magazines have overplayed the story, too, but most still had space to report the other news, whereas evening television shows are limited to about 21 minutes of air time.

David Shaw, media critic of the *Los Angeles Times,* called it the "surrender of the gatekeepers." He wrote,

A few years ago, there were essentially seven gatekeepers in the American news business—executive editors of the *New York Times* and *Washington Post,* executive producers or anchors of the ABC, CBS, and NBC news shows, and the editors of *Time* and *Newsweek.* Occasionally someone else—"60 Minutes," the *Wall Street Journal,* the *Los Angeles Times,* or the *New Yorker*—would break a big story that would force everyone to take notice. If a story didn't make it past one of these it didn't fly, and often the *New York Times* editor was the one who decided. Now all that has changed. Well, almost all. Now the *NY Times* and the other six no longer decide. There are dozens of gatekeepers or none at all. Today there is a weekly network magazine show on every night—"60 Minutes," "Day One," "Turning Point," "Dateline NBC,"—plus the syndicated shows "Inside Edition," "Hard Copy," or "A Current Affair," are on every night. That's a vast maw craving information—infotainment—around the clock. Add to it CNN with its big appetite, and once a CNN story comes at any time, everyone scrambles for it. And once a story like the Gennifer Flowers/Bill Clinton story comes along, it takes on a life of its own and the media succumb to it. Once it's out there, the big seven cannot resist the pressures to use the story.[19]

One journalist said there used to be a fire wall between the responsible media and the sensational media. But not any more. How long this trend toward tabloidization, so pronounced today, will last is difficult to predict. There are signs that due to intermedia criticism the fire wall between serious and trivial journalism may be reconstructed.

The seven gatekeepers that Shaw mentioned were the ones who formerly decided which foreign news stories were important and should be played—and other media followed suit. Anyone watching network news shows recently cannot fail to notice the neglect of foreign news, especially on CBS and NBC, which are deliberately emphasizing "softer" and more trivial stories. Triviality and sensationalism have long been present in American media but usually limited to some feature sections. Today the virus of entertainment values seems to permeate the whole body of journalism and contributes to the public's cynicism and disdain for journalism.

Aside from the distractions of celebrity murder trials, studies of journalists and newspapers have found American newspapers generally lax in their coverage of international news. Only about a dozen of the major metropolitan dailies make a serious effort to report world news; the majority of the 1,750 or so dailies rely entirely on AP for world news. Most dailies print little more than the bare essentials, not enough to provide any clear and coherent view of what is going on in the rest of the world.

Research shows that most Americans get most of their news from the 21-minute evening broadcasts (not counting commercials) of the three major television networks, plus CNN. In the limited time available, television can do little more than provide a summary of the major foreign stories. One critic said that foreign news now often seems to be thrown into a network's regular news productions as a kind of afterthought.

Further, television tends to concentrate for days running (or, as in the Simpson trial, for months running) on the "big story," such as the hijacking of a TWA plane and the taking of U.S. hostages in Beirut, while ignoring significant events elsewhere in the world. Foreign news has been likened to a giant searchlight that highlights one big event while keeping the rest of the world in the dark. Perhaps this is inevitable in a "headline service," as Walter Cronkite called television news, but it does not help to provide the public, which relies on television as its major source of news, with a rounded picture of the world.

One public opinion survey by ABC news found agreement with this crisis-oriented criticism of foreign coverage. Of viewers polled, 55 percent said, "Television news only does stories about foreign countries when there's a war or some other violent crisis going on."[20] Media critic Hodding Carter said the networks "concentrate on showing kids throwing rocks at troops or guns going off or planes bombing or rubble falling. These are the repetitive images that block out the complexities." In addition, he cited the "extraordinary lack of continuity and perspective, which is the shadow of all television news."[21]

There is no doubting, however, the tremendous capacity of television news to focus world attention on particular foreign events. President Bush's address to the nation on Wednesday, January 16, 1991, the fateful evening the Gulf War began, attracted the largest audience in the history of American television. About 78.8 percent of the people in homes with television sets were watching. Much of television may be trivial and banal, but on rare occasions it can enable a vast nation to share a solemn event.

Another example of television's impact concerns the Ethiopian famine. Ethiopians had been suffering and enduring hardships for many months while the world largely ignored them. But after dramatic color television coverage of their plight appeared on the NBC Evening News night after night, Americans were galvanized to generously support relief efforts. To paraphrase a propaganda maxim, the color television report of an event may be as important as the event itself. The obverse is true as well: an unreported event will have little impact.

Inevitably, much of what happens in the world will go unnoted. Wherever he or she may be, the average person obviously does not have the time or interest to follow all the news from everywhere. As one editor asked, "Who wants to read about Zaire if there is nothing going on there?" Gerald Long of Reuters explained more fully: "The prevalent school of journalism throughout the world is a 'journalism of exception.' In other words, you don't report that everything is fine in Pakistan. You report that there has been an air crash."[22] This approach contributes to an inevitable imbalance and distortion of reality.

Hostility Toward Western Journalists

The journalism of exception—reporting civil unrest, the coup d'état, the train wreck, the drought—is at the root of much hostility and antagonism toward Western reporting. Journalists who work abroad say it is difficult to gain access to many parts of the world, particularly Africa, the Middle East, and Asia. Typically, the first measures that authorities take in a political upheaval is to close their borders. Even when journalists do manage to get in to some non-Western countries, many report they are faced with tight restrictions on their ability to travel, to witness events, and to speak freely with officials and local citizens.

Journalists have had particular difficulty in reporting the eight-year conflict between Iran and Iraq and the prolonged civil war involving Serbia, Bosnia, Croatia, and now Kosovo.

In India, the foreign cable networks, CNN and BBC's World Service Television, have become a target for Indian politicians looking for scapegoats to blame for secessionist movements, religious strife, and natural disasters. India's own television network, Doordarshan, owned and controlled by the government, is well known for delaying and sanitizing news broadcasts. CNN and BBC came to India in 1991 and aggressively reported the razing of the Babri Mosque in late 1993 by Hindu fundamentalists, which led to national riots in which 1,800 died. In response, Indian political leaders of both left and right demanded strong action against the networks. However, when things go in favor of the politicians, they praise foreign coverage.[23]

The field of activity for foreign reporters is being narrowed increasingly by both formal and informal methods of official controls. Mort Rosenblum categorized four forms that such methods can take: The "Blackout" approach, which seems to be gaining popularity, takes the view that no news at all is better than critical or unflattering reports abroad, so reporters are simply kept out. "Reluctant Coverage" means that reporters are permitted in, but access to news sources or officials is severely limited. China and various Middle Eastern countries are examples. Rosenblum said the "Subtle Squeeze" occurs in countries that appear to permit open coverage, but actually apply indirect restraints on particular stories. Sometimes correspondents are censored by excessive hospitality that keeps them occupied at some distance from a potentially embarrassing story. The fourth method is "Friendly Persuasion," wherein reporters are not restricted, but efforts are made to influence them in a positive way. American officials have been known to use this method, typified by the press junket—taking reporters to the scene of a news story in hopes they will report favorably on it. Much of what is termed "enlightened public relations" falls within this category.[24]

After months of protest and violence in South Africa that claimed over 1,000 lives—and all fully reported by Western reporters—the South African government on November 2, 1985, imposed sweeping restraints on foreign press coverage. All reporters, print and broadcast, could only cover scenes of unrest while under police supervision. And, most tellingly, pictures and sound recordings of the unrest were banned. If the purpose of the ban was to remove images of violence from foreign television screens, most broadcast journalists agreed, then it worked. "Nobody wants to be in the position of saying that what the South Africans did has worked," said Peter Jennings of ABC news, "but it has."[25]

A major point of contention is that most governments believe the press, including foreign reporters, should serve the host country's national aims, whereas the Western press believes it must decide for itself what news to report. All governments want favorable publicity in the world's media and do not want negative news published.

Physical Danger

Foreign correspondents often risk their lives to cover wars, civil unrest, and other forms of violence. Within unstable nations, journalists, both foreign and domestic, are often singled out as targets for arrest, beatings, or assassination. Sometimes they are just in the wrong place at the wrong time.

Algeria, beset by a long struggle between an authoritarian government and militant Islamic opposition, has proved a deadly place to report the news: As of January 1998, 70,000 to 80,000 people have been massacred.

Since 1993, 60 Algerian journalists have been murdered because of their profession. In 1997, no journalist was slain, but that was because so many Algerian journalists had gone underground, fled into exile, or left the profession.

The Committee to Protect Journalists keeps track of such violence and reported in 1998 that 474 journalists had been killed worldwide between 1987 and 1996. After Algeria, the most hazardous countries and the numbers killed were Colombia, 41; the Philippines, 30; Russia, 29; Tajikistan, 29; Croatia, 26; Bosnia, 21; Turkey, 20; Peru, 19; India, 17; and Rwanda, 15.

Some 182 journalists were in jail in 1996, and here the worst offenders and numbers jailed were Turkey, 53; Ethiopia, 31; China, 20; and Kuwait, 18.

Governments and warring armies are not the only foes of press freedom; sometimes terrorists and thugs attack the press. Louis Boccardi, president of AP, said, "On the international scene, the world continues to grow more difficult to cover. The physical dangers abound. Dozens of journalists have been killed in the last few years ... and many more injured in the pursuit of a story, their story, wherever it was."[26]

Shortcomings of the Western System

In summary, it may be useful to list some of the shortcomings and inadequacies of the Western system of foreign news gathering.

Too few Western journalists and bureaus are deployed in enough of the right locations to provide adequate coverage of world news events. Sparsity and inadequacies of local news media in many nations of Africa, Asia, and Latin America compound the difficulties because those media are themselves unable to make significant contributions to the world news flow. In time, however, the improvement of regional and alternative news services may help alleviate this problem.

Authoritarian countries obstruct news flow by instituting measures such as denial of visas to foreign journalists, censorship, lack of access, and harassment of reporters. Ten or 15 years ago, most reporters covering the less-developed countries would have said that their major problems were logistical—getting to the story and then getting the story out to the world. More recently, better air travel, satellite telephones, the Internet, fax, and even video reports via satellites have markedly improved the logistical aspects of international communication, but the political and cultural barriers to news gathering have not lessened, except in Central and Eastern Europe. It is ironic that at a time when travel and communications technology have made even the most distant corners of the world more accessible, foreign reporting has become ever more difficult and dangerous in many fringe areas.

The limitations and subjectivity of news itself mean that many people in many places are going to be dissatisfied with how the news is reported. For example, a reporter for the *Los Angeles Times* based in Cairo, Egypt, is writing for readers some 12,000 miles away in California. His or her stories will be chosen and later edited, not according to what Egyptians would prefer to read but according to what editors in Los Angeles think their local readers will be interested in knowing.

For news, besides being perishable, is relative and subjective as well as fragmentary and incomplete. Sometimes even the reporting of a mere sports event can cause international repercussions. In the 1988 Olympic Games at Seoul, charges that U.S. television was unfairly focusing on South Korea's dark side prompted a spasm of anti-Americanism. The uproar began after U.S. television audiences watched a Korean crowd explode after a referee penalized a Korean boxer. To U.S. television reporters, this was a good story, and it was played accordingly. Sensitive to their global image, South Koreans were angry about negative coverage because they saw the Olympics more as a public relations bonanza than a sports event.

In some situations, it is true, unfortunately, that ethnicity or racism does directly affect news values. (The fate of two Americans arrested in Iraq is a bigger story than a bomb explosion killing 100 Pakistanis in Karachi.)

In death and disaster, where people reside does seem to affect media coverage directly. Compare the coverage of two air crashes: A U.S. jet plunged into New York's East River, with two dead and seven hospitalized. In Chad on the same day, a French UTA jet exploded, killing all 171 on board, and a terrorist bomb was suspected. The New York crash received far more coverage than the Africa crash in the U.S. media and showed that proximity and American lives counted for the difference in emphasis.[27]

Also, Western news media, although relatively independent of their own governments, still tend to report foreign news from the viewpoint of their country's foreign-policy concerns. This is not the result of any conspiratorial link between journalists and a state department or a foreign ministry. Rather, the unsurprising fact is that events abroad are of interest to readers or viewers in proportion to the ways their own national concerns are involved. Nonetheless, foreign news coverage too often responds to U.S. domestic politics; this means that occasionally important foreign stories do not get covered because they lack the "local angle" of high reader interest. (Yet reader interest is a very fickle matter; during late 1989, network news directors said the public was losing interest in the biggest "good news" story of the modern age, the fall of Communist regimes in East Europe. Perhaps the viewers just became satiated.)

The Western practice of "journalism of exception" continues to rankle critics of the press everywhere. In America, many feel the media report far too much negative news. But as Daniel Patrick Moynihan said, "It is the mark of a democracy that its press is filled with bad news. When one comes to a country where the press is filled with good news, one can be pretty sure that the jails are filled with good men."

The reporting of modern wars—their own wars—have presented special challenges to American and British news media in recent years, and that problem is discussed in the next chapter.

CHAPTER 9

Reporting Today's Wars

The first casualty when war comes is truth.
—Senator Hiram Johnson, 1917

The Persian Gulf War—the short but intense conflict between Iraq and the coalition forces led by the United States—lasted only 42 days, but it changed the ways that future wars will be reported. Television and especially the Cable News Network turned much of the world into a global community witnessing as the conflict evolved from armed confrontation to aerial bombardment to ground invasion. Because of the involvement of Western powers, particularly the United States and Britain, the Gulf War became the biggest-running news story in years, and the telling of it utilized the full resources of the international news system. Eventually, over 1,600 print and broadcast journalists and technicians were in Saudi Arabia alone, with many others in nearby Amman, Baghdad, Tel Aviv, Nicosia, and, of course, Washington and London, two major news hubs.

This avalanche of live global coverage necessarily passed through the prism of deep cultural differences between the West and the Islamic world. Each side viewed the war through quite different lenses. When Iraq's Scud missiles fell on Israeli civilians, for example, Westerners were appalled, while Palestinians and Jordanians were elated. To the West and some Arabs, Saddam Hussein was a dangerous, reckless tyrant; to millions of other Arabs and Muslims, he was a hero who stood up to the West—he was a modern-day Saladin (who recaptured Jerusalem in the twelfth century).

But for both sides, CNN and other television broadcasters made it a "real time" war. After hostilities began early on January 17, 1991 (Baghdad time), reporters described antiaircraft tracers in the night sky of Baghdad and flashes of bomb explosions on the horizon. On succeeding nights, viewers were provided with live video reports from Tel Aviv and Riyadh of Scud missiles, some intercepted by Patriot missiles, exploding against the night sky, and of television reporters donning gas masks on camera.

The press talked of the "CNN effect"—millions anchored hour after

143

hour to their television sets lest they miss the latest dramatic development. Restaurants, movies, hotels, and gaming establishments all suffered business losses. "People are intensely interested in the first real-time war in history and they are just planting themselves in front of their television sets," one expert said. Ratings for CNN soared 5 to 10 times their prewar levels.[1]

The Gulf War was a worldwide media event of astonishing proportions. Global television never had a larger or more interested audience for such a sustained period of time. Television became the first and principal source of news for most people, as well as a major source of military and political intelligence for both sides. CNN telecasts, including military briefings, were viewed in Baghdad as they were being received in Riyadh or Washington, D.C.—as well as in other non-Western countries.

The combatants, particularly the governments of Iraq and the United States, tried to control and manipulate the media with subtle and not-so-subtle propaganda and misinformation messages. Western journalists chafed at the restraints on news coverage of the war itself and complained that there was much news they were not permitted to report. Most coalition news came from military briefings and from carefully controlled and escorted "pools" of reporters. Some official news presented at the briefings was actually disinformation intended to mislead the enemy, not inform the public. For example, viewers were led to believe that Patriot missiles were invariably successful in neutralizing Scud missiles; such was not the case.

Information on the war was tightly controlled on television; one observer called it "the illusion of news." For its own self-defined security reasons, the military often held back or distorted the news it did release. In the opening days of the war, much was made of the "smart bombs" which hit their targets with about 90 percent accuracy. After the war, the U.S. Air Force admitted that smart bombs made up only 7 percent of all U.S. explosives dropped on Iraq and Kuwait. Television scenes (many realistic computer-generated recreations) of precision-guided bombs going down chimneys or in the doors of targets, notwithstanding, the Air Force later said 70 percent of the 88,500 tons of bombs dropped on Kuwait and Iraq missed their targets.[2]

Peter Jennings of ABC News reminded viewers that much of what was revealed in the opening days of war was speculation, mixed with some hard facts and some rumors in the rushing river of information.[3] But whether they were getting hard news or not, many millions of viewers stayed by their television sets. Public opinion polls showed that the overwhelming majority of Americans supported both the war and the military's efforts to control the news; further, some thought there should be more controls on press reporting. A Los Angeles Times Mirror poll found that half of the respondents considered themselves obsessed with war news, but nearly 80 percent felt the military was "telling as much as it can." About the same proportion thought that military censorship may be a "good idea."

But after the war, many in the American press felt that the traditional right of U.S. reporters to accompany their combat forces and report news of war had been severely circumscribed. Michael Getler of the *Washington Post* wrote, "The Pentagon and U.S. Army Central Command conducted what is probably the most thorough and consistent wartime control of American reporters in modern times—a set of restrictions that in its totality and mind-set seemed to go beyond World War II, Korea and Vietnam."[4]

President George Bush and the Pentagon followed a deliberate policy of blocking negative and unflattering news from the U.S. public lest it weaken support for the war. Long after the conflict, the public learned that some Iraqi soldiers had been buried alive in trenches by U.S. plows and earthmovers and that the military had waited months to tell the families of 33 dead soldiers that their loved ones had been killed by friendly fire. Not until a year after the war did the public learn that key weapons like the stealth bomber and the cruise missile had struck only about half of their targets, compared with the 85 to 90 percent rate claimed by the Pentagon at the time.[5]

American casualties were reported, but there were few pictures of dead and wounded. Details of tactical failures and mishaps in the bombing campaign were not released, nor was the information that at least 24 female soldiers had been raped or sexually assaulted by American servicemen.

The older generation of military leaders felt strongly, despite evidence to the contrary, that unrestricted and critical press coverage in Vietnam had contributed to the U.S. defeat there. They were determined it would not happen again. Some journalists blamed their own top editors and news executives for agreeing ahead of time to the field censorship and pool arrangements instead of vigorously opposing them.

Coverage Before Hostilities

Every war is different, and the particular conditions of the Gulf War affected the ways the war was reported and perceived by the public. Most Americans saw it as a "good war" with a quick, decisive victory with amazingly few U.S. and allied casualties. Therefore, press concerns over restrictions on war coverage had little public impact and never became an important issue. And antiwar protests did not have time to develop.

For over five months, from August 2, 1990, when Iraqi troops first invaded Kuwait, to January 17, 1991, when the bombing of Iraq started, television played a central role in reporting all aspects of the major international crisis—the first since the end of the Cold War. The press covered the rapid buildup of coalition forces in Saudi Arabia with television pictures of armed troops arriving with heavy armor and deploying in the desert. This enthusiastic coverage contributed to some Pentagon-inspired misinformation by exaggerating the ability of U.S. troops to repel an invasion. Later, 101st Airborne troops, first to arrive, admitted that during those first weeks they would have been mere road bumps for invading Iraqi forces.

Television played a clear diplomatic role as well by reporting the fate of the thousands of hostages held by Iraq and the international efforts to obtain their freedom. More importantly, the continuing diplomatic efforts by the United Nations and various foreign governments to resolve the conflict were fully aired and analyzed on television. Such international television reports, instantly available in dozens of world capitals, accelerated the often cumbersome processes of diplomacy.

American and British television networks in particular swung into action, at great cost, to boost their ratings by getting their famous anchors into the Gulf, hoping to broadcast live from Baghdad and, better yet, interview Saddam Hussein. A former CBS producer saw the crisis as a "wonderful opportunity for the networks to get out there, to sell themselves, to have great footage and great backdrops for their anchors. Whose interests are being served? The press is serving itself."[6] Nonetheless, the press also serves the public interest at the same time when it aggressively reports how its government conducts a foreign war. This time, television was better equipped than ever before to report the war. Television crews had the newest technology of small, lightweight cameras and portable uplinks that could transmit their video stories home via satellite. Print and radio reporters could call in stories to their newsrooms with suitcase-sized satellite telephones out in the field.

Probably never before have television viewers been exposed to such an endless array of experts—diplomatic, military, political, journalistic—to analyze in excruciating detail each new phase of the unfolding drama. Journalist Elizabeth Drew commented, "Probably in no other prelude to a possible war has the media played such a prominent role as transmission belt—for feelers, for threats, for war scenarios designed to intimidate, and for military information perhaps designed to mislead."[7]

Another impressive facet of network television coverage was its ability to *interconnect* with a variety of news sources thousands of miles apart. When, for example, a new peace proposal was announced in Moscow, Peter Jennings on his ABC news program immediately obtained reactions and comments from ABC reporters and their news sources located at the White House, the State Department, the Pentagon, London, Tel Aviv, Amman, and Paris—an example of television's ability to speed the diplomatic process.

Reporting the War Itself

All this was the prelude to the shooting war, which started just as the evening news programs were beginning at 6:30 Eastern Standard Time (January 16 in the United States; January 17 in the Middle East). The networks and CNN interrupted their prepared news shows to report that aerial bombing had begun in Baghdad. Then followed one of most memorable nights in television history: the opening phases of a major conflict reported in real time by reporters in Iraq, Saudi Arabia, and Washington.

CNN stole the show that night as three CNN correspondents, John Holliman, Peter Arnett, and Bernard Shaw, gave vivid eyewitness descriptions of the U.S. air attack from the windows of their Baghdad hotel room. As in old-time radio, reporters relied on words, not video, that first night. Other networks reported the fireworks, but CNN with its previously arranged leased lines stayed on the longest after the lines were cut for the other networks. The next day, General Colin Powell jokingly said the Pentagon was relying on CNN for military information.

The second night of the war gave prime-time viewers another long, absorbing evening as CNN and NBC reporters in Tel Aviv reported live as Scud missiles landed. Reporters, often wearing gas masks, provided raw and unevaluated information. At one point, NBC reported dramatically that nerve gas had been detected in one Scud attack. Tom Brokaw decried the situation for some minutes, but after the report proved false, NBC apologized. For the first three days of the war, people everywhere stayed glued to television and radio sets, including shortwave receivers. Networks expanded to near 24-hour coverage for the first 36 hours, and even the daytime soap operas were preempted briefly for war coverage. There was not that much to report at that point, and the same facts, theories, and speculations were repeated again and again. Nevertheless, the mesmerized public stayed tuned.

During this early bombing phase of the war, the Pentagon withheld detailed military information, such as the extent of the bombing and destruction within Iraq. Restrictions were placed on interviews with troops and returning pilots. Reporters could cover field combat only in designated pools, groups of reporters accompanied by an escort officer. (One reporter likened a press pool to group of senior citizens on a conducted tour.) All interviews with soldiers were subject to censorship before they could be released.

Most information came from the daily briefings held by military spokespersons in both Riyadh and at the Pentagon in Washington, but much of this was rather general, vague, and lacking in detail. The military had coherent arguments for its restrictive policies. Destroying Iraq's military command and communications capability was a high priority of the bombing strategy, and it was important to withhold useful information, via the media, that would reveal troop movements and intentions of coalition forces. Keeping Iraq's forces off balance and without reliable information was a key part of U.S. strategy.

However, some news executives and critics claimed the press restrictions went well beyond security concerns and appeared aimed at both preventing politically damaging disclosures by soldiers and shielding the American public from seeing the brutal aspects of war. If the war had gone badly, the press would have had difficulty reporting the negative aspects. With over 1,600 reporters in the theater, only about 100 could be accommodated by the pools to report on the 500,000 American force. As the ground war neared, the large press corps became increasingly restive and frustrated at this lack of access.

The response of some reporters was to "freelance"—to avoid the pools and to go off on their own. Malcolm Browne reported, "Some reporters were hiding out in American Marine or Army field units, given GI uniforms and gear to look inconspicuous, enjoying the affection (and protection of the units) they're trying to cover—concealed by the officers and troops from the handful of press-hating commanders who strive to keep the battle field free of wandering journalists."[8] Browne noted that nearly all reporters who tried to reach front-line U.S. troops were arrested at one time or another (including reporters for the *New York Times, Washington Post,* Associated Press, and Cox papers) and sometimes held in field jails for up to 12 hours and threatened with revocation of their press credentials. After the ground war began, these freelancers, particularly John Kifner and

Chris Hedges of the *New York Times,* produced some outstanding reportage. Forrest Sawyer of ABC news, who traveled unofficially with Saudi forces, provided some of the earliest and best reports on the freeing of Kuwait City.

Had the ground war been longer, more heavily contested, and taken a higher toll in U.S. casualties, relations between the military and the freelancing journalists probably would have turned quite acrimonious. But these journalists felt they were doing what they were supposed to do in time of war—maintain the flow of information that Americans need to know when half a million of them are at risk in a foreign war.

Psychological Warfare and Propaganda

Intertwined with the flow of war news was the propaganda war between Iraq and the United States, the principal power in the UN-supported coalition. Each side used information and its own, as well as international, news media to seek advantages in world and regional opinion and to undermine enemy morale. Saudi Arabia and Kuwait, both lacking effective media voices, hired prestigious U.S. public relations firms, such as Hill and Knowlton, to get their views across to Western media and publics.

Saddam Hussein's propaganda was considered crude but effective in a region where rumor and fact are often blurred and conspiracies are easily believed. Iraq's most persistent strategy was to blame the Gulf crisis on an Israeli-American plot to station foreign forces in the region and seize control of Middle Eastern oil.

Saddam's propaganda portrayed American soldiers as foreign invaders who are "drinking alcohol, eating pork and practicing prostitution," according to a broadcast on Holy Mecca Radio, a clandestine station beamed from Iraq into Saudi territory.[9] Iraqi television reported that 40 percent of American soldiers had AIDS. An Indian newspaper with ties to Iraq reported that the Pentagon had sent 5,000 Egyptian women to Saudi Arabia to serve as prostitutes for the American troops. A U.S. Information Agency official commented, "Even though a story can be incredibly preposterous to the Western mind, it can resonate deeply in other parts of the world. The key is the predisposition to believe, not the crudity of the charge."[10] Before the bombing destroyed many of its radio transmitters, Iraq had a greater capability than the West to broadcast in the area, including clandestine radio stations for Egyptian and Saudi Arabian listeners. Even though the Voice of America increased its Arabic broadcasting from 7½ to

13 hours a day, Iraq was largely successful in jamming those and BBC Arabic broadcasts during the first weeks of the crisis.

American and coalition propaganda, because of greater access to international media, probably had higher credibility outside of Arab and Moslem nations. A key aim was to deny Iraq any useful military information as well as to confuse and mislead the enemy; thus, misinformation was dispensed occasionally in military briefings. The most effective misinformation gambit was the threat of U.S. Marine amphibious landings along the Kuwaiti coastline. Western media unwittingly cooperated in reporting the highly publicized practice landings. The assault never occurred, but the story had the effect of pinning down thousands of Iraqi troops who could have been deployed elsewhere.

Main U.S. "psychwar" emphasis was on a psychological campaign designed to shake Iraq's confidence and to undermine the morale of its armed forces. The campaign included broadcasts of antigovernment propaganda into Iraq and the circulation of audiocassette and videocassette tapes depicting U.S. forces as militarily strong and Saddam Hussein's government as corrupt. Allied aircraft dropped a million leaflets into Kuwait urging the Iraqi infantry to surrender. Many who later did give up came in clutching these air-dropped "safe conduct" leaflets.

Several clandestine radio stations were used; the most prominent called itself the Voice of Free Iraq and operated on four frequencies. Propaganda broadcasts backfired against the United States at least once, when on January 7, 1991, the U.S. military reported to U.S. media that six Iraqi helicopters had been flown into Saudi Arabia by defecting pilots. The story was soon denied by the Saudis, and the Pentagon later retracted it. American officials had apparently accepted as fact a disinformation broadcast beamed at Iraq.[11]

The effectiveness of such psychological warfare efforts is always difficult to evaluate. In any case, the propaganda of words always yields to the propaganda of events, and since Saddam Hussein's forces were so soundly defeated, his propaganda of words was also overwhelmed.

The Peter Arnett Controversy

Television, and especially CNN, was the focus of some controversy over accusations that it was being "used" to further Saddam Hussein's propaganda goals. The heaviest criticism was aimed at CNN's Peter Arnett, who for a time was the only American reporter remaining in Baghdad. The question was whether he was working as a professional journalist reporting under difficult conditions or whether he was mainly a conduit for enemy propaganda. Arnett's long, televised interview with Saddam Hussein and his story about a bombed-out factory which Arnett said made powdered milk for infant formula were both controversial. The U.S. military charged that the factory made biological weapons and that Arnett was aiding Iraqi misinformation since such CNN reports are widely viewed and believed throughout the Middle East. However, the U.S. press almost unanimously supported Arnett, a Pulitzer Prize winner for his AP coverage of Vietnam. Even under such restrictive conditions, it was argued, independent reports such as Arnett's widened the amount of information available, and censored reports are worth listening to if only to give the world an idea of what information Iraq wanted distributed. After reporters in Baghdad had left Iraq, they were free of course to write what they wished. Some criticism was directed at CNN for not providing more context and analysis of Arnett's Baghdad reports.

Some critics questioned Arnett's patriotism, implying that an American reporter should support U.S. war aims rather than report the facts as accurately as he could under the circumstances. Arnett's critics failed to understand that Arnett's CNN reports went to a widely dispersed international audience and that CNN's hopes for credibility and acceptance were dependent on the perception of objectivity and truthfulness of its reports.

Triumph of 24-Hour Global News

During the American Civil War, in 1861–65, the demand for news was so great that U.S. newspapers for the first time went to seven-day publication. During the 1963 Kennedy assassination, live television emerged as the preeminent medium for reporting breaking news. The events positioned ABC, CBS, and NBC as major news gatherers but still essentially American media.

During the 42-day Gulf War, CNN established the importance of a 24-hour news network with true global reach. The concept has certainly changed the international news system—especially during times of international crisis and conflict.

The three major U.S. networks were shaken by CNN's success. After CNN's historic scoop on the first night of the war, a number of independent television stations, radio stations, and even several network affiliates relied on CNN in the crisis.[12] Although the three networks had more talented and experienced reporters, they could not compete with CNN either in time on the air or in the vast audiences CNN reached in about 100 countries. The success of CNN has encouraged similar services, such as BBC's World Service Television, but it remains to be seen how well any 24-hour global news network will do financially during peaceful periods when interest in foreign news is low.

The Gulf War certainly conditioned viewers everywhere to keep their television sets tuned to CNN (or its later imitators) during times of high crisis. Perhaps the news business today places too much emphasis on immediate and fast-breaking news "as it happens." Video shots of F15s roaring off runways, of "smart bombs" scoring direct hits, of Tomahawk missiles flying through Baghdad, and tank formations rolling through the desert made memorable viewing. After the fog of war had cleared, though, the press and the public found that the Gulf War was not quite what they thought it was.

The tragic events in the volatile Middle East also reminded the public that wars and political crises are complex and intricate processes that can still best be reported and explained by the printed word. The best and most complete reporting of the Gulf War came ultimately from the print media, which rounded out the picture and provided the context and perspective necessary for understanding. During the first several weeks after the cease-fire, it was the print reporters, not television, who dug out and filled in the details of what actually happened during the air campaign and the brief ground war, details that the military on both sides had so effectively screened from public view.[13]

Lessons for the Press

Wars between nations are by definition major international news stories and should be reported by the press as completely and thoroughly as conditions permit. The American public may be blasé about much foreign news, but it certainly pays close attention when American armed forces go to war. Yet governments at war, even the most democratic, will try to control and manipulate war news to their own strategic advantage. The Gulf War provided ample reminders of this generalization. Censorship and propaganda, the twin arms of political warfare, are integral components of modern warfare, so both sides often deny the press the opportunity to report objectively what has occurred. In numerous modern wars—Uganda versus Tanzania, the Sudanese civil war, Ethiopia's war against Eritrean rebels and Somalia, and the Soviet Union's incursion into Afghanistan—both sides either barred foreign correspondents or discouraged any coverage. The long and bloody Iran/Iraq war, precursor to the Gulf War, was severely underreported.

In the Gulf War, over 1,500 journalists were permitted into the war theater but were allowed little freedom to cover the actual fighting. On the Iraqi side, the few foreign reporters in Baghdad were severely restricted.

From all indications, the U.S. military as well as the Bush administration were pleased with the results of their media policy and would do the same thing again. But among the press, especially American and British journalists, there was a general conclusion that the press had been unduly and even illegally denied access to information about the war.

After the war, a report that called military restrictions in the Gulf War "real censorship" that confirmed "the worst fears of reporters in a democracy" was delivered to Defense Secretary Dick Cheney. It was signed by 17 news executives representing the four networks, AP and UPI, and major newspapers and newsmagazines. The report bitterly complained that the restrictions placed on reporters by the Pentagon were intended to promote a sanitized view of the war. The war was called the first in this century to restrict all official coverage to pools. "By controlling what reporters saw and when they saw it, the military exerted great power to shape and manage the news," the report said. Also criticized were the use of military escorts and "unwarranted delays in transmitting copy."[14]

After more than eight months of talks with news executives, the Pentagon in May 1992 issued a set of principles intended to guarantee that journalists have greater access to future military operations than they had in the Gulf War. However, news media and the government could not agree on whether there should be any official "security review" of news reports before they are published or broadcast. The statement affirmed that "open and independent reporting will be the principal means of coverage of U.S. military operations. The guidelines limited the role of military escorts and said that 'press pools' are not to serve as the standard means of covering operations."[15]

Subsequent military operations in Somalia, Haiti, and Bosnia have not really provided an adequate test of these new principles. But certainly the Gulf War showed that despite all the wonders of rapid, instant, communication (and perhaps in part because of them), the Western news media still can be severely restricted by their own democratic governments in wartime.

The incursion of U.S. Marines into Somalia in December 1992 was

intended to provide military protection to the relief organizations trying to
feed starving Somalis caught in the cross fire of warring clans. Under these
conditions, the Pentagon decided to place no restraints on the media.
Howard Kurtz called what happened the most embarrassing moment ever
in media-military relations: "... the infamous night in December 1992
when Navy SEALS hitting the beach in Somalia were surrounded by a
small army of reporters and photographers who blinded them with television lights, clamored for interviews, and generally acted like obnoxious
adolescents. That sorry performance, turning a humanitarian mission to
aid starving Africans into a Felliniesque photo op, underscored what the
Pentagon had been saying for years: that the press simply could not disci-
pline itself, that reporters would blithely endanger the safety of American
troops for the sake of journalistic drama."[16] It was not one of the media's
finer days.

David Hackworth of *Newsweek* wrote, "[T]o lurch from thought control to no control is plain stupid. When the press corps beats the Marine
Corps to the beach, everyone loses."[17] The Pentagon wanted full coverage
of Somalia, so no controls were placed on the press, and what resulted was
a confused circus. There are those, however, who suspect that the Pentagon
deliberately orchestrated the fiasco to make the media look bad.

Somalia raised the question of whether the media, by its heavy barrage
of pictures and stories of starving Somalis, pushed President Bush in his
last days in office to send troops on their humanitarian mission. The answer is unclear, but Bush did react by committing U.S. armed forces to a
limited and supposedly doable assignment of famine relief. (On the other
hand, despite horrific pictures of death, destruction, and "ethnic cleansing"
from Bosnia, the United States resolutely refused to get militarily involved
until mid-1995.)

When the Somalia assignment expanded in the early Clinton administration to include warlord hunting, it provoked a devastating firefight in
the streets of Mogadishu. When 18 U.S. soldiers were killed and the
pictures shown on U.S. television, the American public was unprepared
to accept casualties when vital U.S. interests were not at stake. The
White House soon announced the United States was getting out of
Somalia.

James Hoge, editor of *Foreign Affairs,* commented, "From its understanding of Vietnam came the military's subsequent emphasis on quick so-
lutions, limited media access and selective release of 'smart' weapons im-
agery. The public, however, will not remain dazzled when interventions
become difficult. As in Vietnam, public attitudes ultimately hinge on ques-

tions about the rightness, purpose and costs of policy—not television images."[18]

The "peaceful" landing in Haiti in September 1994 provided more perspective on military/media relations. When it appeared earlier that a full-scale military invasion to oust the military rulers would take place, U.S. media were planning the most minutely documented war coverage ever. Several hundred reporters and photographers from television networks, newspapers, and magazines were already in Haiti, with the most-advanced equipment ever brought to a war zone. The Pentagon had promised more cooperation than ever, and reporters said they would not be relying on the military for primary access.[19]

However, White House and Pentagon officials, in a meeting with television representatives, asked for a broadcast blackout of eight hours. The Clinton administration also wanted to restrict reporters to their hotels until military commanders gave them permission to go to the fighting.

The *New York Times* editorialized, "Journalists and citizens who believe in the free flow of information should take note of this effort to blindfold the press and the public. It shows that the news-management policies that took root in the Reagan-Bush years and reached their full propagandistic flower during Operation Desert Storm are still in place at the Pentagon. Those policies represent a long-term danger to American troops and the ability of voters to judge the wisdom of elected officials who order military attacks."[20]

In this case, a press and military showdown was avoided when U.S. forces landed without incident in Haiti. Nor were there any frictions between press and military in Bosnia when NATO imposed a military truce and thousands of U.S. and NATO peacekeeping troops occupied that troubled land in late 1995. There, Pentagon policy was to encourage friendly relations with reporters and broadcasters. GIs carried a 16-page guide to Bosnia with a section devoted to "Meeting the Media" that instructed a soldier that he or she "can be an excellent unofficial spokesperson."

Background of Restrictions

How did the American press, the freest in the world, arrive at this situation? The Vietnam War, when relations between the American journalists and the U.S. military soured and reached their lowest ebb in history, was the starting point. Reporters and camera crews, working within military guidelines, were given free access without field censorship to roam Vietnam; some called it the best-reported war in history. Yet many in the U.S. military felt press reporting contributed to the defeat by overstressing negative aspects, including graphic pictures of dead and wounded, highlighting scandals such as the My Lai massacre, and misinterpreting such key events as the Tet offensive, which the military considered a defeat for North Vietnam, not a victory as the press reported. Such reportage, it was argued, aided the antiwar movement at home and turned the American public against the war.

The press for its part felt that the U.S. military lied to and misled the press in Vietnam and that officials consistently painted a much rosier picture of the war than was justified. Given the record of deception, the press, it was argued, was correct in being skeptical of the military.

The view prevailed within the military that the free rein given journalists in Vietnam led to reporting that seriously damaged morale and turned the country against its own troops. If news or information is a weapon, then, the generals argued, it should be controlled as a part of the war effort.

The brief war between Britain and Argentina over the Falkland Islands in the South Atlantic in 1982 provided a model for the Pentagon and other governments on how to manage the media in wartime. No reporters other than British were permitted to accompany the task force, and these reporters were apparently carefully selected. The 17 finally accredited had to accept censorship at the source and were given a Ministry of Defense handbook telling them that they would be expected to "help in leading and steadying public opinion in times of national stress or crisis." The Ministry of Defense had effectively imposed censorship at the source, and most war information was released in London from the ministry, which followed a policy of suppression and subtle control of emphasis. Bad news was either not reported or delayed. After the war was over, the British press gave a very different picture of the war, detailing mishaps and failures not previously reported. Philip Knightley wrote,

> Vietnam was an aberration. The freedom given to correspondents to go anywhere, see everything, and write what they liked is not going to be given again. The Falklands was a model of how to make certain that government policy is not undermined by the way a war is reported. The rules turn out to be fairly simple: control access to the fighting, exclude neutral correspondents, censor your own, and muster support both on the field and at home, in the name of patriotism. Objectivity can come back in fashion after the shooting is over.[21]

For America, the press-versus-military issue surfaced again on October 25, 1983, when U.S. forces invaded the tiny island of Grenada. The Defense Department barred all reporters from covering the initial invasion. After two days of vigorous protests by the press, a pool of 12 reporters and a military escort was flown in. By the end of one week with the fighting winding down, 150 reporters were ferried to the island and allowed to stay overnight. The press, however, was not mollified, and Walter Cronkite said the Reagan administration had seriously erred: "This is our foreign policy and we have a right to know what is happening, and there can be no excuse in denying the people that right." Keith Fuller, Associated Press president, said, "Despite the perils, such coverage has historically been the rule. This is no substitute for accurate, factual, first-hand reports. In their absence, only public confusion and misunderstanding can follow."[22]

But, as in the later Gulf War, public opinion polls showed that the American people generally supported the ban on press coverage. Max Frankel of the *New York Times* wrote, "The most astounding thing about the Grenada situation was the quick, facile assumption by some of the public that the press wanted to get in, not to witness the invasion on behalf of the people, but to sabotage it."[23]

As a result of the furor, the Defense Department appointed a commission headed by Winant Sidle, a retired general, which recommended that a select pool of reporters be allowed to cover the early stages of any surprise operation and share its information with other news organizations. This seemed a fair compromise between the military's need for surprise and the public's need for information.

The new guidelines were first tested in December 1989 when U.S. forces invaded Panama. The press arrangements failed miserably. The Pentagon did not get the 16-reporter pool into Panama until four hours after fighting began, and reporters were not allowed to file stories until six hours later. Most critics blamed the Bush White House for the mix-up and for not insisting that the military facilitate press coverage.

Covering the Next War

In February 1998, when the United States and the UN came to the brink of bombing Iraq because of the dispute with Saddam Hussein about inspecting weapons sites, we had a peek at how the next war (at least in the Middle East) would be covered by international news networks. The *Wall Street Journal* reported that as hostilities loomed, European broadcasters were sending in hundreds of correspondents and crews, trained for the bat-

tlefield and outfitted with microphones and hazard suits. Hotels in Baghdad and Kuwait were bristling with new satellite dishes, satellite phones,
computers, generators, and lighting gear. British broadcasters had their
own satellite dish and production room set up on the *HMS Invincible* aircraft carrier, and CNN had made similar arrangements with a U.S. navy
carrier. With 70 people in the region and planeloads of equipment, CNN
said it was their biggest deployment ever.

All news stations, both radio and television, depend more than ever
on such big news events for ratings, and the competition for vivid action
footage from a war zone has been growing. In America, MSNBC and Fox
News have both launched all-news stations in recent years to counter
CNN. Britain now has three round-the-clock news stations—CNN, Sky
News, and BBC News 24—in addition to coverage from other commercial stations, and all were primed to report the fireworks, which were called
off or at least delayed.[24] (President Clinton's four-day air war against Iraq
in December 1998 came up so unexpectedly that the news media could
not fully mobilize their resources.)

Further, by early 1998, signs of improved relations between the press
and the military were evident. With the armed forces increasingly engaged
in peacekeeping and humanitarian operations as in Somalia, Rwanda,
Haiti, and Bosnia, the military seem to have decided that they must treat
the media less as adversaries and more as partners. Warren Strobel argues
in a recent book, *Late-Breaking Foreign Policy*, that the "traditional wartime
relationship between reporters and officials has been virtually turned on its
head. Rather than controlling reporters in peace operations, military commanders and their civilian bosses desperately need them to help build public support, to explain what may be a complex and indistinct picture and
even to gather useful information for them in the field. In return they may
offer access and independence that allow reporters to distance themselves
from their would-be chaperones in the U.S. military."[25] Strobel was dis-
cussing "operations other than war." It remains to be seen what happens to
press/military cooperation the next time we become involved in a full-
blown war in, say, Korea or Iraq.

First Amendment Concerns

From Grenada to Panama to the Persian Gulf, the American press has been
barred from fully covering wars or military incursions that it has historically and traditionally reported before. This is important because the U.S.
Supreme Court has ruled that the press, in order to inform the public, has

a First Amendment right to those places that "historically" and "traditionally" it has had the right to cover, such as trials and town meetings.

The Supreme Court has also ruled that the press has a First Amendment right to be present at all "public" events. Certainly an invasion lasting more than several hours or a full-scale war is a public event.

Perhaps the press's Constitutional rationale for war coverage was best
expressed by Justice Hugo Black in the Pentagon Papers case:

> The Government's power to censor the press was abolished so that the
> press would remain forever free to censure the Government. The press
> was protected so that it could bare the secrets of government and inform
> the people. Only a free and unrestrained press can effectively expose de-
> ception in government. And paramount among the responsibilities of a
> free press is the duty to prevent any part of the government from de-
> ceiving the people and sending them off to distant lands to die of foreign
> fevers and foreign shot and shell.[26]

The press has no "right" to report sensitive military information that
could aid an enemy, and would not want to do so, but it does have a right
to be there, to keep a watchful eye on the military, just as it does on a criminal trial. No modern war has been fought as quickly and effectively and
with as few allied casualties as by the U.S.-led forces in the Gulf War. But
when wars go badly, as they often can, with incompetent leadership, confused tactics, and unnecessary casualties, it is essential that the press, as independent representatives of the public and of the forces themselves, be
there to report then or later what occurred. The citizens of Iraq had no independent press reporting back to them about the military disasters and
political incompetence that led to the battlefield deaths of thousands of
their young men—a basic difference between a democracy and a dictator-
ship.

The Supreme Court is unlikely to come to the defense of the U.S.
press in this matter. Perhaps the best hope of the press is to protest and
complain until a significant portion of the public supports the right to
know. In the Gulf War, it was apparent that the American news media and
their owners did not complain loudly and vehemently enough about the
pool and censorship restrictions before the bombs started dropping. A sitting president is not likely to modify such restrictions of free expression in
wartime until forced to by political pressures.

The solution, according to Hackworth, a retired Army officer, is "for
the Pentagon to go back to a revised version of the system used in World
War II: the military fights the war, the press covers it, and the American

public is told what is happening. But everyone agrees to play by sensible rules."[27]

Ironically, the greatly expanded capability of global television to report instantly on a modern war provides another rationale for governments to control and censor war news. And when American or British journalists are denied access to war news, the rest of the world is denied access as well.

CHAPTER 10

Muted Debate Over News Flow

A future predicated on the free flow of information is the only way that the global village we seek can come about.

—Federico Mayor, UNESCO President

New World Information Order: "the constant reiteration of the forever unclear."

—William Harley

A recurring theme of global news communication since the 1950s has been the perceived need to improve news flow to and from the poor and struggling new nations of the Third World. Many diverse efforts by governments, universities, news media, and international organizations were launched to help attain these goals even though at times such efforts were compromised by politics, ideology, and the exigencies of the Cold War.

Much serious scholarship as well as partisan polemics have been written, discussed, and heatedly argued about the relationship of communication to development efforts.[1] In this chapter, only two facets are addressed: first, the initiatives for a "New World Information Order" as an effort to end perceived imbalances and inequities in global news flow and media capabilities; second, the persisting difficulties of reporting poorer nations to the West—in this case, news about Africa in American news media, well illustrated by President Clinton's March 1998 trip there.

The "great debate" over news flow has ended but not the news imbalances between North and South.

Great Debate Over Global News

This extraordinary controversy over the control of the flow of global news and mass culture was a dispute that aroused the heated concern of journalists, diplomats, and academics in many nations. This "great debate," which usually pitted Western reporters and often their governments against non-Western and Communist political leaders, involved scathing attacks, beginning in the 1970s, on the West's traditional methods of collecting and distributing international news and popular entertainment. This led to repeated calls for a New World Information Order (NWIO)— a vague but radical reordering of the international communication system.

The disagreements and disputes, which flourished into the late 1980s, have slowly but not completely abated and reflected the widening communication disparities between the West and the poor nations of the South that considered themselves recipients of a one-way flow of communication. The controversy was in large part political and ideological, related to East-West rivalries of the Cold War. The USSR and Communist bloc nations were much involved in supporting the worldwide revolution against Western imperialism, which by 1968 was reaching a violent climax in Vietnam. (The call for a New World Information Order was a nonviolent adjunct of the anti-imperialism movement.) Yet another 1968 revolution, *against* the dictatorships of the left, was dramatized by the Prague Spring revolt of the Czech uprising against Soviet domination. (This revolt and the Solidarity movement in Poland were supported by Western opponents of the NWIO, opponents who espoused the free flow of news, press freedom, and democracy.) As Paul Berman points out, "The two revolutions were badly at odds. One of those revolutions was spreading the totalitarianism of Europe to the former colonies; the other was undermining the totalitarianisms of Europe. One was peaking; the other was just getting under way."[2]

The information wars were fought out mainly in the academic arena, in United Nations forums, and, partly, in news media. With the 1989 collapse of Communist states in Europe, the news controversy ended, but, while it lasted, the dispute was lively and raised important issues.

On the one hand, the "information societies" of the West have been expanding their ability to communicate globally. By comparison, underdeveloped nations have inadequate media systems and are largely passive recipients of the increasing flow of global communications. In addition to news, this includes a deluge of mass-culture products—motion pictures, television programs, videocassettes and audiocassettes, records, and various publications—much of them coming from the United States and Britain. Communist bloc nations as well as other nations were sensitive to this influx as well.

This widening breach results from differences in political and economic structures, as well as from conflicting concepts of media control. The 1960s and early 1970s marked the high tide of nonaligned socialism and the emergence of the one-party state and the developmental concept of the press. Such political structures favored centralized government control of mass communication.

The Western model of journalism was sharply criticized and largely rejected by Communist nations and the new autocracies of what was then called the Third World.

Since 1948, though, the Western approach to news gathering was embodied in Article 19 of the UN's "Universal Declaration of Human Rights," which stated in part, "Everyone has the right to freedom of opinion and expression—and to seek, receive, and impart information and ideas through any medium and regardless of frontiers." Western journalists have long insisted that a free flow of communication was necessary to accomplish this. Peoples everywhere, they said, should have access to information, especially information that affects their security, their well-being, their destinies; therefore, journalists must have an unimpeded right to collect and distribute news anywhere in the world.

This view, for a considerable time, had been the official position of the United Nations and especially UNESCO, which has a special concern with international communication. By 1972, though, the concept of free flow of information was under attack, as typified by declarations both by the UNESCO General Conference and the UN General Assembly concerning direct-broadcast satellites. That technology enabled television programming to be sent by satellites directly to an individual television receiver, bypassing ground receiving stations. The UNESCO group, by a vote of 55 to 7, with the United States voting against and 22 nations abstaining, adopted a draft resolution on satellite broadcasting which subscribed to the necessity of prior agreements between nations before direct satellite broadcasting occurs. This was the first significant retreat from unqualified support for global free flow and was of interest because of the recent growth of satellite telecommunications.

This action set the pattern for what was to come. These international bodies, with a majority of Third World nations, were modifying the principle of free flow by espousing the view that international communicators must obtain prior consent of the nation into which their journalists and news reports may move. In the Western view, this is but a short step to the authoritarian principle that each government has the inherent right to control news entering and leaving its borders.

UNESCO was a leading forum, but not the only one, for this ongoing controversy which involved UNESCO representatives, communications scholars and their associations and journals, and professional journalists and their organizations such as the International Press Institute, Inter American Press Association, International Organization of Journalists, and World Press Freedom Committee. Much was written and many speeches delivered as the controversy swelled at times with increasing passion and acrimony.

Arguments for a New World Information Order

The vague term "New World Information Order" includes both a wide-ranging critique of the Western news system and a rather obscure "program" with few specifics and no timetable for rectifying the situation. One critic called it a "slogan in search of a program."

NWIO advocates point out that a few Western nations provide most of the world's news coverage, entertainment, and advertising. Much of the news coverage, they say, is controlled by a few multinational news agencies. This is unacceptable because the agencies (AP, UPI, Reuters, and AFP) devote too little attention to the domestic affairs of developing nations and foster a negative image of those countries. This they do, the argument runs, by focusing on sensational and disastrous occurrences while ignoring positive events, particularly development issues. In addition, NWIO advocates charge that commercial advertising and mass-culture products foster biases in favor of the industrialized world and multinational corporations, thereby threatening the cultural integrity of developing nations.

For some of the more radical critics, the remedy was to restrict the transnational flow of information, particularly by curbing the activities of Western news agencies. Proposals were made to license journalists, impose international codes of journalistic ethics, inhibit advertising, and extend government control over the press. In this way, they hoped to limit outside influences and keep a tighter control over news and information flowing in and out of their countries.

Not all developing nations saw the situation in such negative terms. Some believed that the gaps in news and communications capacity were real and should be addressed by practical development efforts, including more aid from the West. These countries sought cooperation, not confrontation, with the industrialized nations.

After the early concern with direct-broadcast satellites, the controversy zeroed in on international news flow and the Western media themselves. One of the most widely quoted advocates was Mustapha Masmoudi of Tunisia.[3]

Information in the world, Masmoudi said, is characterized by basic imbalances, reflecting the general economic and social inequities that affect the international community. First, there is a flagrant quantitative imbalance between North and South, created by the disparity between the volume of news and information emanating from the developed world and intended for the developing countries and the volume of the flow in the opposite direction. Masmoudi charged that 80 percent of the world news flow comes from the four major Western nations by way of AP, UPI, Reuters, and AFP, but that these agencies devote too little attention to the Third World. So, without news agencies of their own, the former Third World is dependent on the "big four" for news about themselves and their neighbors.

But the Western media, he said, are oblivious to the real concerns of the less-developed nations, which are relegated to the status of mere consumers of news and information that are sold to them like any other commodity. Masmoudi said the Western media tend to stress the most unfavorable news about poor nations—crises, coups, civil wars, terrorism, street demonstrations— "even holding them up to ridicule."

The present-day information system, Masmoudi said, "enshrines a form of political, economic, and cultural colonialism which is reflected in the often tendentious interpretation of news concerning the developing countries. The Western media are selective in what they report and the criteria used are based on the political and economic interests of the transnational system and the countries where those multinational corporations are located."

Disparities in communication capability, then—and not the disastrous economic policies, political corruption, and misguided rule of some nations involved—were blamed for the former Third World's plight.

Among some of the NWIO advocates, a conspiracy was clearly evident: the Western media were accused of being malevolently and cynically manipulated by their own governments to keep poor developing nations deliberately in a perpetual state of dependence and economic servitude. Other proponents of the new order wanted to restructure the world's media systems to help achieve a more just and equitable economic system and thus to aid and help achieve social justice.

Arguments Opposed to a New
Information Order

But to the West, where the media are largely privately owned (and, in the case of broadcasting, often publicly owned), the press exists to inform the people and to protect liberty against the abuses of governments. Liberty is not the same as social justice, and Western journalists say that when press freedom is sacrificed for some vague social goal, then political liberty and human rights are in jeopardy.

Journalists and political leaders in Western democracies reacted in various ways to this verbal assault on Western mass communication. Some rejected it out of hand as a cynical effort to politicize international news and to justify and gain international respectability for government control of news and censorship. Others conceded a few of the charges and rejected others, but very few journalists in the West, and not many independent journalists in the Third World either, bought the whole argument for a revamped news system.

Many thoughtful journalists and others conceded that there are real bases for Third World complaints but were opposed to the proposals to implement the "order." It was agreed that real disparities in news flow do exist, that non-Western nations do receive a lot more news and information than they send out, and that much of their entertainment and mass culture come from the West. Certainly the poorer nations are being largely bypassed by new technology in telecommunications. Many in the West agree that news media should report more non-Western news and do it with more understanding and regard for the views of other nations.

Yet the coups, the economic disasters, the corruption, and the civil wars must also be reported regardless of where they occur. Agreed, the Western press should provide more comprehensive, sustained reporting of foreign regions and with more historical perspective. This is necessary also because the former Third World must often rely on Western media to find out what is happening in its own and neighboring countries. Further, people in the West would benefit from a better-balanced flow of news from more of the world.

Rosemary Righter agreed that critics of the existing system have a point when they say their affairs are badly reported and that Western media either ignore them or ignore the news they consider important, stressing instead the "bad news." But the Western agencies, she said, "cannot and do not force their wares on unwilling buyers."[4] In many less-developed nations, individual newspapers and broadcasters are not permitted to subscribe directly to Western news agencies; rather, government news agencies buy the foreign services and then redistribute the agency news to local media, thereby acting as real or potential censors. Governments, too, were the principal purchasers of incoming movies and television programs. Western news and entertainment are not imposed on unwilling nations but are usually sought out and paid for by official agencies. The picture of the millions in poor nations being inundated by unwanted alien information is fanciful. The governments were very much in control.

Western critics, then, see the New World Information Order as more than a critique of certain news practices—as essentially an attack on free and independent journalism. An independent press, they argue, makes self-government and democracy possible, and a central problem of journalism around the world is to establish and maintain independent news media that are able to report and criticize their own governments without retaliation or suppression of their freedoms. Few countries have such media, so the free, Western international media play a surrogate role of providing reliable information to people living in nations without independent newspapers and broadcasters. Further, as groups such as Amnesty International attest, a free press plays a particularly useful role in publicizing the plight of political prisoners worldwide and of reporting violations of human rights. Yet the whole thrust of the NWIO is to provide legitimacy for government control of information.

Declarations and policy statements made in the UN or UNESCO are, of course, nonbinding on members, but some nations otherwise hesitant to take a repressive action may find courage in numbers or feel morally justified if a declaration or code adopted by a hundred other nations existed. The end effect, some feel, would be to justify and provide international approbation to repressive actions by authoritarian regimes. That is why many have opposed the NWIO.

A move toward reconciliation of differences was made by UNESCO's International Commission for the Study of Communication Problems.[5] Chaired by Sean MacBride, the report recommended that journalists have free access to all news sources, both official and unofficial, and that all censorship be abolished. While supporting journalists' rights of access to news, the report accepted the former Third World's concerns about the "colonial domination" of news distribution. Private ownership of media came in for some harsh words: "Special attention should be devoted to obstacles and restrictions which derive from the concentration of ownership, public and private, from commercial influences on the press and broadcasting or from private and governmental advertising. The problem of financial conditions under which the media operate should be critically reviewed, and measures elaborated to strengthen editorial independence."[6] The MacBride commission did not resolve the issues and was in fact criticized by both sides.

Concerned at this turn of events, some 60 leaders of print and broadcasting media from 20 countries met at Talloires, France, and pledged to fight efforts of UNESCO to set up the information order. The "Declaration of Talloires" called press freedom a "basic right," and participants said they were resolved to resist any encroachment on it. UNESCO was urged to "abandon attempts to regulate news content and formulate rules for press conduct," insisting this violated its own charter, the Universal Declaration of Human Rights, and the Helsinki Declaration on Human Rights, and was inconsistent with the United Nations Charter.

The declaration attacked the NWIO as politically motivated and specifically opposed plans to license journalists through the device of identity cards and opposed calls for an international code of ethics, saying such codes could only be drawn up by the press itself and must be voluntary. The "abolition of all censorship and other forms of arbitrary control of information and opinion" was called for on the basis that "peoples' rights to news and information must not be abridged." The demand was made that journalists have access by right to all sources of news and information, including people who disagree with a government's policy.[7]

Efforts at Conciliation and Compromise

The controversy continued but in a more moderate tone. The late 1980s ushered in yet another dramatic swing in the world's political economy. A seminal event was the widespread recognition of the failure of socialism as a viable economic system. The economist Robert Heilbroner wrote, "Less than 75 years after it officially began, the contest between capitalism and socialism is over: capitalism has won. The Soviet Union, China, and Eastern Europe have given us the clearest possible proof that capitalism organizes the material affairs of mankind more satisfactorily than socialism."[8] This changing worldview weakened the arguments of NWIO proponents who espoused state socialism while their Western opponents espoused independent media operating in market economies, an increasingly attractive prospect for many non-Western peoples.

Among Western critics of the NWIO, a growing consensus developed that the basic problems were those of both improving the media systems of less-developed nations and providing more diversity and variety of news outlets for the global dissemination of news and entertainment. These remedies, it was argued, would help break down centralized government monopolies of mass communication.

Both sides seemed more willing to find ways to reconcile their differences. UNESCO policy makers said the organization was shifting its activities toward concrete projects that would improve communication media and technical training for journalists in developing nations. To accomplish this, the new International Program for Development of Communications (IPDC), the brainchild of William Harley, a U.S. State Department consultant, was launched. The industrialized nations were to provide concrete financial assistance for projects that would improve the former Third World's ability to communicate.

For their part, U.S. news agencies and other media have shown a willingness to report more non-Western news and to do so with more sensitivity. Moreover, Western journalists joined efforts to help train journalists of the former Third World. At a second Talloires conference of 90 representatives of media from 25 countries, a "List of Talloires" was released, enumerating more than 300 programs, in over 70 countries, that included training, educational, exchange, intern, and fellowship programs for journalists. The American Society of Newspaper Editors launched a series of internship programs for journalists of the former Third World. Other U.S. programs were the Center for Foreign Journalists and the Alfred Friendly Fellowship Program.

Alternative News Agencies

Another significant development has been the expansion of alternative and regional news agencies that can supplement and add variety to news coming from Western news organizations. The oldest alternative agency is the Non-Aligned News Agencies Pool (NANAP), which dates from the Fourth Non-Aligned Summit in Algiers in 1973. Although about 80 nations were involved, it has had little impact even in the media of its strongest supporters.

A more important example is the Inter Press Service Third World News Agency (IPS).[9] IPS is a nonprofit cooperative based in Rome and specializing in non-Western news, which it distributes to media in Europe and North America. With bureaus or correspondents in 60 countries, two-thirds of them in the former Third World, IPS maintains exchanges with 30 national news agencies. The focus is on news relating to development instead of spot news.

Other alternative agencies that have been adding diversity to global news flow include Depthnews, Gemini, and South-North News Service.[10] South-North, based in Hanover, New Hampshire, and run by U.S. journalists, has recruited correspondents to report from 62 countries, and their stories are edited and sent out to the service's subscribers. The purpose of the service is to cultivate reporters from the former Third World and to provide Western media with more news from a non-Western viewpoint. Emphasis is on stories that are insightful and unusual; not hard news or world exclusives.[11]

After 20 years of planning and consultations among African nations after the birth of the Organization of African Unity in 1963, the Pan African News Agency (PANA) was finally inaugurated in May 1983 with the major objective "to promote an effective exchange of political, economic, social, and cultural information among member states" and to "liberate African information from imperialist domination, foreign monopolies and resolutely gear it towards the promotion of development."[12] PANA can provide an important service for African journalism if it can overcome the built-in problems of lack of professionalism, shortage of funds and inadequate telecommunications, low credibility due to the heavy involvement of government news agencies, and political differences between African nations. PANA's average output was 14,000 words a day compared with Reuters' 800,000 words. Moreover, political factors impaired its operations. For example, when the president of Burkina Faso was shot to death in a coup, PANA's member agency in Burkina Faso waited days before filing. And in Burundi, after members of the ruling Tutsi tribe massacred thousands of Hutu, the story was front-page news around the world, but PANA didn't have the story because its member agency in Burundi remained silent.[13] In 1993, PANA said it would shift from reliance on national agencies to more independent reporting and try to make use of the Internet to distribute news.

The Caribbean News Agency (CANA) and Pacnews for the Pacific Ocean area have had some success in filling gaps left by the world agencies. Their success seems to be due to their independence from government and their professionalism.

Alternative and regional agencies certainly should be encouraged and supported but, according to Jonathan Fenby,

> It is clear that none of the efforts, neither the state agencies like TASS or Hsinhua of China nor the domestic agencies of countries like Germany, Japan, Spain or Italy (much less the alternative agencies) come anywhere near to attracting an international clientele similar to that taken for

granted by the Big Four. The question, therefore, is not whether major new sources of international news will emerge, but whether the existing four major services will continue in the role they have played so far.[14]

Another indication of the new conciliatory tone of the discussion was that the cries of "cultural imperialism" (i.e., the one-way flooding of American news and mass culture around the world), so widely heard in the 1970s, have receded as more and more nations have begun producing and exporting their own mass-culture products. In particular, nations such as Mexico, Brazil, Egypt, Hong Kong, and India have become major exporters of entertainment programming for their own regions. The world has available an increasing variety of programming, sold more and more across international markets.[15] The impact of new media technology, especially the revolutionary videocassette recorder and more locally produced media products, has brought about a rethinking of the cultural imperialism thesis.[16] The United States, long the arch-villain of media imperialism, is now on the receiving end of communication flows. Mexico is probably the largest exporter of media products into the United States. Millions of Spanish-speaking consumers in the United States read, watch, or listen to Mexican newspapers, magazines, and movies, as well as radio and television programs, on a daily basis.

One of the major underpinnings of the cultural imperialism thesis was the 1974 study of international television flows by Tapio Varis and Kaarle Nordenstreng, who argued that global television traffic was largely a one-way flow. A 1988 study by Michael Tracey disagreed with their findings: he wrote that national cultural preferences play a much larger part in determining what audiences actually choose to watch than many like to believe. U.S. television, he concluded, does not exert the inevitable dominance that is often assumed.[17]

The diplomatic event that distinctly quieted the information controversy was the decision of the U.S. government to withdraw from UNESCO on January 1, 1985. Britain and Singapore followed suit. Principal reasons given were that the 160-nation organization had been become politicized, focusing on ideological concerns rather than the global problems of literacy, education, science, and media development. The Reagan administration argued it would not support an organization espousing positions that ran counter to U.S. citizens' basic principles and values. UNESCO was also accused of being a bloated, inefficient bureaucracy, as 80 percent of its budget of $347 million was spent on its Paris headquarters rather than in developing nations. Most U.S. media supported the action.

However, a number of U.S. journalists and diplomats who had followed the controversy and had worked closely with UNESCO took strong exception to the U.S. withdrawal, arguing that Western influence in international communication issues would be seriously diminished. Ironically, the U.S. withdrawal came at a time when Western influence on the NWIO controversy was reasserting itself.

The American news media were accused of being one-sided and biased in reporting the role of UNESCO in the long controversy over a new information order. The American public, it was said, did not receive a fair and balanced report of the issues. A careful study by Anthony Giffard indicated that the U.S. news agencies and major newspapers were strongly and consistently anti-UNESCO in both news coverage and commentary. And once withdrawal took place, UNESCO largely disappeared from the news.[18]

The United States has not yet returned to UNESCO, although the Clinton administration had promised to do so. In January 1995, the White House quietly dropped the funds needed for a return from a budget review, saying the decision was financial. The outlook for return was not good even though critics have said UNESCO had met all U.S. conditions for rejoining.

The U.S. government's boycott of UNESCO certainly contributed to the winding down of the NWIO dispute, but there were other reasons as well.

A Changing World

With the collapse of communism in Eastern Europe and the end of the Cold War in 1989, much of the support for the new information order in the UN and UNESCO withered away.

In May 1990, after more than a decade of ideological struggle within international organizations, a United Nations committee dealing with information policy unanimously approved a resolution that put to rest the policy of a new world information order. Western diplomats welcomed the resolution and said it marked the end of the controversy at the UN. Diplomats attributed the agreement to political changes in the Soviet Union and Eastern Europe and said those countries wanted to end the dispute and reach a unanimous agreement.[19] Andrew J. Radolf, a UNESCO spokesman at UN headquarters in New York, said, "The world information order is a thing of the past."[20]

Significantly important too was the worldwide surge of support for the concepts of press freedom, human rights, democracy, and market economies. The protesting crowds in East Berlin, Prague, Beijing, and elsewhere were calling for more open societies, not continued government controls over information. And the alacrity with which non-Western peoples everywhere adopted Western mass culture made the calls of "media imperialism" seem dated and outmoded.[21] People watched Western videos and movies and listened to BBC and VOA and to audiocassettes in increasing numbers. The Western model of independent journalism was no longer on the defensive as it was in the 1970s.

The erstwhile Communist leaders may have voted for controls on global flow of news and entertainment, but the consumers, viewers, and readers of Central and Eastern Europe seemed to welcome it.

At the same time, throughout the former Third World, and especially in Africa, people were calling for, and sometimes getting, multiparty elections and market economies, which imply, in fact require, competing news media and a free flow of information. The view that government should keep its hands off the mass media had, at least for a time in recent years, gained wide acceptance in the world.

Once reigning as the "great debate" that resounded through the halls of UNESCO and the United Nations and involved high-level diplomatic concern and widespread attention in the world's news media, the New World Information Order had become clearly moribund in most nations. William Harley summed it up well:

> All parties have come to recognize that the relationship between the free flow of information and a better balanced flow of information requires that the developing world acquire the skills and equipment it needs to produce such a balance. All parties, too, seem to accept the conclusion that the improvement of the world's communication system lies not in international interference but in international cooperation—in a common effort to adapt communication techniques and technology to the needs of the developing countries, who, in turn, must contribute their own efforts to improve their capabilities through national communication policies of their own.[22]

Yet, in various university outposts, a number of academic and nongovernmental organizations and a few scholarly publications are keeping the great debate going.[23] If no longer a compelling issue between nations great and small, the New World Information Order has become strictly "academic"—in two meanings of the word.

In May 1997, a proposed world conference on communication gaps between developed and former Third World nations was strongly opposed by press-freedom groups concerned that the United Nations and UNESCO might be drawn into yet another "great debate." A spokesperson for the World Press Freedom Committee said, "Governments have no role in dictating to the press what the role of the press will be. That's what this whole thing is about." A number of developing nations, led by Nigeria and Algeria, were leading the effort. The initiative was opposed in part because it was sponsored by Nigeria's late Gen. Sani Abacha, who had harshly suppressed his own press. Leonard Sussman of Freedom House commented, "There are valid objections to the way the news is handled in the West and elsewhere. But there are also some very bad cures that I now see coming up in somewhat sugar-coated form."[24]

Although the great public debate over a world communication "order" has clearly been winding down during this period of rapid technological change in global communication, some of the disparities have not markedly changed. The two dozen or so rich industrialized nations still have a preponderance of media resources and capabilities, while the great majority of people in nonindustrialized nations, many of them poor and impotent, sorely lack both media facilities and the freedom to develop them. What has changed are the terms of the arguments as to how these inequities can be best addressed.

Africa in and out of the News Spotlight

For 12 days in March 1998, American newspapers and television news were full of stories and vivid video about Ghana, Uganda, Rwanda, South Africa, Botswana, and Senegal—all stops on President Bill Clinton's tour of the continent, with an entourage of 800 including over 200 journalists. For that brief time, the public was deluged with considerable information about that complex and troubled region.

But after the President returned to Washington, D.C., the news spigot from Africa was abruptly shut off. This reaffirmed a journalistic truism about Africa: the continent usually makes news when a famous person comes calling, such as President Carter did in 1978 or Pope John Paul II did in 1982 and 1998. Africa gets our attention as well when American soldiers' lives are at risk, as in 1992 when U.S. Marines landed in Somalia. (See Chapter 9, "Reporting Today's Wars.")

Yet most of the time, sub-Saharan Africa, except for South Africa, continues to be the least reported region of the world. One reason is that

Africa's own news media, weak and often government controlled, have not been effective in reporting reliable news to Africans, much less to the outside world, and generally are not much help either to foreign journalists trying to report from Africa.

During the 1960s and 1970s, independent black Africa received special attention in the Western press as some 40 new nations with promising futures stepped onto the world's stage. But as many of these countries foundered and regressed and the Cold War waned, the media's interest in Africa dropped sharply. Today, there is a grudging consensus among journalists that Africa is badly neglected in the news. Jim Hoagland of the *Washington Post* said Africa has gotten short shrift in the media for a long time, and David Gergen of *U.S. News* commented, "The history of American media has been one of general inattention to Africa, except when there's been a major famine or conflict."[25]

Africa's Media Image, a book edited by Beverly Hawk, with contributions by Africanists and journalists with African experience, gives detailed analyses of shortcomings of Western reporting of major African news stories over the past generation—confirming a near unanimous view of African specialists that U.S. news media need to do better.

News flows out of Africa to Europe and America in much the same ways it does from other developing nations in Latin America, Asia, and the Middle East with many of the same traits.

Parachute journalism. A story breaks that captures the world's attention—widespread famine in Somalia or Ethiopia, genocidal warfare in Rwanda, civil war in Congo (Zaire). The foreign press arrives in large numbers, covers the story, shoots pictures and video, and then abruptly leaves. This kind of reporting, typically seen on television, fails to provide needed context and follow-up that such stories require for public understanding.

Declining coverage. Since the end of the Cold War, much less news has been coming out of Africa as many civil wars and upheavals ended. Many small nations, among them Benin, Botswana, Burkino Faso, Mali, Burundi, Guinea, Niger, Lesotho, and Togo, not only have rarely had resident correspondents, but are seldom visited by Western reporters passing through the region. A few years ago, armed conflicts were going on at the same time in Angola, Chad, Djibouti, Ethiopia, Liberia, Rwanda, Somalia, Sudan, and Western Sahara, but little reporting about them appeared in the U.S. news media. On June 8, 1998, Nigeria's military dictator, Sani Abacha, died suddenly. This major story from Africa's most populous nation received only brief mention on the evening television news. The next day, the *New York Times* and *Washington Post* both gave the story several pages of coverage.

Barriers to reporting. Journalists in Africa face barriers not found elsewhere. Few correspondents know the many local languages, although knowledge of English or French is usually sufficient for dealing with officials and educated Africans. Distances are greater, communications less reliable, and air travel inconvenient and often haphazard. Reporters sometimes have to fly through London or Paris to get from one African capital to another. African governments often treat reporters badly; some at times just bar all foreign reporters as Guinea did for many years and Nigeria for a shorter time. Often, reporters may be permitted in, but access to news sources or officials is severely limited.

Failures to report bad news. By gathering news that authorities do not want reported, correspondents face the threat of expulsion. Over the years, many Western reporters have been forced out of Africa and refused visas when they sought reentry. Because of this possibility, some journalists believe that sometimes the bad news does not get reported. A British journalist, Ian Smiley, suggested that such self-censorship was a standard feature of reporting throughout the Third World and was nowhere more rigorously observed than in Africa. Critics charged that U.S. television networks had softened their coverage of South Africa's apartheid regime and avoided stories too critical of the ruling Afrikaners during the turbulent 1980s in order to maintain their bureaus in Johannesburg.[26]

Because of this reluctance to report fully, a darker side of Africa may be ignored. True, the coverage has been thin and violence prone, but the need may not be just to provide more positive, cheerful, and sympathetic coverage. The need may be for more realistic coverage of the continent's deepening crisis. Not much of this gloomy scenario gets into the daily news reports and certainly not during Clinton's upbeat African tour.

Two respected journalists have sounded warnings. Robert Kaplan painted a disturbing picture of West Africa which, he said, is "becoming the symbol of worldwide demographic, environmental, and societal stress, in which criminal anarchy emerges as the real 'strategic' danger. Disease, overpopulation, unprovoked crime, scarcity of resources, refugee migrations, the increasing erosion of nation-states and international borders, and the empowerment of private armies, security firms, and international drug cartels are now most tellingly demonstrated through a West African prism."[27]

Columnist William Pfaff voiced similar concerns: "The destitution of

Africa has been an all but forbidden topic in political discourse. ... The time has arrived, however, for honest and dispassionate discussion of this immense human tragedy, for which the Western countries bear a grave, if partial, responsibility and which will worsen if not addressed. Much of Africa needs, to put it plainly, what one could call a disinterested neocolonialism.[28]

These are controversial views and some argue they show a lack of belief in the survival skills of ordinary people and may convince the concerned and sympathetic outsiders to give up on Africa. This reflects a central quandary about reporting Africa. Despite the steady decline in news about Africa, the U.S. media's selective, violence-ridden reports have painted a negative and discouraging picture of Africa. Yet, if Kaplan and Pfaff are correct, the reality may be bleaker than we believed, and there indeed may be a need for Western nations to intervene. That is not something the American public wants to hear.

Finally, considering the erratic and sparse coverage of Africa on television and the newsmagazines, it is imperative that the handful of prestige newspapers not dilute their African coverage. Three papers, the *New York Times,* the *Washington Post,* and the *Los Angeles Times,* continue to produce superior daily reporting out of Africa. So, a handful of news organizations, including the Associated Press and public radio, can at least be an early-warning system that something important or significant has happened to country X or to president Y and that we ought to pay attention.[29]

CHAPTER 11

Western Media to World Media

> Western values and assumptions have been internalized to a remarkable
> degree in almost every other major culture. ... What the West has done
> to the rest of the world has been done indelibly. Nothing can be the same
> again. History has been changed by the West, which has made the world
> One World. ... What seems to be clear is that the story of the western
> civilization is now the story of mankind, its influence so diffused that old
> oppositions and antitheses are now meaningless. "The West" is hardly
> now a meaningful term, except to historians.
>
> —J.M. Roberts[1]

Modern mass communications, from newspapers and television
sets to communication satellites and videocassette recorders, are among the
many devices and cultural artifacts of Western society that have so inexorably spread throughout the world since 1945. Words on paper, electronic
impulses, and images on tape, film, and recordings have penetrated the
minds and cultures of non-Western peoples with tremendous impact.
Along with pop—and classical—music, Hollywood movies, television programs, and youthful lifestyles have also come ideas and ideology: equality,
human rights, democracy, freedom of expression, individual autonomy,
and free enterprise. John Locke, Thomas Jefferson, Abraham Lincoln, and
Adam Smith were Westerners, as was Karl Marx.

International communication, travel, industrialization, commerce,
and trade have all participated in this Westernizing process, which perhaps
should be termed the "modernization" of the world because so many non-
Western societies now contribute to the process. The practices of Western
mass communication have been so widely dispersed and accepted by people everywhere that the adjective "Western" perhaps should be reserved for
historians, as Professor Roberts suggested.

Checklist of Global News Impact

To summarize the main points of this book, let me list some ways that the new global journalism has influenced and, yes, even changed our world, for high-speed, international news communication is something new and different—in matters of degree if not in kind. Some of these effects have been global or geopolitical, others have directly influenced the media themselves, and some impacts have been felt mostly by individuals.

• *Triumph of Western journalism.* Since the fall of the Communist "second" world, the Western concept of journalism and mass communication has become the dominant model throughout the world and is widely emulated. In journalism, non-Western nations have not only adopted the equipment and gadgets of the Western press and broadcasting but also the practices, norms, ethical standards, and ideology. Throughout the developing and former Communist nations, print and broadcast journalists today increasingly seek editorial autonomy and freedom from government interference. These journalists understand and aspire to the professional values of fairness, objectivity, and responsibility as well as the "checking effect"—the role of the press as a watchdog of government and authority. They want to report the news as they see it—not some government's version of events.

• *Mass culture accepted.* For better or worse, Western mass media also have conditioned the world to use the media for entertainment and leisure. (Political indoctrination by media has been rejected by people everywhere.) Ever-growing audiences accept and enjoy the movies, television, pop music, and even the ever-present commercials. Today, the most traditional of parents find it almost impossible to prevent the influence on their children of "the most powerful engine of mass education the West has yet produced, commercial advertising."[2] Parents and others over 30 years old almost everywhere must be offended and repelled by the noisy, brassy music videos of MTV, but there is no doubting their appeal to teenagers literally everywhere.

• *Impact on Cold War.* Today many experts agree that news and mass culture from the West contributed to the demise of the USSR and the Communist regimes in Eastern Europe. It provided news not available otherwise and served the "forbidden fruit" of Western movies, rock music, lifestyles, and the promise of a better life—democracy, market economies, and a higher standard of living.

• *Global audiences growing.* Each year, literally millions more people are being drawn into the global audience mainly through competing satellite and cable services and shortwave radio. With satellite dishes and antennas sprouting everywhere, the lands of Asia, particularly China and India, are flocking to join the global village.

Some Asian nations welcome global television but others see it as a threat to their cultural identity and political stability. Across the former Third World, governments have had only limited success in blocking satellite services. Governments are finding it nearly impossible to prevent people from getting news and entertainment from the skies. Dishes, which are growing smaller, cheaper, and more powerful, are easily put together from imported kits.

• *Vast audiences for global events.* Great events—a regional war in the Persian Gulf, the quadrennial Olympic Games—can attract significant parts of the global audience. About 3.5 billion people watched some of the 1996 Olympics in Atlanta. The biggest share of that audience was in China because more than 900 million Chinese had access to television sets and three channels broadcast events there all day long.

• *History speeded up.* Nations and people react faster to important events because information moves so quickly and widely. A bomb explodes in an airliner and security measures tighten up in airports everywhere. War breaks out in the Middle East and the price of gas at the pump goes up everywhere. Actions that would have been taken later are now taken sooner—thus accelerating the pace of change.

• *"The whole world watching."* The reality that many millions can watch on television as tanks rumble across borders, troops storm ashore in a distant land, or police fire on peaceful protesters gives much greater import and consequences to news reports. A camcorder's report of Los Angeles police beating a man named Rodney King set off repercussions lasting for years.

• *Diplomacy changed.* Foreign relations and the ways that nations react to each other are now affected by public (and world) opinion formed by global communication. Television viewers concerned by watching starving children in Africa can exert pressures on their government to intervene with military force in a place they later regret going to. Media discussions and debate between diplomats and leaders can clarify policy and influence nations or alliances to act.

Nonstop coverage by CNN and BBC does provide the opportunity to monitor news events constantly and disseminate timely diplomatic information. But some politicians are more concerned than elated by global, real-time broadcasting, fearing a loss of control and the absence of quiet time to make deliberate choices, reach private agreements, and mold the public's understanding of events.

• *Autocrats' loss of controls.* Authoritarian regimes can no longer maintain a monopoly over news and censor what their people know. They cannot stop news from coming into their nation or from getting out. Shortwave radio, fax, Internet, telephones, and Comsats have changed all that and blunted the power of censorship. The Chernobyl disaster showed the impossibility of keeping a nation's bad news from its own people and the world.

During times of crisis, dictators can no longer seal their borders and control information. The news will get out.

• *"Revolution" by personalized media.* Internet, desktop publishing, videocassettes, and VCRs have turned individuals into communicators who can reach out to their own audiences. Photocopiers and audiocassettes have shown they can facilitate political upheavals or revolution, as happened in Iran.

• *Surrogate media for fettered people.* Independent media from outside now provide news and information for people who are captives of their own governments. By publicizing human-rights violations, torture, and political imprisonment, independent media help those victims to survive. It has been argued that a famine never occurs in a nation with a free press because the press by reporting incipient food shortages will bring pressures on its government to act before people begin dying.

• *Reporting pariah states.* The foreign press's persistent reporting about pariah states, such as South Africa under apartheid or the Philippines under Marcos, can apparently help to facilitate political change by forming world public opinion, which in turn can lead to actions by governments.

Persistent American and European press reporting of the civil war in Bosnia and growing evidence of genocide by Bosnian Serbs undoubtedly pushed the Clinton administration and NATO to intervene and impose a cease-fire.

• *"Copycat" effect.* With global news so pervasive and widely available, sometimes imitative acts occur that have unexpected consequences. A terrorist's car bombing in one country, widely shown on television, is duplicated 3,000 miles away. Somali clansmen defy U.S. soldiers in Mogadishu, and a few days later, Haitian thugs are encouraged to stage a near-riot as U.S. troops try to land at Port au Prince, causing the U.S. forces to withdraw.

• *Profit-driven media.* The international communication system has grown and expanded so rapidly because there was money to be made. The profit motive is, of course, a powerful force for technological change. The INTELSAT system, a crucial early component in expanding the reach of global news, expanded so rapidly and effectively because there were real profits from a more efficient and cost-effective way to make international telephone calls.

Whatever their faults, the new "media barons"—Rupert Murdoch and Ted Turner, among others—are entrepreneurs who will take risks and are willing to innovate.

Of course, news media have followed, and profited from, the expanding economy as it has become increasingly globalized.

• *Globalization of advertising and public relations.* The two persuasive arms of Western mass communications—advertising and public relations—have become globalized as well. Here again, the Anglo-American model, speaking English, is the world standard. Though often criticized, advertising and public relations are necessary and inevitable components of market economies and open societies. Moreover, advertising and public relations often make news and are, in fact, an aspect of news.

Downside of Global Media Effects

Rapid change causes dislocations and inequities, and global communication certainly has its negative impacts as well.

• *Fragility of democracy.* The worldwide surge of the late 1980s toward democracy and market economies—from Eastern Europe to Tropical Africa and South Asia—provided the promise and possibility of press freedom and independent media in nations long under one-party or military rule. Recently, over half—99 out of 186 countries—held competitive elections and various guarantees of political and individual rights. Yet most efforts to move from authoritarianism to democracy have failed more often than not after most revolutions, wrote Seymour Martin Lipset, who said that cultural factors appear more important than economic ones. Some of the factors that have promoted democracy in the past are capitalism, economic growth, a moderate opposition, British influences, and Protestantism.[3] As a result of ethnic and nationalistic clashes, the democratic outlook for most nations in Eastern Europe, the Middle East, and Africa today is not promising.

The failure to relieve economic misery in the newly democratic governments in Africa has led to discouragement with democracy, and this may lead to new military or civilian dictators. L. Gray Cowan said, "In most of the African countries where they have had elected democratic governments, the fundamental problem is that they are left with precisely the same economic and social problems they had before."[4]

The rise of democracy and a free press has been associated with market economies, but market economies do not guarantee democratic societies. Currently, the capitalist nations of Indonesia, South Korea, Thailand, and Malaysia have modern media systems and rising standards of living but are not yet fully democratic and are facing financial difficulties as well.

• *Poor nations left behind.* Optimism about the trends in international news communication is based mainly on what is happening in the prosperous societies of the United States, Europe, and Japan. Among the poorer nations of the Southern Hemisphere, especially Africa, development and growth of media and their audiences have been painfully slow in large part because the stubborn problems of poverty, overpopulation, poor health, illiteracy, and economic underdevelopment still defy solution. African countries and some other nations are not acquiring the gadgetry and infrastructure needed to travel on the information superhighway. In absolute terms, the poorer nations are falling further behind and becoming further marginalized. In addition, the onrush of rapid technological change is further widening the gap between rich and poor nations. The lack of skilled workers, an industrial base (including investment capital), and a literate and educated middle class precludes the poor nations from participating fully in the information revolution, particularly the Internet. When most of a country's population still live as illiterate peasants on subsistence agriculture, as in much of Africa, Asia, and parts of Latin America, terms like "transnational data flows," "free flow of information," or a "new world information order" have little practical meaning.

The communication revolution is coming about through education, communications, technology, and dynamic free-market economies—all in short supply in many developing countries.

• *Trends toward media monopoly.* The financial activities of the big players in international communication—Murdoch, NBC, Time Warner, Disney/ABC, BBC, Sony, Mutsushita, Bertelsmann, etc.—are moving generally in one direction: toward consolidation and monopoly of the main structures of international communication. Bigger conglomerates and fewer competitors mean greater profits. Rupert Murdoch with his Fox network in America, Sky Channel satellite TV in Europe, and the Star TV satellite system in Hong Kong and Asia has in effect already acquired a global television network. Problems of regulating these transnational entities are already proving formidable, especially in light of recent megamergers among U.S. media giants. Primarily involved with profitable entertainment enterprises, these conglomerates show slight concern with quality news dissemination. Critics fear that consolidation means a loss of diversity and competition among competing news media.

• *Declining standards.* Some ask, "Where in this commercial scramble for profits and power is the concern for serious journalism and quality entertainment?" Europeans, for example, lament the decline of public service broadcasting of quality drama and entertainment. Rupert Murdoch took BBC World Service television and its newscasts off his Star TV satellite system because it annoyed the Chinese government. Serious international news is often pushed aside for stories that are more sensational and celebrity oriented, such as the death of Princess Diana or presidential sex scandals. Entertainment values are degrading news values.

The U.S. news media carry a lot less serious news from abroad in part because the public seems less interested. Such apathy reflects the reality that we live, for now, in fairly quiet and safe, and for most Americans, prosperous times. U.S. involvement in a general war or a global depression would quickly revive interest in foreign news.

• *Shortcomings of audiences.* In the affluent West, the majority of people attending to mass media have only a superficial interest and knowledge of world affairs. They may know that Russia is having economic problems, but they do not understand the reasons. They may feel frustrated that Europe and the United States have not "done something" about the prolonged civil strife in Bosnia, Kosovo, and Serbia, but they do not understand the complexity and implications of military involvement in the Balkans.

In less-affluent nations, most people lack the education and standard of living to pay attention to world events. In many cases, their own inadequate media are incapable of providing much foreign news.

These and other shortcomings concern observers of the Brave New World of international communication. Most, however, agree that freedom and diversity are better than government control of mass communications at whatever level.

Indications of Improvement

The expanding capacity to communicate information rapidly around a world that has become ever more interdependent has begun to erase some differences and perhaps improve understanding among diverse societies. The better-educated and more-affluent people of most nations—the media users—know more about the outside world and have access to more information than ever before. The educated elites of the developing nations, though small in number, travel more and are more conversant with world affairs than were their predecessors under colonialism.

The international news system, despite its inadequacies, moves a great deal of information, data, and pictures much faster than ever before, and there is every indication that this flow will expand in the years ahead. A major world news event, enhanced by color television pictures via Comsats, frequently has immense and dramatic impact.

Walter Goodman, a frequent critic of television, had some good things to say recently about the little box: "Television, that product of the West, is by its nature on the West's side when it comes to freedom of information. Censors may hedge it in and manipulate it, but they cannot contain it; the content flows across boundaries and over the globe. When Communism fell, television, which every East bloc country boss thought was his to run for purposes of celebrating himself and suppressing his critics, was among the forces that gave it a shove. ... Television's natural impulse is to reveal, not conceal."[5]

These are some of the reasons that the West's version of world news, largely gathered and disseminated by American and West European journalists, often antagonizes and annoys non-Western governments and peoples, despite their reliance on these sources of information.

As the preceding chapter indicates, many question the validity of the current system of international news communication and would replace it with a "new order" that would significantly alter the ways that news is exchanged. The poorer nations' frustrations and antagonisms toward Western media cannot be separated from the economic disparities between rich and poor countries.

To deal with their formidable problems of poverty, massive debt, economic stagnation, disease, and sometimes famine, some leaders would harness mass communications to assist governments in dealing with these pressing issues—a clear invocation of the Developmental concept of the press. But under the Western concept, the press must be free of government to maintain liberty, to make democracy possible. Liberty is not the same as social justice or economic equality. History shows that when press freedom is sacrificed for some "greater good," political liberty and human rights usually disappear.

To the Western journalist, the press must be independent of authority, not an instrument of government, so that it can report the news and expose the abuses of governments at home and abroad. Now more than ever, governments (and corporations) need watching. For whether democratic or authoritarian, only governments—not multinational corporations or media conglomerates—have the power to start wars, nuclear or conventional, to conscript soldiers and send them off to dubious wars, to punish dissidents, to establish gulags, to "ethnically cleanse" people with a different religion. Media in both North and South must contend with governments that try and often succeed in controlling, manipulating, and suppressing what the news media wish to report. Democratic government and private ownership give the press a better chance of resisting government control and serving the public interest, but they are no guarantee of independence.

Modern history is replete with regimes marred by incompetence, venality, corruption, and brutality. Some journalists believe the world's free press has done far too little, rather than too much, critical reporting about economic failures and political abuses, especially among developing nations. This basic impasse over the proper purpose of international news communication and the relations between the press and government will continue.

What Can Be Done?

Improvements in international news communication must come from several quarters. Western journalists and mass communicators can do much to improve their own effectiveness. And governments and journalists of the communications-poor non-Western nations can do more to involve themselves in transnational news, both as senders and receivers. Much can be accomplished as well by nations and journalists working together through international organizations to arrive at some consensus on policy questions and proposals for improved news communication.

Western Initiatives

Western media, with their greater resources, should gather and report more news of the non-Western world and do it with more understanding for the problems and concerns of those nations. The coups, the economic disasters, the civil wars, the famines, and other disasters must be reported, of course, but the press also should provide more sustained, comprehensive coverage of social and cultural aspects in a historical perspective. The public requires more general knowledge of the world so that if, say, Algeria or Kosovo, suddenly dominates the news, readers can react more knowledgeably. People in the West would benefit from a better-balanced flow of news.

Television news, still locked into a half-hour format, needs to expand its foreign coverage and, furthermore, do more than provide blanket coverage of a single running story, such as the O.J. Simpson trial, while virtually ignoring other important stories elsewhere. CNN's round-the-clock coverage of the Gulf crisis revealed the inadequacies of the major networks' formats. Commercial networks should revive the hour-long news documentary, which has almost disappeared from television screens, and not leave it entirely to public television. The networks' recent expansion of magazine programs, such as "Dateline NBC," "Prime Time Live," and "20/20," are largely in the infotainment category, not serious news programs. To pay more than just cursory attention to foreign news, broadcasters must downplay the current emphasis on sensation, celebrity, and entertainment. News media in general need to show more responsibility and sense of public service.

More Western media should invest more money and human resources in covering foreign news and not leave the immense task to the few media groups that do maintain correspondents abroad. And newspapers and broadcasters without their own reporters abroad should do a better job of using the considerable amount of foreign news available from news services and syndicates.

Foreign-news editors could make much more use, as well, of academic sources. Hundreds of area specialists who have current and reliable information about every corner of the world are to be found throughout American universities.

Programs to train journalists from abroad should be continued and expanded. Western news organizations have helped to establish national news agencies and trained personnel to run them. For years, a steady stream of journalists and broadcasters have come to Europe and America for training and internships, but training journalists in their home countries or regions still has merit and perhaps priority.

Western media organizations might also consider selectively establishing newspapers in non-Western countries. Although such a course can be fraught with political risks, some previous ventures have been successful and have markedly raised the level of journalism in those countries. Two of the best newspapers in black Africa, the *Daily Times* of Nigeria and the *Daily Nation* of Kenya (now both African owned) were started by foreign publishers as commercial ventures. India has a number of vigorous newspapers today because British interests started newspapers there during colonial rule. Since independence, these papers have been managed completely by Indians and have served that nation well.

Closer Western ties can be established between journalists of different nationalities through professional groups such as the International Press Institute and Inter American Press Association. This can lead to better understanding and cooperation. These organizations and others, such as Amnesty International, often come to the aid of journalists who have become victims of political repression.

Journalists of various nations working together in professional organizations can assist developing nations in such practical matters as subsidies for expensive newsprint, which is almost entirely produced in northern nations, obtaining media equipment such as used presses and broadcast electronics from Western media, and helping to obtain cheaper preferential rates for news transmissions via Comsats and cable.

Non-Western Initiatives

To balance the flow of information better, the news media in the developing nations must be improved and expanded. This is the clearest conclusion of the information-order controversy, but this will not be easy, because any nation's mass media grow and expand along with general economic and social development and the modernization of individuals. Educated and informed individuals are needed for media jobs as well as for media audiences. Although training and technical assistance from outside can be helpful, the impetus for media improvement must come from within.

A few Western news agencies and other media ideally should not dominate global news gathering as they do, but they themselves are incapable of correcting the inequities of the system—nor should it be expected they can. Newspapers and broadcasters in Africa or South Asia should not have to rely upon a news agency based in London or New York City to find out what is happening in their own region. A much greater diversity of news sources for the world's media to draw upon is needed. For that reason alone, the persistent efforts in Asia, Africa, and Latin America to establish regional news agencies and broadcasting exchange agreements should be encouraged, despite the difficulties involved. Happily, some regions are producing more and more of their own movies, television programs, and popular music.

How soon and how effectively the developing nations can improve their news media may well depend on how their governments respond to the following policy questions.

1. Will non-Western nations cooperate effectively in developing regional and continental telecommunications and news exchanges?

In Africa, for example, long-distance telecommunications can have a revolutionary potential for the sub-Sahara by providing a truly continental system of telecommunications where none has previously existed. An integrated system of regional satellites, Internet connections, cable systems, ground stations, improved AM and FM broadcasting, and microwave relays can have important implications for intra-African exchanges of news, educational broadcasting, telephone service, television programming, and high-speed data transfers. Effectiveness of the Pan African News Agency would be greatly enhanced by improved telecommunications.

2. Will non-Western governments show more concern both for their own peoples' right to know and for an unimpeded flow of information throughout the world?

Too much of the world news controversy has involved the claims of professional journalists versus the claims of governments over regulation of news and information. In today's world, any person, whether born in Pakistan, Norway, Peru, or Tanzania, has the right, at least in theory, to acquire information that affects his or her own welfare and future. And the government under which that person lives should respect that right. A hopeless ideal, some will say, since the overwhelming majority of the world's peoples live under authoritarianism and are far removed from information sources. Nevertheless, that is the direction in which the world has been moving and must continue to do so.

To participate in global news flow requires that information, news, technical data, and cultural fare be permitted to move unimpeded across borders. It also requires that journalists be protected by law from government intrusion in their activities.

3. Will non-Western nations encourage more diversity and freedom in news and information?

Regional and alternative news agencies can be helpful and should be actively fostered. A key question is whether the governments will provide their own journalists and broadcasters with greater autonomy and independence. Journalism flourishes best in an atmosphere of freedom from government and corporate interference, but few journalists in non-Western nations enjoy such latitude. Too many, unfortunately, either work for autocratic governments or are at the mercy of arbitrary political interference. Too few governments in the world today permit their own journalists the freedom to probe serious internal problems, much less allow them to criticize even mildly the performance of those in authority. In general, these nations will continue to lag behind the information societies of the West until they evolve into constitutional, democratic societies with market economies. That will take time, and some nations obviously will not opt for that path to development. But to date, few one-party nations have shown the flexibility and dynamism to join the information societies.

In conclusion, what has happened to international news communication in the past quarter-century is, of course, only one aspect of the broad trend of the revolution in information processing and diffusion that has been transforming the modern world. The frictions we have seen between various concepts of journalism—Western, Developmental, Revolutionary, Authoritarian, and Communist—are just aspects of broader issues of international relations.

For the foreseeable future, the current system of international communication will probably retain its present basic structure with the flow of information and news steadily expanding and audiences growing. Modifications will come mainly from the adoption of more technological and economic innovations in the media themselves. In the late twentieth century, communication technology and economic forces have proved powerful forces for change.

But more than that, a reliable flow of global news and other essential information is an absolute necessity for our interdependent world, and the "closed" nations that try to block out that flow will find themselves unable to compete and prosper.

Notes

Chapter 1

1. Lester R. Brown, *World without Borders* (New York: Vintage, 1973), pp. 10–12.
2. United Nations Population Fund, as reported in the *New York Times,* August 18, 1994, p. A4.
3. Edwin Reischauer, *Toward the 21st Century: Education for a Changing World* (New York: Alfred A. Knopf, 1973), pp. 3–4.
4. Harold D. Lasswell, "The Future of World Communication: Quality and Style of Life," Papers of the East-West Communication Institute, Honolulu, no. 4 (September 1972), p. 3.
5. Thomas Griffith, "Newswatch," *Time,* March 17, 1986, p. 72.
6. Walter B. Wriston, "Economic Freedom Receives a Boost," *New York Times,* April 15, 1986, p. 31. See also David Haward Bain, "Letter from Manila: How the Press Helped to Dump a Despot," *Columbia Journalism Review,* May/June 1986, pp. 27–36.
7. Stephen Hess, *International News & Foreign Correspondents* (Washington, D.C.: Brookings Institution, 1996), p.8.
8. Barbara Crossette, "U.S. Likes Its Foreign Affairs in Nontraditional Terms, Polls Say," *New York Times,* December 28, 1997, p. 8.
9. In his widely noted article, "The Coming Anarchy" in the February 1994 issue of *Atlantic Monthly,* Robert Kaplan painted a bleak picture of how scarcity, crime, overpopulation, tribalism, and disease are rapidly destroying the social fabric of African nations.
10. Robert W. Tucker, "World Unity: A Goal Still beyond Reach," *Milwaukee Journal,* March 6, 1977, Accent section, p. 9.
11. Susan Wels, "Global Integration: The Apparent and the Real," *Stanford Magazine,* September 1990, pp. 46–50.
12. David Binder and Barbara Crossette, "As Ethnic Wars Multiply, U.S. Strives for a Policy," *New York Times,* February 7, 1993, p. 1.
13. Arthur C. Clarke, "Beyond Babel: The Century of the Communication Satellite," in *The Process and Effects of Mass Communication,* ed. W. Schramm and D. Roberts (Urbana: University of Illinois Press, 1971), p. 963.

Chapter 2

1. For this analysis, the author owes a debt to that influential book by Fred Siebert, Theodore Peterson, and Wilbur Schramm, *Four Theories of the Press* (Urbana: Uni-

versity of Illinois Press, 1956). For purposes of this transnational comparison of press systems, the Libertarian and Social Responsibility theories are both included within the Western concept.

A fuller analysis of press concepts is provided by Whitney Mundt, "Global Media Philosophies," in *Global Journalism,* second edition, ed. John Merrill (New York: Longman, 1990), pp. 11–27.

2. Quoted in Siebert et al., *Four Theories,* p. 36.

3. "Indonesia Government Bans Correspondent for the Times," *New York Times,* November 27, 1990, p. A7.7

4. Philip Shenon, "Indonesia Bars Foreign Reporters from Disputed East Timor," *New York Times,* November 20, 1994, p. 4.

5. *Associated Press v. United States,* 52 F. Supp. 362, 372 (1943).

6. See Vincent Blasi, "The Checking Value in First Amendment Theory," *American Bar Foundation Research Journal,* no. 3 (Summer 1977): pp. 521–649.

7. Ben H. Bagdikian, "The U.S. Media: Supermarket or Assembly Line," *Journal of Communication* 35, no. 3 (Summer 1985): 97–109. See also Ben Bagdikian, *Media Monopoly* (Boston: Beacon, 1987).

8. Robert Picard, "Revisions of the 'Four Theories of the Press,'" *Mass Comm Review,* Winter/Spring 1982–83, p. 27.

9. Denis McQuail, *Mass Communication Theory: An Introduction* (Beverly Hills: Sage, 1983), pp. 96–97.

10. Mark Hopkins, *Mass Media in the Soviet Union* (New York: Pegasus, 1970), p. 55.

11. McQuail, *Mass Communication Theory,* pp. 93–94.

12. Raymond Anderson, "USSR: How Lenin's Guidelines Shape the News," *Columbia Journalism Review,* September/October 1984, pp. 40–43.

13. See Donald Shanor, *Behind the Lines: The Private War against Soviet Censorship* (New York: St. Martin's, 1985).

14. Felicity Barringer, "Four Years Later, Kremlin Speaks Candidly on Chernobyl's Horrors," *New York Times,* April 28, 1990, p. 1.

15. Roger Cohen, "Propaganda to Journalism: Europe's Latest Revolution," *New York Times,* December 27, 1992, p. 5.

16. Steven Erlanger, "Russians Watch War on Uncensored TV," *New York Times,* December 20, 1994, p. 3.

17. Michael Gordon, "Russian Media, Free of One Master, Greet Another," *New York Times,* March 16, 1997, p. 3

18. E. Lloyd Murphy, "Nationalism and the Press in British West Africa" (Master's thesis, University of Wisconsin–Madison, 1967).

19. William A. Hachten, "Broadcasting and Political Crisis," in *Broadcasting in Africa: A Continental Survey of Radio and Television,* ed. Sydney Head (Philadelphia: Temple University Press, 1974), pp. 395–98.

20. Anthony Sampson, "Rebel Poli-Techs," *New York Times,* May 6, 1979, opposite editorial page.

21. Rosemary Righter, *Whose News? Politics, the Press and the Third World* (New York: Times, 1978), pp. 14–15.

Chapter 3

1. Colin Cherry, *World Communication: Threat or Promise?* (New York: Wiley Interscience, 1971), pp. 57–58.
2. Joseph Pelton, "Heading for Information Overload," *Inter-Media,* Autumn 1988, p. 19.
3. Robert L. Stevenson, *Global Communication in the 21st Century* (New York: Longman, 1994), pp. 22, 293.
4. Jonathan Fenby, *The International News Services* (New York: Shocken, 1986), p. 108.
5. Mark D. Alleyne and Janet Wagner, "Stability and Change at the Big Five News Agencies," *Journalism Quarterly,* Spring 1993, pp. 40–50.
6. Ed Frede, "AP's Foreign News Desk: They're the Gatekeepers," *AP World,* 1985, p. 3.
7. Martin Woollacott, "Western News-gathering: Why the Third World Has Reacted," *Journalism Studies Review* 1, no. 1 (June 1976): 14.
8. Stevenson, *Global Communication,* p. 289.
9. "Happy Birthday to Agence France-Presse," *Editor & Publisher,* October 12, 1985, p. 52.
10. Louise Lief, "French News Agency Struggles to Keep Its Head above Water," *Christian Science Monitor,* February 2, 1987, p. 15.
11. Hank Whittemore, *CNN: The Inside Story* (Boston: Little, Brown, 1990), p. 301.
12. Ibid., p. 268
13. Tom Rosenstiel, "The Myth of CNN," *New Republic,* August 22 and 29, 1994, pp. 27–28.
14. Ibid., p. 28.
15. Hess, *International News & Foreign Correspondents,* p. 61.
16. William Hachten, *The Troubles of Journalism* (Mahwah, N.J.: Lawrence Erlbaum, 1998) p. 119.
17. Ibid.

Chapter 4

1. Stuart Loory, "News from the Global Village," *Gannett Center Journal,* Fall 1989, p. 167.
2. Ibid.
3. Pelton, "Heading for Information Overload," p. 19.
4. Ibid.
5. Joseph Fitchett, "Europe Sits by the Phone, Awaiting a Revolution," *International Herald Tribune,* December 4, 1985, p. 1.
6. Ibid.
7. Clarke, "Beyond Babel," pp. 952–65.
8. Pelton, "Heading for Information Overload," p. 20.

9. Peter Passell, "Fast Money," *New York Times Magazine,* October 18, 1992, p. 42.

10. Hal Uplinger, "Global TV: What Follows Live Aid?" *Inter-Media,* December 1989, p. 17.

11. Ibid.

12. Rolf T. Wigand, "The Direct Satellite Connection: Definitions and Prospects," *Journal of Communication* 30, no. 2 (Spring 1980): 140–41.

13. Stevenson, *Global Communication in the 21st Century,* p. 322.

14. See Marcellus Snow, "Arguments for and against Competition in International Satellite Facilities and Services: A U.S. Perspective," *Journal of Communication* 35, no. 3 (Summer 1985), pp. 51–79.

15. William K. Stevens, "India TV Boom, Reruns and Politics," *New York Times,* September 27, 1984, p. 5.

16. "China Expands Satellite Effort," *New York Times,* May 11, 1994, p. C6.

17. "TV Mushrooms in the Backyard," *Time,* September 16, 1985, p. 56.

18. Edmund Andrews, "Betting Big on Small-Dish TV," *New York Times,* December 15, 1993, p. C1.

19. Whittemore, *CNN: The Inside Story,* p. 273.

20. Brenda Maddox, "The Telecommunications Revolution," *World Press Review,* December 1981, p. 22.

21. Keith Bradsher, "Science Fiction Nears Reality: Pocket Phone for Global Calls," *New York Times,* June 26, 1990, p. C5.

22. Steve Lohr, "Who Will Control the Digital Flow?" *New York Times,* October 17, 1993, News Review, p. 1

23. John V. Pavlik, "The Future of On-Line Journalism: Bonanza or Black Hole?" *Columbia Journalism Review,* July/August 1997, pp. 30–36.

24. Eric Eckholm, "China Cracks Down on Dissent in Cyberspace, *New York Times,* December 31, 1997, p. A3.

25. Michiko Kakutani, "Data, Data, Everywhere, and All the World Did Shrink," *New York Times,* July 8, 1997, p. B6.

26. Loory, "News from the Global Village," p. 174.

27. Pelton, "Heading for Information Overload," p. 21.

Chapter 5

1. Peter H. Lewis, *New York Times,* June 5, 1994, news review section, p. 18.

2. George Steiner, "B.B.," *New Yorker,* September 10, 1990, p. 113.

3. Bernard Gwertzman and Michael T. Kaufman, eds., *The Collapse of Communism* (New York: St. Martin's, 1990), pp. 352–53.

4. Otto Friedrich, "1984, Meet 1989," *Dateline,* May 7, 1990, p. 7.

5. William A. Henry III, "The Television Screen Is Mightier Than the Sword," *Dateline,* May 10, 1990, p. 51.

6. "How Resistance Spread the Word," *Newsweek,* September 2, 1991, p. 39

7. Alvin Toffler, *PowerShift* (New York: Bantam, 1990), pp. 357–58.

8. He Zhou and Jian Hua Zhu, "The 'Voice of America' and China," *Journalism Monographs,* no. 143 (February 1994): 1, 35.

9. Nicholas D. Kristof, "Via Satellite, Information Revolution Stirs China," *New York Times,* April 11, 1993, p. 1.

10. Even computer viruses have been reportedly used to express disapproval of China's Communist leaders. One "virus" appears on a computer screen to ask whether the user likes Prime Minister Li Peng. If the person at the keyboard says no, regular work can continue. But if the user says yes, the virus wipes out all of the computer's memory.

11. Patrick Tyler, "Satellite Dishes Must Go, Chinese Leaders Maintain," *Wisconsin State Journal,* November 22, 1993, p. 3.

12. Philip Shenon, "A Race to Satisfy TV Appetites in Asia," *New York Times,* May 23, 1993, p. 12.

13. Warren Hoge, "Murdoch Halts a Book Critical of China," *New York Times,* February 28, 1998, p. A5.

14. Philip Shenon, "A Repressed World Says, 'Beam Me Up,'" *New York Times,* September 11, 1994, p. 4E.

15. Neil Hickey, "Terrorism and Television," *TV Guide,* August 7, 1976, p. 2.

16. Ibid.

17. Tony Atwater, "Network Evening News Coverage of the TWA Hostage Crisis," *Journalism Quarterly,* Summer/Autumn 1987, p. 522.

18. "Terror Coverage Is Criticized," *New York Times,* July 31, 1985, p. 3.

19. Ibid.

20. Tom Wicker, "Not a Pseudo-Event," *New York Times,* July 9, 1985, p. 27.

21. E.J. Dionne, Jr., "The U.S. Is No Longer Captive to the Hostage Ploy," *Washington Post* (National Weekly Edition), December 24–30, 1990, p. 14.

22. Daniel Lerner, "Notes on Communication and the Nation State," *Public Opinion Quarterly,* Winter 1973–74, p. 541.

23. John Naisbitt and Patricia Aburdene, *Megatrends 2000* (New York: Avon, 1990), p. 133; and Daniel Pederson, "Boom on the Tube," *Newsweek,* October 9, 1989, p. 40.

24. John Rockwell, "The New Colossus: American Culture as Power Export," *New York Times,* January 30, 1994, section 2, p. 1.

25. Naisbitt and Aburdene, *Megatrends 2000,* p. 135.

26. John Naisbitt, *Global Paradox* (New York: Avon, 1993), p. 28.

27. Naisbitt and Aburdene, *Megatrends 2000,* p. 136.

28. Pico Iyer, *Video Night in Kathmandu* (New York: Alfred Knopf, 1988), pp. 29–30.

29. Naisbitt and Aburdene, *Megatrends 2000,* p. 134.

30. Stuart Elliott, "Whether in Asia, Latin America, or the United States, Teen-agers in a Study Dress and Think Alike," *New York Times,* December 23, 1994, p. C6.

31. Quoted by Naisbitt and Aburdene, *Megatrends 2000,* p. 153.

32. John Seabrook, "Rocking in Shangri-La," *New Yorker,* October 10, 1994, p. 76.

33. Douglas Boyd, Joseph Straubhaar, and John Lent, *Videocassette Recorders in the Third World* (New York: Addison, Wesley and Longman, 1989), p. ix.

34. Ibid., p. 11.

35. Barbara Crossette, "In India, News Videotapes Fill a Void," *New York Times,* January 2, 1991.

36. Michiko Kakutani, "Taking Out the Trash," *New York Times Magazine,* June 8, 1997, p. 31.

Chapter 6

1. "*International Herald Tribune* Begins Singapore Satellite Edition," *Editor & Publisher,* October 9, 1982, p. 28.
2. Richard Chesnoff, "The Global Newspaper Game," *U.S. News & World Report,* May 25, 1987, p. 53.
3. William Read, *America's Mass Media Merchants* (Baltimore: Johns Hopkins University Press, 1976), p. 14.
4. Ibid.
5. Ibid.
6. Deirdre Carmody, "Magazines Find Green Pastures Abroad," *New York Times,* March 20, 1995, p. C5.
7. Read, *America's Mass Media Merchants,* p. 136.
8. 1986 IMS Directory of Publications (Ft. Washington, Pa.: IMS, 1986), pp. 727–28.
9. Read, *America's Mass Media Merchants,* p. 124.
10. Alex Jones, "Journal's Apology Troubles the Press," *International Herald Tribune,* November 30, 1985, p. 1.
11. For a fuller discussion of the *Journal's* difficulties with Lee Kuan Yew, see William A. Hachten, "Media Development without Press Freedom: Lee Kuan Yew's Singapore," *Journalism Quarterly,* Winter 1989, pp. 822–27.
12. "Despite Glitches, the First European *Wall Street Journal* Gets out on Time," *Editor & Publisher,* February 12, 1983, p. 31.
13. Chesnoff, "Global Newspaper Game," p. 53.
14. Al Hester, "The Collection and Flow of World News," in Merrill, *Global Journalism,* p. 37.
15. Richard W. Stevenson, "Ad Agency Mergers Changing the Business," *New York Times,* May 13, 1986, p. 1.
16. Ibid.
17. Toffler, *PowerShift,* p. 340.
18. Toffler, *PowerShift,* p. 341.
19. For a perceptive discussion of the issues, see Jay G. Blumler, ed., *Television and the Public Interest: Vulnerable Values in West European Broadcasting* (Newbury Park, Calif.: Sage, 1992).
20. Daniel Pederson, "Boom on the Tube," *Newsweek,* October 9, 1989, p. 40.
21. Richard W. Stevenson, "Lights! Camera! Europe!" *New York Times,* February 6, 1994, section 3, p. 1.
22. Jane Perlez, "Poland Exercises the Right to Channel Surf," *New York Times,* November 14, 1993, p. 12.
23. Toffler, *PowerShift,* p. 342.
24. Richard W. Stevenson, "Mondo Murdoch," *New York Times,* May 29, 1994, section 4, p. 2.

25. Hachten, *Troubles of Journalism*, p. 68.

26. Toffler, *PowerShift*, p. 343.

27. Doreen Carvajal, "German Media Giant Will Buy Random House for $1.4 Billion," *New York Times,* March 24, 1998, p. A1.

28. Roger Cohen, "The Ethics of Cross-Ownership," *Gannett Center Journal,* Spring 1990, pp. 112–13.

29. David Sanger, "Politics and Multinational Movies," *New York Times,* December 27, 1990, p. C1.

30. Jan Arnold, "U.S. to Study Media 'Globalization,'" *Wisconsin State Journal,* February 15, 1990, p. 7B.

31. Naisbitt and Aburdene, *Megatrends 2000,* p. 139.

32. Ibid., p. 140.

33. Donald R. Browne, *International Radio Broadcasting* (New York: Praeger, 1982), p. 4.

34. Jeremy Tunstall, *The Media Are American: Anglo-American Media in the World* (London: Constable, 1977), p. 128.

35. Deirdre Carmody, "Increasingly, British Editors Are Setting Tone in U.S.," *New York Times,* October 5, 1992, p. 6C.

Chapter 7

1. David Binder, "Shortwave Radio: More Preachers, Less Propaganda," *New York Times,* August 28, 1994, p. 5E.

2. For some of these definitions and distinctions, I have relied on the still relevant views of W. Phillips Davison, *International Political Communication* (New York: Praeger, 1965), pp. 9–10.

3. Binder, "Shortwave Radio," p. 6E.

4. Ibid.

5. For a scholarly and authoritative study of this broad and complex subject, see Browne, *International Radio Broadcasting.*

6. "Candor Becoming a Staple of Shortwave," *New York Times,* March 13, 1989, p. 18.

7. Browne, *International Radio Broadcasting,* p. 4.

8. Ibid., p. 359.

9. "Candor Becoming a Staple of Shortwave," p. 18.

10. Ibid.

11. Binder, "Shortwave Radio," p. 6.

12. Alex S. Jones, "In a Crisis, Whom to Tune in, in the Soviet Bloc, Probably Western Radio," *New York Times,* May 3, 1986, p. 4.

13. Deborah Stead, "BBC Is Expanding Its Arabic Radio Broadcasts," *New York Times,* February 18, 1991, p. 27.

14. Ibid., p. 358.

15. Carolyn Weaver, "When the Voice of America Ignores Its Charter," *Columbia Journalism Review,* November/December 1988, pp. 36–43.

16. Robin Grey, "Inside the Voice of America," *Columbia Journalism Review,* May/June 1982, p. 25.

17. Neil Lewis, "Wick Is Surviving the Criticism," *New York Times,* June 26, 1985, p. 12.

18. "The Broadcast Wars, Continued," *New York Times,* October 23, 1993, p. 15.

19. "The Propaganda Sweepstakes," *Time,* March 9, 1981, p. 34.

20. Morton Kondracke, "Fine Tuning," *New Republic,* May 28, 1990, p. 10.

21. Quoted in "The Wall Comes Down" (report of a Reuters conference in New York City, July 25, 1990), p. 8.

22. Craig R. Whitney, "U.S.-Financed Radio Stations Packing Up for Move to Prague," *New York Times,* August 21, 1994, p. 9.

23. Walter Laqueur, "Save Public Diplomacy," *Foreign Affairs,* September/October 1994, p. 19.

Chapter 8

1. Alicia C. Shepard, "An American in Paris (and Moscow and Berlin and Tokyo)," *American Journalism Review,* April 1994, p. 22.

2. Leon Hadar, "Covering the New World Disorder," *Columbia Journalism Review,* July/August 1994, p. 27.

3. Ibid.

4. Hess, *International News & Foreign Correspondents,* p. 61.

5. Righter, *Whose News?* p. 70.

6. Mort Rosenblum, *Who Stole the News?* (New York: John Wiley, 1993), p. 20.

7. Scott Schuster, "Foreign Competition Hits the News," *Columbia Journalism Review,* May/June 1988, p. 45.

8. Stephen Hess, "The Cheaper Solution," *American Journalism Review,* April 1994, p. 27.

9. Rosenblum, *Who Stole the News?* p. 18. Rosenblum was drawing on periodic surveys conducted by Prof. Ralph Kliesch of Ohio University.

10. Hess, "The Cheaper Solution," p. 29.

11. Rosenblum, *Who Stole the News?* pp. 19–20.

12. Bill Carter, "3 Networks Retrench after War," *New York Times,* March 4, 1991, p. C1.

13. Hess, "The Cheaper Solution," p. 100.

14. Ibid.

15. Lynn Ludlow, "They Commute to the World," *Et Cetera,* Spring 1987, p. 38.

16. "World News: Truth and Consequences," *Columbia Journalism Review,* January/February 1995, p. 4.

17. Sally Bedell Smith, "New TV Technologies Are Starting to Change the Nation's Viewing Habits," *New York Times,* October 9, 1985, p. 10.

18. Ibid.

19. David Shaw, "Surrender of the Gatekeepers," *Nieman Reports,* Spring 1994, pp. 3–5.

20. Sally Bedell, "Why TV News Can't Be a Complete View of the World," *New York Times,* August 8, 1982, Entertainment section, p. 1.

21. Ibid.

22. Righter, *Whose News?* p. 70.

23. Arthur J. Pais, "Anger in India," *Columbia Journalism Review,* May/June 1993, p. 17.

24. Rosenblum, *Coups and Earthquakes: Reporting the Third World for America* (New York: Harper and Row, 1979), pp. 98 ff.

25. Peter J. Boyer, "South Africa and TV: The Coverage Changes," *New York Times,* December 29, 1985, p. 1.

26. Mark Fitzgerald, "A Dangerous Affair," *Editor & Publisher,* November 2, 1985, p. 18.

27. William A. Henry III, "Who Cares about Foreigners?" *Time,* October 9, 1989, p. 106.

Chapter 9

1. "Tourism Shaken by 'CNN Effect,'" *New York Times,* January 28, 1991, p. 8.

2. Tom Wicker, "An Unknown Casualty," *New York Times,* March 20, 1991, p. A15.

3. Alex S. Jones, "Feast of Viewing but Little Nourishment," *New York Times,* January 19, 1991, p. 8.

4. Michael Getler, "The Gulf War 'Good News' Policy Is a Dangerous Precedent," *Washington Post National Weekly Edition,* March 25–31, 1991, p. 24.

5. Howard Kurtz, *Media Circus* (New York: Times, 1993), p. 215.

6. E.J. Dionne, Jr., "Are the Media Beating the War Drums or Just Dancing to Them?" *Washington Post National Weekly,* September 10–16, 1990, p. 22.

7. Elizabeth Drew, "Letter from Washington," *New Yorker,* December 31, 1990, p. 92.

8. Malcolm W. Browne, "The Military vs. the Press," *New York Times Magazine,* March 3, 1991, p. 45.

9. Elaine Sciolino, "Iraq's Propaganda May Seem Crude but It's Effective," *New York Times,* September 16, 1990, p. E3.

10. Ibid.

11. Michael Wines, "C.I.A. Joins Military Move to Sap Iraqi Confidence," *New York Times,* January 19, 1991, p. 7.

12. Jonathan Alter, "When CNN Hit Its Target," *Newsweek,* January 28, 1991, p. 41.

13. See Robert E. Denton, *Media and the Persian Gulf War* (Westport, Conn.: Greenwood, 1992); and John R. MacArthur, *Second Front: Censorship and Propaganda in the Gulf War* (Berkeley: University of California Press, 1992).

14. Jason DeParle, "17 News Executives Criticize U.S. for 'Censorship' of Gulf Coverage," *New York Times,* July 3, 1991, p. A4.

15. Robert Pear, "Military Revises Rules to Assure Reporters Access to Battle Areas," *New York Times,* May 22, 1992, p. A8.

16. Kurtz, *Media Circus,* p. 214.

17. David Hackworth, "Learning How to Cover a War," *Newsweek,* December 21, 1992, p. 32.
18. James F. Hoge, Jr., "Media Pervasiveness," *Foreign Affairs,* July/August 1994, pp. 139–40.
19. Bill Carter, "TV Ready for Battle, with High-Tech Access," *New York Times,* September 18, 1994, p. 11.
20. "Military Censorship Lives," *New York Times,* September 21, 1994, p. A18.
21. Philip Knightley, "The Falklands: How Britannia Ruled the News," *Columbia Journalism Review,* September/October 1982, p. 53.
22. "Media Access to Grenada Stirs Controversy," *AP Log,* October 31, 1991, p. 1.
23. "Journalism under Fire," *Time,* December 12, 1983, p. 76.
24. Robert Frank, "News Networks, Led by CNN and BBC, Gear Up to Broadcast Fighting in Iraq," *Wall Street Journal,* February 19, 1998, p. A19.
25. Seymour Topping, "The Military and the Media Suspend Hostilities," *Columbia Journalism Review,* March/April 1998, p. 58.
26. *New York Times v. United States,* 403 U.S. 713, 717 (1971).
27. Hackworth, "Learning How to Cover a War."

Chapter 10

1. See Frederick W. Frey, "Communication and Development, in Ithiel de Sola Pool and Wilbur Schramm eds., *Handbook of Communication* (Chicago: Rand McNally, 1973), pp. 337–461, for an overview on communication and development.
2. Paul Berman, *A Tale of Two Utopias* (New York: W.W. Norton, 1996), pp. 11–12.
3. Masmoudi's remarks are from a 1978 UNESCO paper he prepared for UNESCO's International Commission for the Study of Communication Problems, chaired by Sean MacBride.
4. Rosemary Righter, "The Roots of the Controversy," *World Press Review,* October 1981, p. 42.
5. The MacBride Commission report was published as a book, *Many Voices, One World* (Paris: UNESCO, 1980).
6. Ibid., p. 217.
7. Paul Lewis, "West's News Organizations Vow to Fight Unesco on Press Curbs," *New York Times,* May 15, 1981, p. 1.
8. Robert Heilbroner, "The Triumph of Capitalism," *New Yorker,* January 23, 1989, p. 98.
9. C. Anthony Giffard, "The Inter Press Service: New Information for a New Order," *Journalism Quarterly* 62, no. 1 (Spring 1985): 17.
10. Elise Burroughs, "Fledgling News Services Cover the Third World," *Presstime,* August 1983, pp. 14–16.
11. Douglas Wilhelm, "Journalism's Little Giant," *Boston Globe,* February 8, 1987, p. A1.
12. Paul A.V. Ansah, "The Pan-African News Agency: A Preliminary Profile" (a paper prepared for the 14th IAMCR Conference in Prague, August 1984), p. 1.
13. James Brooke, "Africans Find Freeing News Isn't So Easy," *New York Times,* November 8, 1988, p. 3.

14. Fenby, *International News Services*, p. 22.

15. Philip S. Gutis, "American TV Isn't Traveling So Well," *New York Times,* February 2, 1986, section E, p. 5.

16. Christine Ogan, "Media Imperialism and the Videocassette Recorder: The Case of Turkey," *Journal of Communication,* Spring 1988, p. 93.

17. Michael Tracey, "Popular Culture and the Economics of Global Television," *Inter-Media,* March 1988, p. 8.

18. C. Anthony Giffard, *UNESCO and the Media* (New York: Longman, 1989), pp. 268–69.

19. Paul Lewis, "Proposal on Press Fades in the U.N.," *New York Times,* May 6, 1990, p. 4.

20. Robert Pear, "U.S. Won't Rejoin UNESCO, Deriding Agency as Inept," *New York Times,* April 17, 1990, p. 1.

21. See Iyer, *Video Night in Kathmandu,* for an entertaining view of Western mass culture throughout Asia.

22. William G. Harley, *Creative Compromise: The MacBride Commission* (Lanham, Mass.: University Press of America, 1993), p. 222.

23. See Paul Grosswiler, "Continuing Media Controversies," in Merrill, *Global Journalism,* pp. 117–99. See also George Gerbner, Hanid Mowlana, and Kaarle Nordenstreng, *The Global Media Debate: Its Rise, Fall and Renewal* (Norwood, N.J.: Ablex, 1993).

24. Barbara Crossette, "A Media Panel That the Media Shy From," *New York Times,* May 4, 1997, p. 10.

25. Beverly Hawk, ed., *Africa's Media Image* (New York: Praeger, 1992), p. 224.

26. Hachten, *Troubles of Journalism,* pp. 132–33.

27. Robert Kaplan, "The Coming Anarchy," *Atlantic Monthly,* February 1994, pp. 44–76. He views were expanded in his book, *The Ends of the Earth* (New York: Random House, 1996).

28. William Pfaff, "A New Colonialism?" *Foreign Affairs,* January/February 1995, pp. 2–6.

29. Hachten, *Troubles of Journalism*, pp. 134–35.

Chapter 11

1. J.M. Roberts, *The Triumph of the West* (Boston: Little, Brown, 1985). pp. 278, 290, 291.

2. Ibid.

3. "New Democracies Face Long Odds for Survival," *Stanford Alumni Review,* September 1993, p. 5.

4. Howard W. French, "African Democracies Worry Aid Will Dry Up," *New York Times,* March 19, 1995, p. 1.

5. Walter Goodman, "Even If Used as Weapon, TV is True to Its Nature," *New York Times,* January 20, 1998, p. B3.

Selected Bibliography

ALISKY, MARVIN. *Latin American Media: Guidance and Censorship.* Ames: Iowa State University Press, 1981.

ALLEYNE, MARK D. *News Revolution: Political and Economic Decisions About Global Informat ion.* New York: St. Martin's, 1997.

ALTSCHULL, J. HERBERT. *Agents of Power.* New York: Longman, 1984.

ASANTE, MOLEFI, and WILLIAM GUDYKUNST. *Handbook of International and Intercultural Communication.* Newbury Park, Calif.: Sage, 1989.

BISHOP, ROBERT L. *Qi Lai! Mobilizing One Billion Chinese: The Chinese Communication System.* Ames: Iowa State University Press, 1989.

BLUMLER, JAY (ed.). *Television and the Public Interest.* Newbury Park, Calif.: Sage, 1992.

BOYD, DOUGLAS A. *Broadcasting in the Arab World.* 2d ed. Ames: Iowa State University Press, 1993.

BOYD, DOUGLAS A., JOSEPH STRAUBHAAR, and JOHN LENT. *Videocassette Recorders in the Third World.* New York: Addison, Wesley and Longman, 1989.

BOYD-BARRETT, OLIVER. *International News Agencies.* Beverly Hills: Sage, 1980.

BOYD-BARRETT, OLIVER, and DAYA KISHAN THUSSU. *Contra-Flow in Global News.* London: John Libbey, 1992.

BROWNE, DONALD R. *International Radio Broadcasting: The Limits of the Limitless Medium.* New York: Praeger, 1982.

———. *Comparing Broadcast Systems.* Ames: Iowa State University Press, 1989.

COLE, RICHARD R. (ed.). *Communication in Latin America: Journalism, Mass Media and Society.* Wilmington, Del.: Scholarly Resources, 1996.

CURRY, JANE, and J. DASSIN (eds.). *All the News Not Fit to Print: Press Control around the World.* New York: Praeger, 1982.

DESMOND, ROBERT. *Crisis and Conflict: World News Reporting between Two Wars, 1920–40.* Iowa City: University of Iowa Press, 1982.

———. *Tides of War: World News Reporting, 1931–45.* Iowa City: University of Iowa Press, 1984.

DIZARD, WILSON P. *The Coming Information Age.* 3d ed. New York: Longman, 1989.

———. *Meganet: How the Global Communications Network Will Connect Everyone on Earth.* Boulder, Colo.: Westview, 1997.

———. *Old Media New Media.* New York: Longman, 1994

DORDICK, HERBERT, and GEORGETTE WANG. *The Information Society.* Newbury Park, Calif.: Sage, 1993.

EDELSTEIN, ALEX. *Total Propaganda: From Mass Culture to Popular Culture.* Mahwah, N.J.: Lawrence Erlbaum, 1997

FENBY, JONATHAN. *The International News Services.* New York: Shocken, 1986.

FLOURNOY, DON M. *CNN World Report: Ted Turner's International News Coup.* London: Jon Libbey, 1992.

FLOURNOY, DON M. and ROBERT K. STEWART. *Making News in the Global Market.* Luton, U.K.: University of Luton, 1997.

FORTNER, ROBERT S. *International Communication.* Belmont, Calif.: Wadsworth, 1992.

FREDERICK, HOWARD H. *Global Communication and International Relations.* Belmont, Calif.: Wadsworth, 1992.

FRIEDLAND, LEWIS A. *Covering the World: International Television News Services.* New York: Twentieth Century Fund, 1992.

GERBNER, GEORGE, and MARSHA SEIFERT. *World Communications: A Handbook.* New York: Longman, 1984.

GERBNER, GEORGE, HAMID MOWLANA, and KAARLE NORDENSTRENG. *The Global Media Debate: Its Rise, Fall and Renewal.* Norwood, N.J.: Ablex, 1993.

GEYER, GEORGIE ANNE. *Buying the Night Flight.* Washington, D.C.: Brassey's, 1996.

GIFFARD, C. ANTHONY. *UNESCO and the Media.* New York: Longman, 1989.

GWERTZMAN, BERNARD, and MICHAEL T. KAUFMAN (eds.). *The Collapse of Communism.* New York: St. Martin's, 1990.

HACHTEN, WILLIAM A. *Growth of Media in the Third World: African Failures, Asian Successes.* Ames: Iowa State University Press, 1991.

————. *The Troubles of Journalism: A Critical Look at What's Right and Wrong with the Press.* Mahwah, N.J.: Lawrence Erlbaum, 1998.

HACHTEN, WILLIAM, and C.A. GIFFARD. *The Press and Apartheid: Repression and Propaganda in South Africa.* Madison: University of Wisconsin Press, 1984.

HARASIM, LINDA. *Global Networks: Computers and International Communication.* Cambridge, Mass.: MIT Press, 1993.

HARLEY, WILLIAM G. *Creative Compromise: The MacBride Commission.* Lanham, Mass.: University Press of America, 1993.

HAWK, BEVERLY G. *Africa's Media Image.* New York: Praeger, 1992.

HEAD, SYDNEY W. *World Broadcasting Systems: A Comparative Analysis.* Belmont, Calif.: Wadsworth, 1985.

HESS, STEPHEN. *International News & Foreign Correspondents.* Washington, D.C.: Brookings Institution, 1996.

HOPKINS, MARK. *Russia's Underground Press.* New York: Praeger, 1983.

HOWKINS, JOHN. *Mass Communications in China.* New York: Longman, 1982.

IYER, PICO. *Video Night in Kathmandu.* New York: Alfred Knopf, 1988.

KAPLAN, ROBERT D. *The Ends of the Earth.* New York: Vintage, 1996.

KURIAN, GEORGE (ed.). *World Press Encyclopedia.* 2 vols. New York: Facts on File, 1982.

KURTZ, HOWARD. *Spin Cycle: Inside the Clinton Propaganda Machine.* New York: Free Press, 1998.

Many Voices, One World. Paris: UNESCO, 1980, 1984.

MARTIN, L. JOHN, and RAY HIEBERT. *Current Issues in International Communication.* New York: Longman, 1990.

MCPHAIL, THOMAS. *Electronic Colonialism: The Future of International Broadcasting and Communication.* 2d rev. ed. Beverly Hills: Sage, 1987.

MCQUAIL, DENIS. *Mass Communication Theory.* 3d ed. Newbury Park, Calif.: Sage, 1994.

MERRILL, JOHN C. *Global Journalism: Survey of International Communication.* 3d ed. New York: Longman, 1995.

MICKELSON, SIG. *America's Other Voice: The Story of Radio Free Europe and Radio Liberty.* New York: Praeger, 1983.

MICKIEWICZ, ELLEN. *Changing Channels: Television and the Struggle for Power in Russia.* New York: Oxford University Press, 1997.

MOHAMMADI, ALI. *International Communication and Globalization.* Thousand Oaks, Calif.: Sage, 1997.

MOWLANA, HAMID. *Global Information and World Communication.* New York: Longman, 1986.

MUELLER, BARBARA. *International Advertising: Communicating Across Cultures.* Belmont, Calif.: Wadsworth, 1996.

MYTTON, GRAHAM. *Mass Communication in Africa.* London: Arnold, 1983.

———. *Global Audiences: Research for World Broadcasting, 1993.* London: BBC World Service/John Libbey, 1993.

NAISBITT, JOHN, and PATRICIA ABURDENE. *Megatrends 2000.* New York: Avon, 1990.

NELSON, MICHAEL. *War of the Black Heavens: The Battle of Western Broadcasting in the Cold War.* Syracuse: Syracuse University Press, 1997.

NORDENSTRENG, KAARLE. *The Mass Media Declaration of UNESCO.* Norwood, N.J.: Ablex, 1984.

POOL, ITHIEL DE SOLA. *Technologies of Freedom.* Cambridge, Mass. [2]: Belknap, 1983.

POSTMAN, NEIL. *Amusing Ourselves to Death.* New York: Penguin, 1986.

RIGHTER, ROSEMARY. *Whose News? Politics, the Press and the Third World.* New York: Times, 1978.

ROGERS, EVERETT. *Communication Technology: The New Media Society.* New York: Free Press, 1986.

ROSENBLUM, MORT. *Coups and Earthquakes: Reporting the Third World for America.* New York: Harper and Row, 1979.

———. *Who Stole the News?* New York: John Wiley, 1993.

SCHRAMM, WILBUR, and ERWIN ATWOOD. *Circulation of News in the Third World.* Hong Kong: Chinese University Press, 1981.

SCHWARZLOSE, RICHARD A. *The Nation's Newsbrokers.* 2 vols. Evanston, Ill.: Northwestern University Press, 1990.

SEIB, PHILIP. *How News Coverage Affects Foreign Policy.* Westport, Conn.: Praeger, 1997.

SHANOR, DONALD. *Behind the Lines: The Private War against Soviet Censorship.* New York: St. Martin's, 1985.

SHENK, DAVID. *Data Smog: Surviving the Information Glut.* New York: Harper Edge/Harper Collins, 1997.

SINGHAL, ARVIND, and EVERETT ROGERS. *India's Information Revolution.* Newbury Park, Calif.: Sage, 1989.

SMITH, ANTHONY. *The Age of Behemoths: The Globalization of Mass Media Firms.* New York: Priority, 1991.

STEVENSON, ROBERT L. *Communication, Development and the Third World.* New York: Longman, 1988.

————. *Global Communication in the Twenty-first Century.* New York: Longman, 1994.

STEVENSON, ROBERT L., and DONALD SHAW. *Foreign News and the New World Information Order.* Ames: Iowa State University Press, 1984.

STROBEL, WARREN. *Late-Breaking Foreign Policy: The News Media's Influence on Peace Operations.* Washington, D.C.: U.S. Institute of Peace Press, 1997.

SUSSMAN, GERALD, and JOHN LENT. *Transnational Communications: Wiring the Third World.* Newbury Park, Calif.: Sage, 1991.

TOFFLER, ALVIN. *PowerShift.* New York: Bantam, 1990.

VAN GINNEKEN, JAAP. *Understanding Global News.* Thousand Oaks, Calif.: Sage, 1998.

WALKER, ANDREW. *A Skyfull of Freedom: Sixty Years of the BBC World Service.* London: Broadside, 1992.

WHITTEMORE, HANK. *CNN: The Inside Story.* Boston: Little, Brown, 1990.

WILHELM, DONALD. *Global Communication and Political Power.* New Brunswick, N.J.: Transaction, 1990.

WOLFSFELD, GADI. *Media and Political Conflict: News from the Middle East.* New York: Cambridge University Press, 1997.

ZHOU, HE, and JIAN HUA ZHU. The 'Voice of America' and China. *Journalism Monographs,* no. 143 (February 1994).

Index

209